AN OLD VIRGINIA COURT

Being a Transcript of the Records of the First Court

of

FRANKLIN COUNTY, VIRGINIA

1786-1789

With Biographies of the Justices and Stories of Famous Cases
Transcribed, Annotated, Glossarized and Indexed

by

MARSHALL WINGFIELD, D. D.

A Native of the County

CLEARFIELD

Originally published
Memphis, Tennessee, 1948

Reprinted for
Clearfield Company, Inc., by
Genealogical Publishing Co., Inc.
Baltimore, Maryland
1996

International Standard Book Number 0-8063-4618-3

Made in the United States of America

DEDICATION

Mr. J. Thomas DeWitt
Knoxville, Tennessee

Dear Tom:

Your ancestors and mine have lived in Franklin County, side by side, through many generations. You have been away from the hills of Franklin all of this century and I have been away all of it save the first nine years. But we have kept a little of the quietness of the hills in our hearts and something of their strength in our purposes. Your success has not affected you adversely. On the contrary, you have made many people happy by your generosity. As I dedicate to you these earliest records of our native county, let me say that of all my friends you have done most for me and hold first place in my heart.

Affectionately,

MARSHALL

3

INTRODUCTION AND ACKNOWLEDGMENTS

The earliest volume of court records of my native Franklin County, Virginia, has fascinated me ever since that day, more than forty years ago, when an indulgent county clerk pointed out some of its sidelights on history to my history-loving mind. I had resolved to make a copy of the book for my own use long before I thought of giving it to the public in this form. That resolution I carried out many years ago. Painstaking effort has been made to reproduce the book as it is—spelling, punctuation, abbreviation, pagination and all the rest. I have personally checked and re-checked puzzling words and phrases and when, in a few instances, I have been unable to make sense out of them, I have set them down as they appear.

The records alone constitute a treasure trove for the geneaologist. But to give the volume wider appeal, I have written biographical sketches of the justices of one hundred and sixty-three years ago, and stories of some famous cases of record in the Clerk's Office which holds the record-book herein reproduced.

Grateful acknowledgments are hereby made to Miss Doris Garrett, (now Mrs. Richard Dickinson) who assisted in the transcribing; to Mr. Carl Hefton who, in setting the type, followed the copy so perfectly that proof-reading was hardly necessary; to Mr. I. P. Wortham of the Superior Press who designed the book and gave it his personal attention during the process of printing; to Mr. Russell L. Davis, Franklin County lawyer, who found that in transcribing the record book, I had missed pages 126 and 127, and had the same transcribed for me; and to my wife, Marie Gregson Wingfield, who typed the transcriptions, biographical sketches and case histories, helped read the galley proofs and page proofs, made the index and contributed so much by way of encouragement that her name should be on the title page.

In days to come, when I am in "the realm of the unreplying," some antiquarian may point out words that more time and patience might have deciphered. Let me answer, while I can, that accuracy has been my goal and I have done my best to attain it.

MARSHALL WINGFIELD

A NOTE ON THE AUTHOR

Born in Franklin County, Virginia, February 19, 1893, Dr. Marshall Wingfield went to Tennessee at the age of sixteen and entered college there. Subsequent studies took him to Texas Christian University, Union Theological Seminary, Vanderbilt and Chicago universities and to summer lectures at Oxford. His continuing academic interests have kept him in touch with colleges and universities where he frequently serves as visiting lecturer, critic judge for debates, leader of Religious Emphasis Week exercises and commencement speaker. He has given as many as three baccalaureate addresses in a single year.

Pastor of First Congregational Church of Memphis for many years, Dr. Wingfield's religious activities have not been confined to his parish. He has served, or is now serving, as interchange preacher between England and America, as summer preacher for interdenominational union services of Boston, as special preacher in many noted Congregational and Presbyterian Churches of America, as moderator of the state conference to which his church belongs, as president of the Interdenominational Ministers Association of Memphis, as president of the Memphis Council of Churches, as director of the Atlanta Theological Seminary Foundation of Vanderbilt University, as staff correspondent of the Christian Century, as Mid-South correspondent for Religious News Service, as conductor of a radio program of religious news since 1945 and as member of a trio (priest, rabbi and minister) visiting army and navy installations under the auspices of the National Conference of Christians and Jews.

To Memphis civic, cultural and fraternal groups Dr. Wingfield has given generous support and leadership. Through his services as president of the Memphis Council of Social Workers, president of the Memphis Co-Operative Club, and president of the Crosscut Club, his social sympathies won city-wide recognition and approval. As founder of the Memphis Round Table he was given a citation. Co-founder of the Memphis Inter-racial Commission, he was adjudged the white citizen who contributed most to good inter-racial relationships in 1944, and awarded the Pro Bono Publico plaque of the Negro Chamber of Commerce. Baccalaureate speaker in 1947 at Tuskegee Institute (founded by Booker T. Washington), Dr. Wingfield was chosen to deliver the dedicatory address at the dedication of the memorial to Booker T. Washington at his birthplace in Franklin County, Virginia. As a reviewer of books over radio and before various Memphis groups and for The Memphis COMMERCIAL APPEAL since 1930, Dr. Wingfield has gained distinction as a literary critic of ability and integrity. His own activity as an author is suggested by his dozen or more volumes listed on a preceding page of this work.

With an interest in international affairs made intelligential by the extensive foreign travel incident to conducting study groups overseas, Dr. Wingfield was chosen as a delegate to the Conference on the Bases of a Just and Durable Peace held at Delaware, Ohio, in 1942, and to the National Study Conference on the same issue, held in Cleveland, Ohio, in 1945. More recently he was appointed by the State Department of the United States as a delegate to the second national conference of the United Nations Educational Scientific Cultural Organization. He has been a member of the national panel of the American Arbitration Association since 1942.

Deeply interested in history, especially American history, Dr. Wingfield for many years has served as president of the West Tennessee Historical Society which, though an old organization, issued its first publication under his administration. He is a member of the executive committee and of the editorial committee of the Tennessee Historical Commission.

Dr. Wingfield has served as speaker on many notable occasions, including Memorial Day exercises in the Amphitheatre of Arlington National Cemetery, the dedication exercises of the Jefferson Davis Highway, numerous addresses for state and general conventions of the United Daughters of the Confederacy and Sons of Confederate Veterans, and the address at Elmira, New York, in 1946, at the first celebration of Confederate Memorial Day ever held at the North under the auspices of Northern people. Two of these addresses were read into the *Congressional Record*.

Venerating his grandfather, Pinckney Greene Wingfield, who served four years in the Tenth Virginia Calvary, C. S. A., Dr. Wingfield has given much time to the work of the general organization of Sons of Confederate Veterans in order to preserve some of the things which were dear to his grandfather's heart. He has served the organization as camp commander, state commander, commander-in-chief, chaplain-in-chief and historian-in-chief. In the last named office he was succeeded by the noted authority on Confederate matters, Douglas Southall Freeman and with Dr. Freeman holds the SCV Distinguished Service Award. Dr. Wingfield's devotion to Southern history and traditions gave added significance to the action of Lincoln Memorial University in conferring upon him an honorary doctorate, since that University holds no Confederate traditions and observances. Governor McCord of Tennessee carried Dr. Wingfield on his staff, with the rank of colonel, during both terms of his administration. Dr. Wingfield has received other recognitions which are usually thought of as limited to non-clergymen. He is listed in numerous biographical dictionaries including WHO's WHO IN AMERICA.

Though he has not made his home in Franklin County since 1909, Dr. Wingfield is still a land-owner there, as he has been since attaining his majority, and he returned to his old home for a visit every year until the death of his mother in 1945. He and his wife are planning even now to spend the days of their retirement amid the scenes of his childhood.

KARL F. EAHEART, JR.
Minister, First Presbyterian Church (USA)
Clifton, Tennessee

PAGE ONE

Feb. 1786—Ordered that John Smith be App'd Const. for the County. Ord. that John Stewart be App'd Const for this County Who Qual. Accg. to Law. Ord. That John Terry be App'd Const. for this County who Qual. Accd'g to Law. Ord. that Edw'd Steuart be App'd Const. for this County who Qual. Accd'g to Law. Present: Swinfield Hill, Gent. Ord. That Geo. Wright be App'd Const. for this County. Ord that William Canady be App'd Const. for this County who Qual. Accdg. to Law. Ord. that William Rentfro be App'd Surveyor of the Rd. from Tho. Webbs to the X-Roads with the usual hands. * * * William Walton be App'd Surv. of the Rd. from the Cross-Rds. to Little Creek with the usual hands. Ord. that Tobias Miller be App'd Sur. of the Rd. from Little Creek to Maggotty Creek with the foll'g hands * * * Jacob Cradle, Rich'd Richards, Will Dodd, Ira Landes, Ro. West, Jno. French, Danl. French, Jr., Rich'd McLary, Jacob McNeal, Jacob Dillmon, Geo. Price, John Altick, John Bowman, Daniel Rudy, Steph. Potter, Will Thomas, Wm. Clay, * * * Delany, Chris. Chas. Long & Mich'l Peters which are Ord'd to * * *

PAGE TWO

Feb. 1786: Attend S'd Surveyor to Clear & Keep S'd Road * * *. George Turnbull App'd Surveyor of the R'd from Magotty Creek to Gills Creek with the usual hands. Thomas Charter App'd Surveyor of the Road from Gills Creek to Radfords ford on Staunton River the usual Hands. Shores Price App'd Surveyor of the road from the * * * Speer to Theo. Webbs, With the usual Hands. A Deed Fuson to Sheridan, Ack'd & O. R'd. Ord. that Will Marin be App'd Surv. of the R'd from Greers ford to Gills Creek to Black Water with the usual * * *. Ord. that Joel Cheetwood be App'd Surveyor of the road from Blackwater to Hartwells Old Place with the usual Hands. Ord. that the Clerk Transmit to the Governor & Atto. Genel. of the Courts Choosing Robert Williams States Atto. for Franklin County. A Deed Fuson to Sloan Ack'd & O. R'd. A Deed Fuson to McAlary Ack'd & O. R'd.

---

* * * Missing.

7

PAGE ONE-A

At A Court held for Franklin County at the House of Colo. James Callaway * * * February 1786. Present: Peter Saunders, Thomas * * *, Jonathan Richardson, John Smith, & Moses Greer. Stephen Smith, Clerk of this County Co * * *   * * * * * * entered into & Ack'd Bond with Surity * * * Qual. Accdg. to Law. John Rentfro Qualif'd as a Jus. of the Peace for County Accg. to Law. Present: John Rentfro Gent. Thomas Prunty, Hugh Woods & John Ferguson Qual. as Deputy Sheriff by the Approb. Of Rob. Woods Sherif of this County. Ord. that John Rentfro, Thomas Arthur & Spencer Clack be Appointed Commissioners for this County to meet the Commissioners of Henry County to Superintend the running the Dividing Line between the s'd Counties. Ord. that John Dickinson be Appointed to run the Dividing line Between the Counties of Franklin & Henry according to Law And make return thereof to next Court. Robert Williams & George Hancock Gen: Qualif'd as Atto's According to Law. Orderd that William Rentfro, Will Mavity & Thomas Hail be App'd to review a Rd. from the House of Colo. Peter Saunders the Nearest & best Way to the Washin'g Iron Works and Make rep. Acc'd to Law.

PAGE TWO-A

At a Court held for Franklin County * * * Thomas Callaway at   * * *   * * *   Monday the Second day of February * * *   * * *   Commission of the Peace and of Oyer & * * *   * * *   The Twelfth Day of December 1786 under * * *   * * *   the Common Wealth directed to Hugh Innes * * * Hairston, Robert Wood, Peter Saunders, Thomas * * * Jonathan Richardson, John Smith, Moses Greer, * * * Clack, John Gipson, Swinfield Hill and John Rentfro Gent: Justices of the County of Franklin, was Presented and read, of which the first Seven Named the said Commission were Appointed to be of the * * *. Whereupon Peter Saunders and Thomas Arthur * * * the above mentioned Gent. Justices Administered the * * * Oath a Justice of the Peace & to the Above named Robert Hairston and the Said Robert Hairston Administered the Oath of a Justice of the Peace & eaa to Peter Saunders, Thomas Arthur, Jonathan Richardson, John Smith, Moses Greer, John Gibson &

* * * Missing.

8

Swinfield Hill Gents * * * The Court being thus Constituted: Present the above Justices. A Commission under the Seal of the Comm. Wealth Appointing Robert Woods Shereff of this County * * * the Twelfth day of December 1785. Was presented and read whereupon the Said Robert Woods entered into Bond with Security and Qualified According to Law. William Ryan is with the Approbation of Robert Woods Sheriff Appointed & Qualified as a Deputy Sheriff. Stephen Smith is Appointed Clerk of this Court who Qualified Accordingly. Ordered that Court be Adj'd till Next * * * (Signed) ROBERT HAIRSTON.

PAGE THREE

Feb. 1786—A Deed Jona. Richardson to Stephen Farler Ack. & O. R. Ordered that the Overseers of the Poor do bind out Jesse & James Turpin, Orphans of James Turpin, accorg. to Law. Present: Robert Hairston, Gent. Hugh Innes & Spencer Clack Two of the Gent. Named in the Commissior of the Peace for this County Came Into Court & took the Usual Oathes to the Common Wealth & the Oath of a Justice of the Peace. On the Petition of Sundries the Inhabitants of the North Fork of Black Water, Leave is Granted to James McVey to build a Saw Mill & Grist Mill on the Said Fork. George Robinson is Exemped from the Payment of County Levies for the Future. A Deed George Griffith to John Ferguson Prov'd by their Witnesses & O. R. A Deed Thomas Black to Samuel Calland Acknowgd & O. R. Ordered that Peter Wood be Appointed Surveyor of the Road from the Fork Roads Below Peter Hollands to Hails Ford & from thence to the Oposite Shore with the following hands, to wit, Joel Meadow Sr. & his hands, John Hook & his hands, Henry Guthrie & his hands & Drury Allen & that they Clear & keep the same in Repair Accordg to Law Peter H. vs Jones, John Hook Spl. Bl. & Impl. James Prunty sworn Constable. Present: Hugh Innis & Spencer Clack Gent.

PAGE FOUR

Feb. 1786—Order that Thomas Charter be Appo. Surveyor of the Road from Gills Creek to Rich'd Wattses. Order'd that Asa Holland be App'd Surveyor of the Road from Rich'd Wattses to the fork of the R'd below Peter Hollands. Ordered that John

---

* * * Missing.

9

Booth Sr. by App'd Surveyor of the Road from the fork Near Peter Hollands to Radford Foard on Staunton. Ordered that the Sheriff Summon Twenty four Friends to Appear here at May Court, to Serve as a Grand Jury of Inquest for the Body of this County. Robert Hairston Gent. is Appointed to take the Tithables & Taxable Property in the Company of Militia Commanded by Owen Ruble. Peter Saunders Gent Is Appointed Also to Capt. Hietts Company. John Rentfro Esq. Also to his Own Company. Swinfield Hill Esq. to his Company. Hugh Innis Esq. to Capt. John Dickinson's Comp'y. Spencer Clack to Cap. William Ryans Comp'y. John Smith to his Own & Capt. Reeves Comp'y. Moses Greer to Capt. William Rentfros Comp'y. Moses Greer to Capt. William Rentfro's Comp'y. Thomas Arthur to his Own Company. Jonathan Richardson to his Own Company. John Gipson to Capt. Earlys Company.

PAGE FIVE

Feb. 1786—Ordered that Swinf'd Hill, John Smith, Israel Standifer and John Robertson be App'd to review a Road from the Place the nearest & best way into Rd near Marcums Shop and make Report thereof to the Next Court. Holden McGee having offered an Contempt to this Court. It is Considered that he be find 5 pounds & Pay the Costs & It is Ord. that the Sheriff Receive him into his Custody until he Pay the Same. Ord. that the fine Imposed on Holden McGee for Off'g an Insult to this Court be remited. Orderd that Holden McGee be find Accg. to Law for Profeng Luncy in the face of the Court & Giting Drunk & to Pay Costs. On the Compt. of Eliza. Archer vs William Archer her Husband for a Breach of the Peace. On hearing the Parties & Sundry Witness's Sworn & Exam'd it is Consider'd by the Court that he be Discharged. On the Complaint of Will Archer vs Edw'd Richard for a Breach of the Peace it is Considered by the Court that he be Dischagd on hearing. Black vs Hubard—Leave Granted to Am'd Writ. Richards Assee vs Edwards Same. Same Assee vs Same Same. Smiths Exetr. vs Same. Spencer Clack Spl. Bl. & Jud. by Nihil Driet Acc'g To T & Co: & leave to Amend Writ. Robert Woods Gen. Sher, of this County entered into & Ack'd Bond with Security Accorg. to Law for the Collection of Officers fees w'ch is Orderd to be recorded. Orderd that Court be Adjurnd till Court in Course. P * * * S * * *

---

* * * Missing, but evidently Peter Saunders.

PAGE SIX

Mar. 1876—At a Court held for Franklin County at the House of Colo. James Callaway the Sixth day of March 1786. Present: Peter Saunders, Tho. Arthur, John Smith, Swinfield Hill, Moses Greer, John Gipson, John Rentfro. A Deed from James Prunty to William Boon Ackn'd & O. to be Rc'd. Also Robert Boulton to Lodwick Tuggle Ackn'd & O. R. Also Joseph Davis to William Stephenson Ack'd & O. R. Also the Same to Peter Hickman the same. Thorp vs Woodson Tho. Prunty Sp. Bl. A Deed Joel Chitwood to Skelton Taylor. Ackn'd & O. R. Also the Same to James Greer the Same. Also Benja. Greer to James Greer the same. Ordered that the Overseers of the Poor to Bind out Alley Musgrove Accordg. to Law. John Dickenson Surveyor hath Agreeable to an Order of the Court Returned a Plat of the Division Line between this & Henry County which is O. Re.

PAGE SEVEN

Bartee vs Pinkard Extrs. referd to Anthony Pate & John Spencer &, in Case they Disagree, the S'd Referces to Choose an umpire. Pursuant to an Act of Assembly in that Case made & Provided the Court doth Set & Rate the following Liquers, Diet, Lodging, Pasuage, Stablage, & Provender which the Several Ordinary Keepers in this County Are to Entertain & Sell for the ensuing Year, Viz, For Good West India Rum, 12 P Gallon. Continent Rum, 8/ Do. Peach Brandy, 10/ Do. Whiskey, 8/ Do. Wine, 16/ Do. Strong Beer P Quart, 1/6. Cider, P. Do, 7/2. Dinner If hott, 1/6. Breakfast If hott, 1/3. Lodging for each Person, 6. Corn or Oats & Gallon, 1/. Stablage & Fodder & Night, 9. Pasturage & Night, 6. And So in Proportion for a Greater or Lesser Qty. Hill vs Martin Atta. John Payne into Court & Prayed Garnishment of the Attached Effects & Issue. An Instrument of writing Containing the Belief of John Early Respecting Dism'is & O. R'd. Dickinson is Recommended to his excellency the Governor as a Proper Person to execute the Office of Surveyor for this County. Trammell vs Bartee, Sam'l Webb Spl. Bl. & Impl.

PAGE EIGHT

Mar. 1786—Black vs Hubbard, Judgt Confst Accordl to Specially Stay of Execution till May & the Defst not to take an Advantage of a Replevy. The Court are of Opinion that This Place is the Center of this County. Court is Adj'd till Tomorrow Ten o'clock—HUGH INNES. At a Court held at the House of Colo. James Callaway on Monday the Sixth Day of March '86 for the Examination of William Dillingham on Suspicion of Feloniously Stealing a Mare the Property of Walter Bernard, & Colt the Property of Vilet Hill & also for Stealing from Edw'd Richards one Steer & other Misdemeanors. Present: Hugh Innes, Peter Saunders, Robert Hairston, Thomas Arthur, Jonathan Richards, Moses Greer, Gent. Robert Williams Att'o for the Sale enters a None Proe Quy as to the Tryal of the S'd Dillingham, the States Witnesses not Appearing, and the said Dillingham being led to the Barr in Custody of Robert Woods Gent. Shrif of the County said to whose Custody for the Cause afores'd he was Committed & it being demanded of the said Dillingham whether he is Guilty of the Fact where with he stands Charged, answered that he is in no Wise Guilty. Whareupon the Court Proceeded to Examine divers Witnesses as well on behalf of the Commonwealth as the Prison at the Barr. On Consideration Whereof the Court are of Opinion that the s'd Dillingham is not Guilty of the Fact wherewith he stands Charged, Therefore his discharge Out of Custody. HUGH INNES.

PAGE NINE

At a Court held for Franklin County the Nineth day of March * * * at the House of Colo. James Callaway. Present: Robert Hairston, Thos Arthur, Jno. Rentfro, Spencer Clack & Hugh Innes. Richardson Asee vs Edwards C. O. Same vs Same Same. Archer vs. Richards Spl. Impl. Callaway &c vs Willson C. O. Cooper vs Robertson Cont'd for Defet. Calland vs Jones Juddg for Mch Int & Costs. Ferguson vs Bartee & other Alisas Cap't. Hill vs Ferguson Cont'd. Geo. Hancock vs Willis. Jud Auy Specially & Costs. Richards vs Archer Spl. Impl. Sloan vs Underwood, N. Summon. Richardson vs Lockmire Alias Caps. Standifer vs Stoaks, Atta. Stone Assee vs Aday & Craighead C. O. Slone vs Vanover N Sum. Taylor vs Stewart Alias Caps.

* * * Missing.

12

Trent vs Webb Cont'd for Deft. Watt vs Martin Jr. N Sum. Woods vs Willis C Order.

PAGE TEN

March 1786—Austin Asee vs Prather & others Ind. Aul into Spu. Same vs Miller C. O. Defdt & Pd. Same to Livsey Same. Tho. Prunty Bl & Sl. Thorp vs Woodson Spl vs Impl. Graham vs Dougger Impl. Likins vs Davis Continued. Griffith vs Greer Dismis'd on the Plfs Cost. Edings vs Davis Continued. Patterson vs King C. Order. John Dickinson vs Binion Perryman, Indg & Atta Agst Garnishee. Hugh Innes Absent & is recommended to his excellency the Governor as a Proper Person to act as Corner for this County. Present: Hugh Innis, Gent. James Callaway Entered into Bond with Security Conditioned as the Law Directs for Keeping an Ordinary at this Place. Cap Thomas Arthur Is Appointed Surveyor of the road from the fork of the Roads near Isaac Rentfroes to Blackwater leading to Washington Iron Works with usual hands to be kept in repair According to Law. Isaac Rentfroe Esq. Is Appointed Surveyor of the road from the Above Named fork Road to Doggets foard on Blackwater with the usual hands to be Kept in Repair Agreeable to Law. Robert Hairston Esq. and Moses Greer Esq. are Appointed as Commissioners of the Land Tax for this County.

PAGE ELEVEN

March 1786—Isaac Rentfro, William Rentfro, Frederick Rives, John Dickenson, George Turnbull, Thomas Hale & John Martin & Frances Graves are Recommended to his Excellency the Governor as Proper Persons to serve in the Commissior of the Peace for this County. Ordered that Daniel Richardson be Appt'd Surveyor of the road from the Pittsylv'a Line to Cap. William Ryans & his former List be his Gang w'ch he is to Keep in Repair accordg. to Law. James Beaver is Appt'd Surveyor of the Road from William Ryans to Colo. Gordon Quartee & that his former list be his Gang & that they Clear & Keep the Same in Repair According to Law. Ordered That James Dillion, Charles Lumsden, Jas. Burns, John Robinson, Or any Three of them, do View a Way for A Road the Nearest & Most Convineint Way from Dillions Old Mill On Blackwater Into the Wagg'n Road at

John Liveys & Make report thereof to the Court. Orderd That Thomas Hill, David Stewart, Edward Choat Sen'r & Edward Choat Jun'r, or any three of them, Do View a Way for a Road from David Stewart to this Place & make a report to the Court. Orderd That Samuel Webb be Appt'd Surveyor of the Road from Gills Creek to Dillions Old Mill on Blackwater the usual Hands. Orderd that John Divers be Appt'd Surveyor of the Road from Gills Creek to the Waggon Road near Peter Holland Old Place with the usual hands. On the Motion of Robert Woods Gent, of this County Obediah Richardson is admitted as a Deputy Sherf, whereupon he took the usual oths to the ComWealth & also the Oath of a Deputy Sherif.

PAGE TWELVE

April 1786—Orderd. That William Dodd, Patrick Sloan, Lute Abshire & Christian Chas. Long be Appt'd to View a Road from Sloans Mill to Patrick Sloan on B. Water & Make report thereof to the Court. Court is Adjourned to Court in Course. HUGH INNES. At a Court held for Franklin County the Third Day of April 1786. Present: Hugh Innis, Thomas Arthur, Jonathan Richardson, Moses Greer & Swinfield Hill, Gent. A Deed James Hubard to Levi Shockley Proved by Two Witnesses & O. Certifi-cate. Bailey Carter Sworn Constable. A Deed Thomas & Robert Bowlton to David Shockly Proved by Three Witnesses & O. R'd. Also John Ellis to the same, the same. Lewis Davis Sworn Constable. A Deed James Sloan to George Kelly Ac'd & O. R'd. Also William Young to Allen Ridley Young the Same. Israel Standifer, John Law, Jesse Law & Henry Law, Or any three of them, are Appointed to View & make the Nearest & Best Way for a Road from Harwell's Cabbins to the Pittsylv'a Line into the New Road leading from Major Witchers. A Deed Edmund Swiney to Nathl' Dikson Ack'd & O. Rd'd. Also John Hoff to Peter Lukmon the Same.

PAGE THIRTEEN

April 1786—Robert Hairston & Moses Greer Gen. Commis-sioners for the Land Tax Came into Court & took the Oath as Comm's of the Said Tax Accordg. to Law. Court is Adjourned till Tomorrow Ten O'Clock.—HUGH INNES. At a Court held & Continued for Franklin County the 4th. day of April 1786.

Present: Peter Saunders, Thomas Arthur, Jonathan Richardson, Swinfield Hill and Moses Greer, Gent. Sam'l Patterson vs Sam'l Randolph, Judgl for Six Pounds fifteen Shillings & Costs Condim'a. Taylor vs Stewarts Dismissed on the Pltfs Cost. Cowan & the vs Martin & Swanson Judg. Confessed by Swanson with Stay of Execution Three Months Accordl to Sply & Costs. Alis Cap's vs Martin. Ogle vs Martin Dismissed the Pltf. not further Proseu. Ordered that David Stewart be Appointed Surveyor of the road from the Said Stewarts to Franklin Courthouse with the List fil'd to be his Gang &c. Orderd That Thomas Hill, Thomas Hale, David Barton & Joseph Davis or any 3 be Appointed to View a Road from the Spring Branch of Peter Saunders to this Courthouse & make report thereof to this Court. Lovell vs Wyne, George Ramsey Spl. Bl & Delivered him & the Court Orderd the Defedt. into the Custody of the Sherf. Lockart Ex'd & C vs Jones, Jud. for One Pound * * * from Feb. 9 1774 & Cost.

PAGE FOURTEEN

April 1786—Sam'l Collard vs Francis Quarles Jud for £3.17.1 & Cost Att. affects Conden'd & Order for Sale. Cook vs. Perryman Dismissed at the Pllfs Cost on hearing. Ordered that Moses Greer be App'd Surv. of the Road from Blackwater Across the Grassy Hill to this Courthouse & list filed to his gang & ca. Trent vs Webb Jud for £2.2&4 & Costs. A Deed William Vincent to Anna Praddy Pv'd by Two Witness & O. C. A Deed William Young to Dan'l Richardson the Same. Estes vs Hubbard, Robt. Prunty Garn, being Swo. saith he Owes the Deft. £1.14.5 Subjected to Collards attachmt. vs the Deft Trans Kearby another Garn saith he owes the Deft £2-5-0. John Kearby another Gran, saith he owes the Deft. Nothing. Jud grn for £2.5.0 & Co & Or Conda Callaway & Early's vs Robert Hodgkins, Jud for £1.14.5 & Cost & O Conda. Callaway & Early's vs John McCoy Judmt for £78.7.3 & Costs, with Interest from the first of August 1782 till P & Order of Condena. Same vs John Cary Jud. for £35.10.5 & Costs with Int. from the first of October 1784 till Paid & Order Condema. Same vs Lebanus Maberry for £55-9-14 & Costs with Interest from the first of October 1783 till Paid & Order Condema. Same vs David Evans for £98.11.92 & Costs with Int from the first of June 1782 till Paid & Order

* * * Missing.

15

Condmnation * * * * * * John Wagnor for £17.1.7 & Costs
with Int from * * * April 1782 till Pd & Order Condema.

PAGE FIFTEEN

April 1786—Callaway & Early vs Edmund Spencer Jud. for
£5.0.0 & Cost With Interest from Decem. 1782 till paid & Order
Conden. Dickinson vs Perryman, James Prunty a Garsee being
Sworn, Sayth he has in his hands £1.10.7 Subject to Three
Orders from the S'd Perryman to Robert Perryman, Robt. Boulton
& Thomas Hammonds & Continued for Further Service Atta
vs Parrott Garnishee. Present: John Rentfro Esq. Peter Saunders
Gent. is Appointed to Purchase Three Record Books for the use
of the Clerks Office & that he Bring in his Account for the same
at the laying of the next County Levies. Austin Assee &c vs
Stewart, New Summons. Court is Adjourned till Court in
Course.—PETER SAUNDERS. At a Court held at Franklin
Courthouse on Tuesday the 4th Day of April 1786 for the Examination of William Weaks on Suspicion of Felony. Present:
Thomas Arthur, Swinfield Hill, Moses Greer & John Rentfro,
Gent. The said William Weakes was led to the Barr in Custody of Robert Woods Gent. Shf. of the said County, to whose
custody for the Cause afores'd he was Committed & it being
demanded of the said Prisoner whether he was guilty of the fact
wherewith he stands Charged or not guilty, answered that he is
in no wise guilty. Whereupon the Court Proceeded to Examine
divers Witnesses as well on behalf of the Commonwealth as the
Prisoner at the Barr. On Consideration whereof the Court are
of Opinion that the said Prisoner is Guilty of the Fact wherewith
he stands Charged

PAGE SIXTEEN

April 1786—And that he ought to receive a further Tryal
before the Honorabel the Court of Oyer & Tumnener on the 2nd
Tuesday in June Next. Therefore he is remanded into the Custody of the Sherirf afores'd. Whereupon the s'd Prisoner Threw
himself on the Mercy of the Court & it is ordered that he receive on his bare back 16 lashes well laid. Peter Saunders Severally indebted to the Commonwealth of Virginia in the Sum
of £100 each, to be levied on their respective Goods & Chattles,
Lands & Tenaments, On Condition they do not Appear before

* * * Missing.

16

the Honourable the Court of Oyer & Tuminer on the 2nd Tues-day in June next to give Testimony against the Williams Weakes & that he ought to give Suriety for his Good Behaviour. Where-upon he with William Ferguson & William Mavity Acknowl-edged themselves Severally indebted to the Comwealth of Vir-ginia, that is to say, the said Wm Weaks in the Sum of £100, & his Securities in the Sum of £50 each, to be levied on their respective Goods & Chattels, Lands & Tenements on Condition the said William Weaks be not of Good Behaviour One Year & a day & especially towards Peter Saunders Gl.—T. ARTHUR.*

PAGE SEVENTEEN

May 1786—At a Court held for Franklin County the first day of May: 1786 * * * Present: Peter Saunders, Thomas Ar-thur, John Rentfro, John Gipson, John Smith, Gent. Hill vs Forsythe. Dismis'd. Same vs McDonald the Same. Leave is Granted to Robert Lilley to Build a Water Grist Mill on Prathers Run he being Proprietor of the Land on both Sides of Said Run. A Deed William Kelly to Jacob Kingery Ack & O. R. A Deed John Langdon to Jacob Boon Ack'd & O. R'd. Hook vs Wood Jas. Callaway Spl. Bl. Impl. & O R. Hunt vs Clardy Wm. Rob-ertson Spl Bail & Spl Impl. Thorp vs Thomas Miller Sr. Thomas Miller Jr. Spl. Bl & Spl. Impl. A Deed Daniel Shumate to Jacob Miller Prov'd & O R. Also a Deed from Wm. Akers to Jacob Wemmer Ack'd & O R. Also the Same to Jacob Miller the Same. Also A Deed from Tho. Hunt to John Hook Ack'd & O R. James Callaway vs Lewis Thompson, Isham Hall & William Davis Spl. Bail, Never Absconded & Issue. A Bond from John Cook to Daniel Richardson for the Conveyance of Land. Proved & O. R.**

PAGE TWENTY

May 1786—Orderd that the Overseers of the Poor &ca the Parish of Patrick, do bind Ellenor Jones According to Law. Also that they Bind out Edith Jones Agreeable to the Same. Ander-son vs Griffith Dismiss'd by Information of Clk. Barton vs Liv-sey Spl Impl. Demoss vs Markham &c Comm Order Agst Tho Markham And Atta Agst the Other. Edings vs Davis, Abates by return. Ferguson vs Bartee &c Alias Cap's. Marcus Likins

---

* Across this page, written large, are the letters E X X.
* * Pages 18 & 19 are blank.

vs Davis, Abates by Return. Lovell vs Markham Atta. Same vs Wyne C. Order & Dism'd Out of Custody. Same vs Swanson Plur Caps. Pincard vs Randal Atta. Patterson vs King Jud. for £1.13.9 & Costs. John Dickinson Foreman, Benjamin Cook, William Jamison, Sam'l Patterson, Owen Rubil, Isaac Bates, Theo Webb, Danl. Spangler Sr., Danl Spangler Jr., Alex'dr Ferguson, Isaiah Willis, Tho. Hill, Nathan Swanson, James Greer, John Woods, John Martin & James Coleman, Were Sworn as A Grand Jury of Inquest for the Body of this County & withdrew to Consult on their Presentments. Livsey vs Ramsey Dismissed with Costs. Thorp vs Stout, Judgt, Confessed accorl to Sply & Cost Stay Exeon 2 Months.

PAGE TWENTY-ONE

May 1786—Thorp vs Chitwood Judgt Confess'd Accordl. to Splly & Cost stay Exor one Month. John Peek is appointed Surveyor of the Road from Shooting Creek to Oyler Creek & a List filed to his Gang &c. Richardson vs Hundley & N. P. Standifer vs Stokes Contin'd. Snuffer vs Bibly &c C. O. Deft & Bl. & A. C. Sloan vs Vandover Jud for £1.14.0 & Costs. Thorp vs Brower Jud Confesed Accordg to Specialty & Cost Stay of Execn Three Months. Walton vs Kelley & Miller William Kelly Spl &c. Same vs Same the Same. Willson vs Hale Dismiss'd the Pllf not further Pross'g. Jones vs Clardy Rich'd Booth Spl. Bail, Impl &c. Teal vs Farley's Spl. Impl. David Prewit is exempt from the Payment of County Levies for the future. Austin Assee vs Livsey. Dismiss'd. Richards vs Archer and Archer vs Richards Refer'd to Hugh Innis, Spencer Clack, William Ryan & Robert Mason & in case they Disagree to Choose an Umpire & this as their Award to be the Judgment of the Court. Scott vs Martin Jr. Dismiss'd at Pltfs Costs. Watts vs Martin Jr Dismissed at Pltfs Costs. The Grand Jury Return'd into Court & made Several Presentments whereof Process in Orderd to Issue.

PAGE TWENTY-TWO

May 1786—Sloan vs Underwood Atta With Proelam . . a. Willson vs Rentfro Impl. Harkrader vs Arthur, Continued. David Godall exempt. from agst. Paymt. of Co. Levies. Hook vs Grifffith, Jud. Confessed Accordg to Specially & Cost. James Mills is Appointed Sur'v of the road Down Maggotty from the

18

fork of the road Leading to Lute Abshires to the Black Water Road Above Tho. Wattses Xing Ayletts Creek & List filed to his Gang &c. Luke Abshire is appointed Surveyor of the Road Down Maggotty from the Caroline Road to the fork of the Road leading to the Said Abshire & A List fil'd to his Gang &c. Miller vs Griffith Thomas Livsey Sr. Spl. Bail & Impl. Richardson vs Lockmire Danl Spangler Spl Bl & Sl Imp. Thomas Prunty vs Jones Adminiss rs Spl Impl. Austin Asee vs Stewart, Continued. Ordered that the Shereff he find 50/. & Costs for his non Attendance on the Court Terry Assee vs Rentfro. Jud Confess'd Accordg to Splly with Stay of Excu four Months. Clyborn vs Parker Atta. Thorp vs Altick Jud Conf'd Accorg to Specially & Costs with Stay of Eccu 2 Months. Same vs Rudy the Same. Absent John Smith. Present H. Innis.

PAGE TWENTY-THREE

May 1786—Thomas vs. Levsey, C. Order Agst Defft & Bail. Arthur vs. Jones & Martin Atta. Johnson vs. Doggett Spl. Impl. Markham vs. Ready C. Order. Present: Spencer Clack. Thorp vs. Duvall Jud Confess Accorg to Specity & Stay. Execn One Month. Clardy vs. Hunt Atta. Hancock vs. Livsey Dismiss'd Agreed. Black vs. Saunders Com Order. Cole vs. Tho Doggett heir of Evans Wm Miller Sl Bl & Impl. Sherdan vs. Stewart Jud. Accog. to Sply & Costs. Griffith vs. McDowall Atta Agst Garshee. A Deed from William Weeks to William Mavity, e. Proved by Two Witnesses & O. C. Pratt vs. Sheridan Jud. Conf'd for £. & Costs. Stephenson vs. Grymes, Sam'l Calland A Garshee being Sworn Sayith that he hath in his hands Sufficient to Satisfy the Pllfs Demand w'ch will be Disi. in Feb next Jud. for £6.8.0 & Costs & O. Condin. John Dickinson Gent. Produced a Commission from the Masters of the College of William & Mary whereupon he took the usual Oaths to the Comm. Wealth of the Oath of a Surveyor of this County & with James Callaway & Thomas Hill his Securities Ented into Bond & Acknowledg'd the Same According to Law.

PAGE TWENTY-FOUR

May 1786—Thorp vs. Bates Jno to Specially & Costs Stay Excun. Three Months. Ferguson vs Stewart Contin'd. Ordered that Edw'd Choat Sr., & Edward Choat Jr., William Bartee &

Sam'l Patteson be Appointed to Review a Road from David Stewarts in Chesnut to Franklin Courthouse the nearest & best Way & that they make report thereof to Court. Kelly vs Williams, Ebenezer Pyatt a Garshee being Sworn Sayith that he hath in has hands £1.19.11, Jud for £5.0.0 Ord. O. Condimin'd & Costs. On the Motion of John Dickinson Surveyor of this County William Cavanaugh is Admited as A Deputy Surve'r whereupon he took the usual Oaths to the Common Wealth & Also the Oath of Dept Surveyor. Ordered that the overseers of the Poor do Bind out Jesse Thompson A Poor Orphan of John Thompson Dec'd. Dickinson vs Perryman, Nathl' Parrot a Garshee being Sworn Saith he hath in his hands a Book (the Whole Duty of Man) the Property of the Deftt & O. C. & Cont'd. William Weeks Asse vs Isaac Jenny, Jud for Sply & Costs. Thomas Hale vs Joseph Miller Jud. Accg to Sply & Costs. Bates vs Rentfro, Dismissed At Deftts Costs. Cooper vs Robertson, Dismiss'd with Costs. Court is Adjournd till Tomorrow Ten O'Clock. HUGH INNES.

PAGE TWENTY-FIVE

May 1786—At A Court held & Continued for Franklin County on Tuesday the Second Day of May 1786. Present: Hugh Innis, Jonathan Richardson, John Smith & John Rentfro, Peter Saunders, Gent. Boyd vs Miller Jud Accdl to Specially & Costs. Cowan & the vs Martin C. O. Defett & Sherff. Maviety vs Innes Admrs C. Order. Lovell vs Swanson C. Order. Saunders vs Weeks Spl. Impl. Thomas Miller vs Geo. Griffith Spl Impl. Thorp vs Tench's C. Order. Same vs Toney the Same. Same vs Walker the Same. Same vs Miller &c C. O. Same vs Miller & Street the Same. Same vs Rentfro Same. Same vs Bell Same. Same vs Blackburn, Jud & Costs. Same vs Harkrider C. Order. Same vs Livsey Jr. Jud & Costs Jud for 21/. Wade vs Ferguson Cont'd at Plfs Costs. Watson vs Miller Dismis'd Want of Prosse. Isaac Bates vs Rentfro C. Order. Watson vs Hynes Dismis'd by Pltfs Order. Ferguson vs McDonald Dism'd.

PAGE TWENTY-SIX

May 1786—Standifer vs Rentfro Dismiss at Pllfs Costs. Greer vs Webb Spl. Impl. Bartee vs Pincard Exrs Cont'd for Award. Callaway & Earlys vs Willson Jud. Accordl, to Specially & Costs.

Poteet vs Jones Genl. Issue with Leave. Stone Assee vs Aday &
Craighead Spl. Impl. Trammel vs Bartee & Tunstal. Austin Assee
vs William Miller, C. O. conf'd Jud w'th Costs. Graham vs
Dugger Genl Issue. Thorp vs Woodson. Genl Issue. Woods vs
Willis C. O. Conf'd W. Engn. Orderd that the Sheriff Appear
at Next Court to give Security for the Collection of the Certifi-
cate Tax for the Year 1786. Richardson vs Edwards H. Innis &
S. Clack Spl. Bl. & Co. Order. Same vs the Same the Same.
Usebus Stone is Allowed Two Day Attendance & One Coming
& Reting 23 miles as a Witness for Jno. Ferguson ads Bartlet
Wade. John Hunter is Allowed Two Days Attendance for Y
Same. Ordered that the Surveyor of this County do lay off &
Survey Ten Acres of Land for a Prison Bounds to Include, Spring,
Prison, Ordinary & Courthouse, & that he return a Plot of the
same to this Court & that Thomas Arthur, Swinfield Hill &
Stephen Smith are Appointed to Superintend the S'd Surveyor
in laying of the Said Bounds.

PAGE TWENTY-SEVEN

Present: Spencer Clack, Thos. Arthur. Moses Greer & Jona-
than Richardson, Gent. Ordered that Robert Shewood, William
Jamison, James Majors & James Beavers, or any Three of them,
Are App'd to view a Road from the County Road Leadg to
Henry C. House the Nearest & best Way to David Stewarts on
Chesnut Creek & Make Rept. to the Court. The order Yesterday
for Impos'g a fine on the Shiff of this County for neglect of
Duty the Same is Remited he having Shewn Cause for the Same
he Paying Costs. Peter Saunders Gent. Is Appointed & Recom-
mended to his Excellency the Governor As A Proper Person to
excute the Office as a County Lieutenant for this County. Hugh
Innis Genl. is also Appointed & Recommended as a Colo. Commander for the said County. Thomas Arthur Genl. is Also Recommend to his Excell'cy the Governor as A Proper Person to
excute the Office of first Major for the Said County. John
Rentfro Gent. is also Recom'd as a Proper Person to execute the
Office of 2nd Major for this County. Court is Adjourned till
Court is Con. HUGH INNES.

PAGE TWENTY-EIGHT

June 1786—At a Court held at Franklin Courthouse on Tues' day the Thirteenth day of June 1786 for the examination of James Stokes on Suspicion of Felony. Present: Thomas Arthur, Swinfield Hill, Moses Greer & John Rentfro Gent. The said James Stokes was led to the Bar in Custody of Robert Woods Genl, Sheriff of the Said County to whose Custody for the Cause Aforesaid he was Commited & waved his Priviledge and it Being Demanded of the Said Prisoner whether he was Guilty of the fact wherewith he Stands Charged or not Guilty, answered that he is no Wise Guilty whereupon the Court Proceeded to examine Divers Witnesses as well on Behalf of the Common Wealth as the Prisoner at the Bar, On Consideration Whereon the Court are of Opinion that the Said Prisoner is Not Guilty of the fact where' with he Stands Charged, Therefore he is Discharged Out of Cus' tody. T. ARTHUR. At a Court held for Franklin County on Monday the Third Day of July 1786. Present: Robert Hairston, Thomas Arthur, Jonathan Richardson, Swinfield Hill, John Smith & John Gibson, Gent. William Thompson is Appointed Surveyor of the Road from the Sign Post to Jas Martins W'ch he is to keep in Repair According to Law & the List fil'd to be his Gang. Spencer vs Gibson, Jud Confessed for £300. with Stay of Exeu Three Months.

PAGE TWENTY-NINE

May 1786—A Deed from Josiah Marcum to Robert Napier Proved by Two Witnesses & O. C. James Penn Esq. Produced a Commission to Practice as Attorney at Law, Whereupon he took the Usual Oaths Prescribed by Law. The Last Will & Tes' tament of Henry Guthry Dec'd Was Produced in Court and Proved by the Oaths of Two Witnesses & O' R'd the Heir at Law Agreeing to the Same & John Guthry One of the Witnesses to the Said Will also a Legatee. Agree to relinguish his Interest in the Same. Whereupon James Guthry & Penolepe Guthry took Administration of the Estate with the Will Annexed who made Oath & With John Guthry, David Guthry, John Hook & Richard Booth their Securities, Entered into Bond & Acknowl' edged the Same According to Law. John Booth Sr. Joel Meador Sr. John Wood & Rich'd Watts, Or any Three of them, are Ap' pointed to Appraise the Said Estate & return an Inventory thereof the Court. Cook vs Richardson leave Granted to amend Writ returned to August Court. Hugh Innis Gent Produced a Commission Appointing him Coroner for this County whereupon he took the Oaths Proscribed by Law & with Peter Saunders his Security Entered into Bond & Acknowlged the Same According to Law.

PAGE THIRTY

July 1786—A Deed from Fredrick Reives to Burwell Reeves Ackndg'd & O. R.'d. Also Francis Thorp to Shadrack Woodson Prov'd by Two Witnesses O. C. John Lumsden is Appointed Surveyor of the road from Dillions Old Mill on Blackwater to the Waggon Road at Jno. Livseys which he is to Clear & Keep in Repair Accorg. to Law & the List fild to be his Gang. A Deed Benjamin Clardy & Agness Clardy to John Bozwell. Proved & O. Rcd. Peter Saunders Gent. Produced a Commission from his Excellency the Governor App'd him County Lieutenant of this County, Whereupon he took the Oaths Prescribed by Law. Hugh Innes Gent. Produced a Commission from his Excellcy the Governor appoint'g him Colonel of the Militia of this County Whereupon he took the Oaths Prescribed by Law. Thomas Arthur Gent Produced a Commission from his Excellency the Govenor Appointing him Lieutenant Colonel of the Militia of this County whereupon he took the Oaths Prescribe by Law. John Rentfroe Gent. Produced a Commission from his Excellency the Governor appoint'g him Major of the Mititia of this County, Whereupon he took the Oaths Prescribed by Law. Robert Williams Esq. Produced a Commis'n Appointing him Depy States Atto. for this County Agreeable to an

PAGE THIRTY-ONE

July 1786—Order of Court in January Next Whereupon he took the Oaths Prescribed by Law. Mary Webb Agreeabel to Recognizance taken before John Rentfro Gent. Came into Court & with Theodorick Webb & Jno. Rentfro her Securties the Said Mary Webb Acknowledged herself Indebted to the Common Wealth of Virginia in the Sum of £20 & her Securities in the Sum of Ten Pounds Each to be Levied on their Respective Goods & Chattels, Lands & Tennaments, on Condition that she be not of Good Behaviour One Year and a Day & Especially towards

23

Rachel Jones. Isaih Willis is Appointed Surveyor of the Road from Hatchet Run to William Ferguson Plantation on Pigg River in the Room of William Standifer & the Usual hands to be his Gang. Present: Hugh Innis Gent. William Archer Agreeable to Recognizance taken before Hugh Innis Gent. Came into Court & With Jno. Woods his Security. The said William Archer Acknowledged himself Indebted to the Common Wealth of Virginia in the Sum of Twenty Pounds & his Security also in the Sum of £20 to be Levied on their Respective Goods & Chattles, Lands Tenements on Condition that he be not of Good Behavior One Year & a Day & Especially towards Edward Richards. Luke Standifer Is Appointed Surveyor of the Road from Story Creek into the Road Leading to this Courthouse & the List filed to be his Gang. Crisley Whitmore is Exempted from the Payment of County Levies for the Future. Also Lawrence Lesane the Same.

PAGE THIRTY-TWO

July 1786—Jesse Kerly is Exempt from the Payment of County Levies for the Future. Peter Saunders, Saml Hairston, Spencer James & John Sneed, Or Any Three of them, are Appointed to Review a Way for A Road from Spencer James in the Best & nearest way to this Courthouse. A Report for the Review of a Road from Peter Saunders Spring Branch to this Courthouse, Ret'd & O. R. Court is Adjourn'd till Court in Course. HUGH INNES. At a Court of Quarterly Sessions held for Franklin County on Monday the Seventh Day of August 1786. Present: Hugh Innis, Moses Greer, Jonathan Richardson, John Smith, John Rentfro, Gent. Thorp vs Abshire, Jud. Confessed Accorg. to Specially & Cost Stay of Excon till the 15th Instant. Richards vs Archer, Award Ret. for Defdt & O. R'd. Archer vs Richards, Award Ret for Plff & O. R'd. Archer vs Richards Award Ret for Plff & O. R'd. Price vs Woodson, Jno Rentfro Spl. Bail. Same Asee vs Same the Same. A Deed Benjamin Poteet, to Alexander Ferguson Pro'd & O. R. A Deed Lachlon McGrady to Jacob Flora Same. Also Garrat Fitzerrald to Jacob Boon Ack'd & Eliz'a his wife being priviely Examed & duly Relinguish her Dower & O. R.

PAGE THIRTY-THREE

August 1786—A Deed Nathaniel Ready to Alex Ross Ack'd & O. R.'d. A Deed John Ellis to William Smith Pr'd by Two

Witne & O. R'd. A Deed Lochlan McGrady to Jno. Early Ack'd & O. R'd. Patterson vs King Eusebas Hubard Spl. Bl. A Deed Robert Mason to John Harger Ack'd & Sara his Wife being Privily Examinded freely relinguished her Dower & O. Recordl. A Deed Moses Wray to John Hook Proved & O. R'd. The Tuesday After the first Monday in every Month is Appointed by the Court As the Rule Day. Clardy vs Hunt George Asberry Spl Bl. Wills vs Wallis Jud. Accorg to Specially & O. C. Hale vs McKinzie Joseph Ellis Spl. Bl. Joshua Rentfro Foreman, William Miller, Jesse Law, Stephen Wood, Nathan Swanson, Samuel Hairston, Peter Geerheart, Daniel Spangle, Owen Rubel, William Hunter, John Hunter, William Maviety, Joseph Young, William Toney, David Morgan William Wright, Thomas Hale & Robert Powell, was Sworn a Grand Jury of Inquest for the Body of this County, Whereupon they withdrew to Consult upon their Presentments. Ordered that Charles Bradshaw be Summond to Appear before the Next Succeeding Court of Qty Sessions to Show Cause if Any he Hath why he did not Appear before this Court as a * * * of the Grand Jury.

PAGE THIRTY-FOUR
AUGUST 1786—Trammel vs Bartee Jud. Confessed for £3 & Cost Except Attornees fee to be Paid in Stock &c. Walton Assee vs Webster Jud. Confess'd for Specally & Costs with Stay of Excen till January Court. Same vs Isaac Rentfro the Same. Richard Bailey vs William Mead, James Callaway A Garnishee being Sworn, Sayith, that he hath Sufficient in his hands to Satisfy the Pllfs Demand, to be p'd in Bar Iron, Castings & Steel, Jud. Accordl. to Accol, for £13 10/ With Interest from January 1778 & Costs & O. C. A Deed of Trust from Joseph King Ju. to Samuel Calland Ack'd & O. R'd. Demoss Exet & c v Thomas Marcum Dism'd Defds Cost. Marcum vs Ready Dism's'd at Defets Cost. Trent vs Vaughan, Elexieus Harsten a Garshee being Sworn Sayith he has in hands Six Small Deerskins, One Mattock and a Sheep. Jud for £3.15.6 & Costs & O. C. John Sullivant an Other Garnishee being Sworn Saith he has in his hands Seven Shillings & Six Pence. Bryant Trent Another Garshee Sayth he Owes the Defedt 15/ & Cont. John Ramey is Allowed Two Days Attendance & Twice Coming & Returning 60 Miles, as a Witness for Bartee ads Trammer.

---
* * * Missing.

25

PAGE THIRTY-FIVE

August 1786—Rentfro vs Snuffer Jud Confessed for £12.10 & Int. & Cost With Stay of Excun 3 Months. On the Motion of Geo. Hancock Gent. Jud. is Granted him Against John Willis & Thomas Miller for £4.4.4 with Int. from 16th March 1786 & Costs on Replevy Bond. Austin Assee vs Parther & Miller, Jud. is Granted the Pllf, for Six Pounds five Shillings & Seven Pence with Int. from 28th March 1786 & Costs on Repley Bond. Austin Asee of Trent vs Stewart, Jud Against Wm. Trent for £3.10 & Costs. Ferguson vs Stewart Continued. Thorp vs Campbell Jud Accordl. to Sp & Costs. Same vs Harkrider. Jud. Accordl. to Sp & Costs. Henderson vs Patteson, Benja. Cook & Wm Cowden Spl Bl. Saunders vs Standifer, William Standifer a Garshee being Sworn Sayith that he Owes the Deftt S/6, William Standley another Garishee, Sayith he Oweth the Defdt Nothing, Jud. Accordl. to Specially & Costs & O. C. Holley vs Cockran, Thomas Arthur Spl. Bl. Asberry vs Stoaks Edw'd Choat In Spl. Bl. & Delivered him up & Joseph Young Spl. Bl. Hill vs Ferguson, Jud for £2.5.0 & Costs. Moses Hudgins is allowed One Days to Attend. as a witness Hill vs Ferguson. Joseph Semmons is Allowed 5 days for the Same.

PAGE THIRTY-SIX

August 1786—The Grand Jury Returned into Court & made Several Presentments Whereupon Process is Ordered to Issue. Sherwood vs Edwards Spencer Clack Spl. Bl. Barton vs Livsey Leave to Amend Writ. Arthur vs Willson. Jud for £2.2.6 & Costs. Asberry vs Bollard Jud. Accordl. to Specialty & Costs. Tabitha Arthur is Allowed One Days Attendance & On Coming & returning 45 miles as a Witness for John Hook Assee of Arthur vs Wood. Wade vs Farguson, Dismissed. John Hunter is Allowed One Days Attendance as a Witness for Ferguson Ads Wade. Usebus Stone is Allowed 2 Days Attendance as a Witness for John Ferguson ads Wade & Coming and Returning 23 Miles Jones vs Beard Jud. for £-3 & Costs. Innes vs Tusley. Jud. Confess'd accordl to Specially & Costs. Cockran vs Brummet &c Jud for £2.12.6 & Costs. Samuel Patteson is Allowed Two Days Attendance as a Witness for Rob. Cox Jones vs Sam'l Beard.

PAGE THIRTY-SEVEN

August Sessions—Prunty vs Jones Admr'd Plea filed, Issue & Jud. fen £4.12.6 & Costs, After all Debts of a Superior Dignity are Paid. Richardson vs Hundley &c Jud Accordg. to Spell & Cost. Thorp vs M. Rentfro. Jno Rentfro Apl. B. & Iml. Spl. The Report of a Review of a Road from Spencer James to the Courthouse Ret. & O. R'd. John Sneed is Appointed Surveyor of the Road from Spencer James's to Colo Saunders & the List filed to be his Gang. Court is Adjourn'd till Court In Course. PETER SAUNDERS.

PAGE THIRTY-EIGHT

August Sessions—Jonathan Richeson is Recommend'd to his Excellency the Gov. as a Proper Person to serve as A Capt. of the Militia for this County. Skelton Taylor is Lieut & John Taylor Is Ensign. Also John Smith is Capt. Jno. Davies Lieut; Peter Holland. Also Thomas Hale Capt; Luke Standifer, Lieut; Thos. Hill, Ensign; Swinfield Hill, Capt; Hugh Woods Sen. & Lewis Davis, Ensign; William Rentfro, Capt; Thos. Doggett Jr, Lieut; Wm. Miller, Ensign; William Ryan, Capt; Spencer Clack, Lieut; Nathan Ryan, Ensign; John Dickinson, Capt; Jno. Law, Lieut; Jas. Arthur, Ensign; Burwell Rives, Capt; Kemplin Edmondson Lieut & Israel Standifer; Samuel Hairston, Capt; David Barton, Lieut; Wm. Rentfro, Ensign; Isaac Rentfro, Capt; Geo. Turnbull, Lieut; David Morgan, Ensign; Joshua Rentfro, Capt; Joel Walker, Lieut; Jas. Rentfro, Ensign; John Early, Capt; Jubal Early, Lieut; Wm. Wright, Sr, Ensign. On the Motion of Samuel Calland, Jud. is Granted him, Frances Quarles, & Spencer Clack, for the Sum of £5.12.6 with Interest from 10th April 1786, On Replevy Bond. Houzer vs Jamison, John Bird Spl. Bl. John Dickinson Sur'v of this County Ret'd a Plot of the Prison Bounds Which is O. R'd. Jno. Rentfro Absent. Ingram vs Rentfro, Jud Confess'd for £3 & Costs. Present John Rentfro. Thomas Arthur & Swinfield Hill are Appointed to Employ Persons to Mark out Distinctly the Prison Bounds by fixing Stones at Certain Distance & to bring in their Account for the Same at Laying the County Levis. Absent Hugh Innes. * * * vs McKinzee Thos. Prunty D S of this County who Levied Atta on the Defts Effects is Allowed 20/ for Keeping 4 head * * * 3 Months & G. Issue.

(Pages 39 & 40 missing)

PAGE FORTY-ONE

August 1786—Demoss vs Roberson Dismissed at Pllfs Cost. Cook Assee vs Swanson Jud. Accordg to Specly & Cost & Int. James Callaway & Co. vs Cornelius Vanover Sr. Wm. Cowden Sp Bl. Griffith vs McDowell, Patrick Sloan, A Garshee being Summoned & failing to Appear, Jud. Is Granted him for £3 & costs. Stout vs Terry & Greer. Jud fa £2.18.0 & Costs. Trent vs Allen Jud Accordl to Spl & Cost. Stone vs Aday & Craighead, Henry Lavior Spl. Bl. Court is Adjourned till Tomorrow 10 O'Clock. ROBT INNES. August Rules 1786—Bates vs. Rentfro Not Guilty w'th leave & Issue. Barten vs Livesey Genl. Issue. Cole vs Doggett Genl. Issue. Cowan & Wife vs Martin C. O. Confirm'd.

PAGE FORTY-TWO

August Rules 1786 Con'd Fow'd. Greer vs Webb Not Debt & Issue. Harkrider vs Arthur Gl. Issue. Hook Assee vs Wood Genl. Issue. Hunt vs Clardy Gl. Issue. Johnson vs Doggett Gentl, Issue. Jones vs Clardy Cond. Love; vs Wynne C. O. Conf'd. Mavity vs Jonese Admx Non Asse & Issue. Miller vs Griffith des'd Agreed. Prunty vs Jones Admrx Paymt & Issue. Richardson vs Edwards C. O. Conf'd Same vs Same . . . . . . Same. Jona. Richardson vs Lockman Gl. Issue. Stewart vs Haynes. Cont. Stone vs Adey PaymI. & Issue. Saunders vs Weeks Gl, Issue. Snuffer vs Bybe & Bell C. O. Conf'd. Standifer vs Stokes Cont'd. Thorp vs Bell C. O. Conf'd. Same vs Rentfro John Rentfro Spl. Bl. Pas & Issue. Same vs Miller & C. O. Conf'd. Same vs Walton C. O. Conf'd. Same vs French C. O. Conf'd. Same vs Toney C. O. Conf'd. Same vs Miller Gl. Issue. Tcal vs Trarley Gl. Issue.

PAGE FORTY-THREE

August Rules 1786 Con'd Fow'd. Thomas vs Livesey C. O. Conf'd. Woods vs Willis Cont'd. Weeks vs Saunders. Not Guilty with Leave & Issue. Willison vs Rentfro Non Ass. & Issue. Walton vs Kelley Y Miller Net Debett & Issue. Same vs Same Same. Con, Wealth vs Ellis N. P. Same vs the Cleborne N. P. Same vs the Surveyor of Roads. Same vs Hieth N. P.

Arthur vs Jones & Martin Jud. Accordl. to Splly & Att'a Afect Reliat. Black vs Swanson Same. Chitwood vs Williams Spc. Imp. C. Callaway vs Price C. O. Dep & Bo. Clardy vs Hunt C. O. Clybourne vs Parker C. O. Cook asse vs Richardson Spl. Impl. & Oyer. Callaway & Early vs Stewart C. O. Dillion vs Blanken- ship Spl. Impl. Same vs Key N. Atta. Same vs Preston C. O. Deff & Shf. Sherewood vs Edwards Spl. Impl. Ferguson vs Bartee & Thompson Abates by Retn. Griffith vs Kelly Cont. Harris vs Storm Cont'd. Huckaby vs Patterson Impl. Same vs Hodges Same. Same vs Wilis.

PAGE FORTY-FOUR

August Rules 1786 bro. forw'd. Houser vs Jamerson C. O. Deft & Bl. Hall vs Pate Cost. Jones vs Spangler Spl. Impl. Same vs Same Same. Kelly vs Miller, Impl. Lovell vs Markum Jud. Accordl to Spy & Att. a Afect Reliated Thorp vs Woodson Cont'd. Lovell vs Swanson Atta. Miller vs Kelly Cont. Same vs ——— Kelly Cont. Martin vs Raley Atta. Miller Asse of Gib- son vs Kelly C. O. Deff & Bl. Moody Asse of Dimoss vs Booth C. O. Perryman vs Saunders & Impl. Pinkard vs Randall N. Atta. Patterson vs Hubbard C. O. Ramsey vs Livesey dis'd Deff Costs. Ryan vs King Ref'd to Hugh Innes & Saml. Collard in C.— does Not Agree to Choose an Umpire. Sloan vs Underwood. N. Publica. Standifer vs Rentfro Defts Costs. Snuffer vs Bybee Atta. Stokes vs Bartee dis'd Plf Costs. Storm vs Harris Cont'd. Swanson vs Haynes Atta. Stokes vs Goggins, Impl.

PAGE FORTY-FIVE

August Session 1786—At a Court of Quarterly Session Cont'd & Held for Franklin County On Tuesday the 8th. Day of Au- gust 1786. Present: Peter Saunders, Thomas Arthur, John Rent- fro, Hugh Innes, John Smith, Spencer Clack, Gent. Callaway & Early vs Thompson, Jud. for £22.9.0 & Cost & O. Conda. Dick- inson vs Perryman, Jud. for £1.7.0 & Cost & Atta. Effets Cond & Conten'd for Garshees. Grayham vs Danggar, Continued. Poteet vs Jones, Cont'd. ConWealth vs Huckaby. Jud. Accordl to Law & Costs. Same vs Webb . . . Same. Same vs Millam Same. Same vs Hall Cont. Same vs Keen Jud. Accorl. to Law & Costs. Same vs Sherwood. Same. Same vs Luttrell. Same. Same vs Huff Same. Same vs Carroll. Same. Same vs Webb.

Same. Same vs Thompson. Same. Same vs Richards. Same. Same vs Archer. Same. Same vs Dillingham Same.

PAGE FORTY-SIX

August Sessions 1786—Com Wealth vs Halcomb. Jud. Accordl. to Law. Same vs Turly. Same. Same vs Hunt. Same. Same vs Laefield. Same. Cook Asse vs Richardson, Ro. Williams Spl. Bl. & Spl. Iml. Calland vs Jamison, Jud. Grnt. Stokes vs Richardson, Judgt. Slone vs Sheredon Jud. for £4.10. & Cost. Spangler vs Miller, Thomas Prunty a Grn. being sworn saith he Owes the Deff £14, Judg accordl. to a former Jud. of Henry Court & Costs deducty. £7. to Rec'd at Jones's Admr's. Miller vs Griffith Dism'd At Defts Cost. Callaway & Co. vs Vanover, Judgt. Accordl to Ans. & Splly & Costs. Freebee & Elliott vs Rentfro, John Rentfro, Spl. Bl. Hilton vs Bryant, Jud. accorg to Spl. & Costs. Miller vs Jones & the Opinion of the Court is the Defts wife no right to assum Y. P. Demand & Dismiss'd with Costs. Walton vs Rentfro. Jud. Conf'd w'th Stay of Excon till Jan. & Cont. Calland vs Turly. Jud. Accoring to Specially & Cost. Hill vs Bartee Judgmt. Same vs Caster Jud. Accordl. to Specially & Cost. Same asee vs Markum, Jud. Accordl, to Sp. & Costs. Harkins vs Turley, Jud. Accordl to Splly. & Costs. Hill vs Webb Atta. Com Wealth vs Marlin. Jud. Agreeable to Recog'd & Cost. Same vs H. Martin Same.

PAGE FORTY-SEVEN

August Rules for 1786 Brought forward. Smith vs Cook. Cont. Walker vs Jones &c. Impl. Williams vs Cheetwood, Imp'l. Welch vs Spencer &c C. O. Defft & Shf. Saunders vs Early dis.'d Deffts. Costs. Hill vs Martin. Dism'd Agreed. Richardson vs Hubbard Att'a vs Garn. Haile vs McKinsey. Gl. Issue. Scott vs McGrady C. O. Deff & Shf. Demoss vs Clardy Spl. Impl. Metter vs Griffith. C. O. Demoss vs Binnion & Ac C. Parris vs Haile Spl. Impl. Asberry vs Stokes Spl. Impl. Welch vs Haile. Impl. Markum vs Hartwell N. P. Hodges vs Bird Cont'd. Sutherland vs Bell. Dism'd Agreed. Patterson vs King, C. O. Bailey vs Stockton Abates by Shfs. Act. Callaway & Early vs McDowell C. O. Clark &c vs Hunt &c C. O. Callaway & Co vs Taylor Atta. Same vs Richardson. N. P. Same vs Barnks. N. P. Smith & Elliott vs Rentfro. John Rentfro Spl. B. & Impl.

Doggett vs Johnson, Spl. Impl. Same vs Anderson &c Same. Haile vs Menifee. Impl. Holley vs Cockran. Impl.

PAGE FORTY-EIGHT

August Rules 1786, Con. forw'd. Ingram vs Rentfro, Cont. Menefee vs Haile. Spl. Impl. Mullender asee vs Bybee A. Capt. Price vs Woodsson, Impl. Same vs Same. Impl. Martin vs Farley. N. P. Trent vs Booth. C. O. Thorp vs Rentfro. A. C. Walton vs Same A. C. Callaway & Co. vs Haynes. Abates by Ret. Same vs Vanover. C. O. Gilliam vs Chitwood. C. O. Huston vs Levicey. C. O. Chitwood vs William. Spl. Impl. Sherwood vs Edwards. Impl. C. Wealth vs Hill N. Sl. Same vs Martin. Marlin vs Coleman. Atta. Woods & wife vs same C. O. Prunty vs Jones. C. O. Gordan vs Heard John Cox. Spl. Bl & Im. Miller vs Willis. C. O. Jenkins vs Ramesey. Doggitt vs Anderson & Wife, Abates by Ret.

PAGE FORTY-NINE

At a Court held at Franklin Courthouse on Wednesday the 30th. Day of August 1786 for the Examination of John Barnett for Stealing a Horse the Property of John Marr. Also One Other Horse the Property of Thomas Hale & Also by force of Arms Robing Samuel Durst of a Great Coat & Sundry Other Goods. Also, William Weeks on Suspicion of & for Aiding, Abeting & harbouring John Barnott & Henry Vincent Two Noted horse thieves & Sundry Other Crimes. ALSO, George Ramsey on Suspicion of Aiding, Abeting & harbouring John Barnott & Henry Vincent Two Noted Horse thieves & Sundry Other Crimes. PRESENT: Hugh Innes, Peter Saunder, Swinfield Hill, Thomas Arthur & Moses Greer Gent. The Said John Barnett being led to the Barr in Custody of Robert Woods Gent Sheriff of the said County to whose Custody for the Crimes aforesaid he was Commited and it being Demanded of the sd. Barnett he Was guilty of the facts wherewith he Stands Charged or not Guilty answered that he is Guilty, Whereupon the Court Proceeded to Examine Divers Witnesses as Well on Behalf of the Common Wealth as the Prisoners at Bar on Consideration whereof the Court are of Opinion that the s'd Barnett is guilty of the fact wherewith he stands Charged & that he Ought to Receive a further Tryal before the Honble the General Court in October Next, therefore he is remanded into the Custody of the Sheriff Aforesaid. Thomas Hale, William Rentfro & Sam'l Durst & Gideon Smith Came before the Court & Acknowledged themselves Severally Indebted to the Common Wealth of Virginia in the Sum of £100 each to be levied On their Respective Goods & Chattles Lands & Tenaments on Consideration they do not Appear before the Honble the Genl Court on the first Day thereof in October Next to give Testament Against the Said John Barnet who is charged with horse-stealing & Robbery.

PAGE FIFTY

The Said William Weeks was led to the Bar in Custody of Robert Woods Gen. Sheriff of the Said County to whose Custody for the Charge Aforesaid he was Committed and it being Demanded of the Said Weeks whether he was Guilty of the wherewith he stands Charged or Not Guilty, Answered that he was in no wise Guilty whereupon the Court Proceeded to Examine Divers Witnesses as well on Behalf of the Common Wealth as the Prisoner at the Bar on Consideration whereof the Court are of Opinion that the Said William Weeks is Guilty of the Crime Wherewith he stands Charged & that he Ought to Receive a further Tryal before the Honble the General Court in October on the first day thereof therefore he is Remanded into the Custody of the Sheriff Aforesaid. John Short & John Randolph Short, Came into Court & Acknowledged themselves Severally Indebted to the Common Wealth of Virginia in the Sum of £100 Each to be Levied on their Respective Goods & Chattles Land & Tenements on Condition they do not Appear before the Honble the Genl Court in October next on the first day thereof give Testimony in Behalf of the Common Wealth Agst the said William Weeks, Accused of Aiding Abeting & harbouring Horse thieves & Sundry Other Crimes.

PAGE FIFTY-ONE

The Said George Ramsay being Led to the Bar in Custody of Robert Woods Gen. Sheriff of the Said County to whose Custody he had been Commited for the Crimes Aforesaid And it being Demanded of the Said George Ramsey whether he was Guilty of the fact wherewith he Stands Charged Or not Guilty, answered that he was in no Wise Guilty. Whereupon the Court

Proceeded to Examine Divers Witnesses as well on Behalf of the Common Wealth as the Prisoner At the Bar in Consideration Whereof the Court are of Opinion that the Said George Ramsey is Guilty of the facts wherewith he stands Charged & that he Ought to Receive a further Tryal before the Honble the General Court in October Next on the first Day thereof, therefore he is Remanded into the Custody of the Sheriff Aforesaid. Thomas Hill & Susannah Ramsey came into Court & acknowledged themselves Severally Indebted to the Common Wealth of Virginia in the Sum of £100, Each to be levied on their Respective Goods & Chattles Land & Tenements on Condition they do not Appear before the Honble the General Court on the Day thereof to give Testimony in Behalf of the Common Wealth Against the Said George Ramsey, who is Accused of aiding & Abeting & harbouring Horsethieves, & Sundry Other Crimes. HUGH INNES.

PAGE FIFTY-TWO

September 1786—At a Court held for Franklin County on Monday the 4th Day of September 1786. Present: Hugh Innes, Thomas Arthur, John Smith, Jonathan Richison, Gent. Huston vs Levsey a Dedimas Awarded the Plff to Take the Deposition of Gabriel Jones, Giving Legal Notice. A Deed Christopher Skillmon to James Rodgers Prov'd & O. R. The Court are Of Opinion that Jud. may be granted on Replevy Bonds in the Intermediate Courts. A Deed Robert Prunty to Peter Finney Ackg'd & Fanney his Wife being Privily Examined Relinguished her Dower & O. R. Same to Francis Kerby the same. Richard N. Vennable Produced a Licence to Practice as an Attorney in this & the Other Inferior Courts of this State Whereupon he took the Oaths of an Attorney at Law. On the Mot. of Thomas Hale Jud. is Granted him Agst Joseph & Thomas Miller on Replevy Bl. & Costs. Also, Will Weeks & Js. Jenny the Same. Also Francis Thorp vs Jacob Blackburn & Jacob Wimmer the same. Also, Same vs Will & Tho Miller, the Same. A Deed Joshua Rentfro to Isaac Jones, Son & Heir of Isaac Jones Dec'd Ack'd & O. R. A Deed Daily Ryan to Isiah Wills Prov'd & O. R'd. Also Jesse Law to Saml Sullevant Ack'd & O. R'd. Also William Warren to John Rodgers Ack'd & Eliza his wife Being Privily Examined Relinguished her right &O. R'd.

September 1786—A Deed Danl Stewart to Edwr'd Winston Ack'd & O. R'd. Also William Weeks to Mich'l Coats Prov'd Webster his wife being Privily Examined Relinguish'd her Right & O. R'd. Also John Webster to Saml Webster Ack'd, Ann of Dower & O. R. Benja. Cook, Robert Prunty, Amos Richardson, Abram Vandevender, Or any three of them, are Appointed to View a way for a Road from Pittsya Old Courthouse Road to James Gap on Chesnut Mountain & from thence to the Road Leading to this Courthouse. Hook vs Slone Ud. Dism'd at Defts Cost. A Dedimus for the Examination of Mary Wife of Abil Edw'ds And a Deed to Danl Jett Ret & O. R'd. Martin vs Coulman Dismiss'd. A Report of a View of a Road from the County Road leading towards Henry Courthouse & from thence to David Stewarts Ret & O. R. And that James Beavers & a Gang belonging to his Road do Clear the Road (above) from the Road that leads to Henry Courthouse to William Jamisons. Also Daniel Richardson & His Gang from William Jamison to David Stewarts on Chesnut. William Sherwood is Appointed Sur'v of the Road from Chesnut Creek to the Road Leading to Tho. Hills & a List filed to be his Gang W'ch he is to Keep in Repair Accordl. to Law. Edward Choat Jr. is Appointed Sur'v of the Road from the fork of the Road that goes by Tho. Hills to this Courthouse & a list fild to be his Gang &c. A Deed George Griffith to Jacob Dillmon Prov'd by One Witness & O. C. Also Aaron Levinson to Jacob Dillmon Prov'd by One Witness & O. C.

PAGE FIFTY-FOUR

September 1786—Cowan to Hook Proved & O. R.'d. A Deed from Jacob Dillmon to Michel Peter Proved & Eliza Dillmon his wife being Privily Examined Reling'd her Right of Dower & O. R'd. The Last Will and Testament of Peter Craighead Dec'd was Exhibited in Court by Rich'd Radford & Mary Craighead the Executor & Exetx of therein Mentioned & Proved who made Oath According to Law & with Richard Compton. Their Surity Entered into Bond & Acknowledg'd the same (No Tax P'd). John Cletcher Came into Court & Craving the Peace of George Asberry & Thomas Parker, It is Ordered that the said Asberry & Parker Give Security for their Good behaviour towards

the Said Cletcher. Whereupon, the said George Asberry &
Thomas Parker Came into Court & with Nathaniel Tate & Jno.
Smith their Surity Severally Acknowledged themselves Indebted
to the Common Wealth of Virginia, that is to say Asberry &
Parker, in the sum of Twenty Pounds Each & the Said Suritys
in the Sum of Ten Pounds each to be Levied on their Respective
Goods & Chattels lands & Tenements, On Condition the said
Asberry & Parker be not of Good Behavior towards the Citizens
of this Common Wealth One Year & a Day & Especially to-
wards the Said John Cletcher. A Bill of Sale from Daniel Farley
to Lawrence McGeorge Proved & O. R'd. The Sheriff of this
County is fined the Sum of 40/ with Costs for non Attendance
on the Court. Philip Sherdan is Exempt from the Payment of
County Levies for the Future.

PAGE FIFTY-FIVE

September 1786—Kinzee Coats & Phillip Sheredan Came into
Court and Acknow'd themselves Severally Indebted to the Common Wealth of Virginia that is to say the Said Costs in the Sum
of £20. & the said Sheredan in the Sum of £10 to be levied on
their respective Goods & Chattles Lands & Tenaments on Condition the Said Kinsey Coats do not Appear before the Grand
Jury in Novem. Next on a Complaint lodged Against him for
leting a Prisoner Escape Out of his Custody. Richard Ballard is
Appointed Surveyor of the Road from James Martin's to the
County Line & List filed to be his Gang. John Johnson is Appoint'd Surveyor of the Road from the Botet. Line to the last
ford of Maggoty & the Former List to be his Gang. David Morgan
is Appointed Surveyor of the Road from the Last ford of Mag-
gotty to Isaac Rentfro & John Langdons List of hands to be his
Gang. Michajah Stone is Appointed Surveyor of the Road from
Town Creek to Chesnut Road & A List filed to be his Gang.
Thomas Hale, Chatten Doggett, George Ferguson & Moses Greer,
Or any three of them, are Appointed to Review a Road from
Said Doggett to Story Creek & Make Report thereof. Luke
Standifer, William Mullins, James Martin & Wm. Standley, Or
any three of them, are Appointed to View a Road from Story
Creek to the County line near Hickeys Cabbins & make report
thereof to the Court. William Thorp is Exempted from the Pay-
ment of County Levies for the future. Shores Price is Appointed

35

Surv. of the Road in the Room of Shadrick Woodson & Woodson's former List to be his Gang. Thomas Hale is Appointed Surveyor of the Road to w'ch he was formerly Appointed by order of Henry Court & his former List to be his Gang.

PAGE FIFTY-SIX

September 1786—A Deed Thomas Prunty to John Fuson Ackg'd & O. R.'d. Jacob Dillmon is Exempted from the Payment of County Levies in future. Edward Sweeny is Also Exempted. Present: Robert Hairston, Moses Greer & Swinfield Hill. Frederick Rives, John Dickenson, Hugh Martin & George Turnbull Gent. Are Recommended to his Excellency the Governor As Proper Persons to serve in the Commission of the Peace for this County. Court is Adjourn'd till Court in Course. HUGH INNES. At a Court held at Franklin Courthouse on * * * the day of September 1786 for the Examination of James Mead and William Ramey Who was Commited on Suspicion of being Confederates & Part Concered in Stealin a Negro Wench & Other Articles. Present: * * * Gent.

PAGE FIFTY-SEVEN

At a Court held at Franklin Courthouse on Wednesday the 13th. of September 1786, for the Examination of Robert Edmonds & Rebecca Edmonds his wife who Was Commited on Suspicion of Stealing from from Charles Doughton a Squirril Skin Purse and in it One doubloon, a Joannis, eight Joanneses, & One Guinea On Monday night the 4th Day of this Inst. at Rocky Mount. Present: Peter Saunders, Thomas Arthur, Jonathan Richeson, Swinfield Hill, John Smith & Moses Greer, Gent. The Said Robert Edmonds & Rebecca his Wife being led to the Bar in Custody of Robert Woods, Genl Sheriff of the Said County to whose Custody for the Cause Aforesaid they were Commited it being Demanded of the said Prisoners Whether they were Guilty of the fact wherewith they Stand Charged or not Guilty the s'd Robert Edmonds answered that he is Guilty of the fact wherewith he Stands Charged & Whereupon the Court Proceeded to Examine Divers Witnesses as well on behalf of the Common Wealth as the Prisoner at the Bar On Consideration whereof the Court are of Opinion that the Said Robert Edmonds

* * * Missing.

is Guilty of the fact wherewith he stands Charged & that he ought to Receive a further Trial before the Honble the Genl Court in October next on the first day thereof he is Remanded into Custody Again, Whereupon the Said Robert Edmonds Threw himself on the Mercy of the Court & it is Ordered that, he Stand One half Hour in the Pillory, receive 39 Lashes on his Bare Back & have Both Ears Croped. And the Said Rebecca is Discharged out of Custody, No Witness Appearing Against her. PETER SAUNDERS.

PAGE FIFTY-EIGHT

October 1786—At a Court held for Franklin County on Monday the 2nd Day of October 1786. Present: Hugh Innes, Spencer Clack, Jonathan Richeson, Swinfield Hill Gent. A Deed James Hubard to Levi Shockley further Prov'd & O. R'd. Allso John Ellis to William Smith . . . . . the Same. Also Josiah Marcum to Robert Napier . . . the Same. Also Joshua Brock to Ashford Napier Ack'd & O. R. Also John Rhea to George Tunbull Proved & O. R. Also John Gillaspy to Benja White Ack'd & Anna the Wife Being Privily Exam'd Reling'd her Dower & O. R'd. Also Darby Ryan to Andrew Reel Prov'd & O. R. Also Adam Teal to Thomas Watts Ack'd & Mary the Wife being Privily Exam'd Reling'd her Dower & O. R. Also William Griffith to John Scruggs Ack & Susannah the Wife being Privily Exam'd Relinguished her Right of Dower & O. R. Also John Jones to Jesse Dillon Ack'd & O. R'd. Also David Beheler to Enock Hodges Ack'd & Eliza the Wife being Privily Exam'd Relinguished her Right of Dower & O. R. Also James Greer to Thomas Quigley Ackn'd & Ellenor the Wife being Privily Examined Reling'd her Right of Dower & O. R'd. Also Saml Randall to Sam'l Lutterel Jr. Prov'd by 2 Witnesses & O. C. Also the Same to Danl. Jones Sr. the Same.

PAGE FIFTY-NINE

October 1786—Isham Hall. Ephraim Hammons & John Smith are Allowed One Days Attendnce Each as Witness to Prove a Deed from Thomas Hammons to Nathl. Parrot. A Deed Frederick Rives to Alex' Rives Ack'd & O. R'd. The last Will and Testament of Jesse Keely Dec'd was Exhibited in Court by John Keely & Frederick Rives the Executors therein named who made Oath Accordingly & with Robert Woods Sr. their Security entered into Bond in the sum of £500 & Acknowledged the Same According to Law—William Graves Sr. John Law Sr. Lewis Jenkins & William Haynes, or any three of them, Are Appointed to Appraise the S'd Estate. William Ramey & James Mead Appearing before this Court on their Recog'ce on Suspicion of Felony & not being further Prossa'd Are Discharged Out of Custody. Isham Blankenship is App'd Surveyor of the Road in the Room of John Lumsden. A Deed William Thompson to Stanhope Richeson Ack'd & Sarah the Wife being Privily Exam'd Relinguished her Right of Dower & O. R'd. Robert Wood Gent. Sheriff of this County Came into Court & with Frederick Rives, John Dikenson, Swinfield Hill Jonathan Richeson William Menefee Jr. & Robert Woods Jr. his Securities entered into Bond and Ack'd the Same for the True & faithful Collection of the Revenue Tax Accordl. to Law. Solomon Davis is Appointed Sur'v of the Pig River Road from Chesnut Creek to the top of the Hill at Grimmits Folley & List filed to be his Gang. A Deed Peter Gilliam to Jonathan Price Ack'd & Anna the Wife Being Privily Examined Reling'd her Right of Dower & O. R.

PAGE SIXTY

October 1786—Philmon Sotherland, William Swanson, Will Greer & Nathan Swanson or any three of them do View a Way the Nearst & Best Way from Anth's ford to the Head of Jacks Creek & make Report thereof. Frederick Rives, William Clay, Jno. Keen, & Elisha Keen Or Any three of them Do View a Way for a Road from the head of Jacks Creek to Intersect the Road that leads to Henry Courthouse by Robert Woodses. William Ferguson, Edm'd Sweney, Jacob Flower & Danl Ross Or any three of them do View a Way for a Road from the Pole Bridge Branch to the County line Near the Mouth of Nicholases Creek & Make Report thereof. John Grimmit is Exempted from the Payment of County Levies for the future. On the Motion of Stephen Smith, Jud is Granted him Against Arthur Edwards & Nathan Ryan for the Sum of £58.6.3. the Interest thereon from the Xth Day of May 1786, till paid & Cost On a Replevy Bond. Swinfield Hill, John Rentfro & Jonathan Richeson are Appointed to Receive the Prison when finished by Colo. Jas. Callaway. Cook vs Richardson Dedimus Awarded the Defendt, to take the

Deposition of Spencer Clack, Giving the Pltf Ten days Previous Notice. Court is Adjourned till Court in Course. HUGH INNES.

PAGE SIXTY-ONE

November Sessions 1786—At a Court of Quarterly Sessions Held at Franklin Courthouse on Monday the Sixth day of November 1786, Present: Hugh Innes, Thomas Arthur, Jonathan Richeson, John Smith & John Gipson & Peter Saunders, Gent. Hunt vs Clardy Refer'd to Wm. Terry & O. H. Trent & in Case on the Award they Disagree to Choose an Umpire & their Award or any 2 of them to be the Jud. of the Court. Clardy vs Hunt— the Same. Cook vs Smith. Jud. Conf'd Accordg. to Spl. & Cost. Same vs Same . . . . the Same. John Dukinson, Foreman. John Martin, Robert Prunty, Saml. Bird, Sam'l Patteson, Philimon Southerland, William Swanson, Benjamin Cook, Robert Hodges, James Stewart, Amos Richardson, Joseph S. Price, Owen Rubel, Peter Gearheart, Joseph Davis, John Willson, John Hunter, Wm. Hunter, Abraham Jones, John Charter & Antho. Pate were Sworn as a Grand Jury of Inquest for the Body of this County whereupon they Withdrew to Consult on their Presentments. Cheetwood vs Gilliam. Dismissed at Defetts Cost. Gilliam vs Cheetwood. Dismissed at Pltfs Cost. Harkrider vs Arthur. Dismissed at Pltfs Cost. Cook vs Warran Dism'd at Pltfs Cost. James Callaway & Co vs John Banks, Jno. Epperson Spl. Bl. & Jud. Confessed Accordl. to Spl. & Costs. Present: Robert Hairston, Gent.

PAGE SIXTY-TWO

November Sessions 1786—Bartee vs Thompson. Jerem. Holliday a Garshee being Sworn Sayeth he Owes the Defdt £3.15.0 Jud. for £2.15.3 & Costs & O. Condem'a & the Garshee Sayeth that the Above Sum of £3.15.0 is not due untill Xmas & then to be Paid In Iron. Wm. Austin vs Stephen Herd, Sam'l Webb a Garnishee being Sworn saith he has Sufficient in his hands of a Horse Of £12. Value which is ordered to be Sold towards Satisfying the Plts, Judmt. for £2.13.6 W'th Int. 27 & Costs. John Cheetwood vs Ashford Napier Jno. Woodall Spl. Bl Grayham vs Hurnt Geo Asberry Spl. Bl. Jud. Confess'd According to Spl. & Costs. Sam Calland vs Robert Kemmins, Jud Accordl. to Spl & Bl. Holliday came into Court & Prays Garnishment of the

Attachm'd Effects & Issue. Samuel Dillion vs Isham Blankenship, Elijah Blankenship & Elisha Blankenship, Dismiss'd at Plffs Costs. Same vs Same & Other. the Same. Cheetwood vs Coleman, Wm. Roberson. Spl. Bl. Law vs Davis, Sam'l Dillion A Garshee being Sworn Sayith he Owes the Defdt. Six Pounds. Jud. for £6 to be paid in Cattle & Ord. Conden'a & Costs. Patteson vs King, Wm. Jenkins Spl. Bl. & Impl. Clerk & Co. vs Hunt, Geo. Asberry Spl. Bl. Jud. Confessed Accordl to Spl. & Costs, Stay Exeon 2 Months. Jas. Callaway & Co. vs Booth. Jud. Cof'd Accg. to Splly & Costs Stay Excon 2 Months.

PAGE SIXTY-THREE

November Sessions 1786—The Grand Jury Returned into Court & made Several Presentments whereon Process is Ordered to Issue Trent vs Asberry & Others Jud. Confessd by Asberry, Pate & Radford for £816.18.11 Specia & £437.17.10. Certificates, Debt & Damages, there Interest & Damages to be remited in Case the Governor & Court Shall Remit the same to the Pltf, and Al. Capts vs Bandy & Abates as to Douglass. Court is Adjourned till Tomorrow 10. O'Clock. HUGH INNES. At a Court of Quarterly Sessions Continued & Held for Franklin County on Tuesday the 7th Day of November 1786. Present: Hugh Innes, Robert Hairston, Spencer Clack, Jonathan Richardson, Moses Greer, Gent. Trent vs Banghan. Jud. for £3.15.6 & Costs & O. Cond'a. Ferguson vs Stewart Cont'd at Defetts, Costs. Dickinson vs Perrymon, Rob. Williams A Garshee, being Sworn Sayith he owes the Def'd Nothing & Cont'd for S. Garshee. Bartee vs Pincards Exetrs, Award Ret for the Defedts & O. R'd. Stewart vs Haynes. Cont'd. Hall vs Pate, Secu'y for Cost to be given at Next Court or be Dis'd.

PAGE SIXTY-FOUR

November Sessions 1786—Hodges vs Bird. Dismiss'd. Demoss & Wife vs Hills Exors on hearing the Court being of Opinion the Pltfs Demand being not due. Same vs Pursey. Thorp vs French. Judgt. Miller vs Griffith Judgt, Award to Spy & Co. Spangler vs Parrott, Judgt, Award & to Ane & Co. Cook vs Hall, Judgt. Same vs Woodall, Judgt. Same vs Jamison, Same. Same vs Swanson. Same. Same vs Young, Same. Holland vs Jones, Judgt. Early vs Bartee, Same. Hook vs Ferguson, Same. Hamock vs Weaks, Same. Crump vs Parrott, Same. Callaway & Trent vs Jones, Same. Danger & Wife vs Sherdon, Did'd at Deft, Costs. Venables Exors vs Young, Judgt. Stewart vs Dillon, Jud. Miller vs Jones Adm'rs Jud. for £3. when Assets. Hunter vs Stogdon, Cont'd Absence Peter Saunders. Saunders Assee vs Bates, Jud. Accordg to Spy.

PAGE SIXTY-FIVE

November Sessions 1786—Young vs Weeks, Cont'd. Dotson vs Campbell Atta. v Garshee. Ferguson. vs Martin, Atta v. Garshee. Hill vs Anderson, Jud. Accordg. to & Co. O. Bond. Same vs McDaniel. Jud. Accordg. Spl & Costs & O Cona. Thorp vs Stout & Woodson, Jud is Granted the Pltf, Agst the S'd Woodson as Security for S'd Stout on Rep. Bond & Costs. Com. Wealth vs the Surveyor of the Road from Foxes Cabbins to Story Creek on Present, Ord. to be Dismiss'd Same. vs. the Surv, of the Road from Story Creek to the Iron Works Road On Prest. the Same. Com. Wealth vs the Surveyor of the Road from Jno. Bratchers on Stanton to Gills Creek, On the Same. Comm. Wealth vs the Sur' of the Road from Gills Creek to the Mouth of Magotty, the Same. Stokes vs Bartee . . . Jud. Confessed for 52/ with Stay of Excon. Demoss vs Bennie & Edwards, Jno Chitwood Spl. Bl. Cook vs Smith Nathan Swanson Spl. Bl. Same vs Same, the Same. Slone vs Vanover & Jamison & Jud. is Granted the Plaintiff Agst the Defedts Security in Replevy Bond & Costs. Bates vs Rentfro. Dism'd. Jones vs Clardy, Dismissed at Deffts Costs. Dillion, vs Mead Jud. for £30 & Jas. Callaway a Garshee being Sworn Sayith he hath in his hands Sufficient to Satisfy the Pltfs Demand R. C. in Bar Iron, Castings & Steel & Spcie & O. Condina.

PAGE SIXTY-SIX

November Sessions 1786—Common Wealth vs Dillingham A Jury Sworn & Returned a True Bill Agst the said Dillingham & O R'd. Cole vs Doggett. A Jury Sworn Verdict Returned for the Defdt & Nonsuit With Costs. Hale vs McKinzee A Jury Sworn. Verdict Ret. for the Pltf for £12. & O. R'd. Greer vs Webb Cont'd at Dfdts Costs. Hale vs McKinzie, Joseph Ellis Spl. Bl. & Delivered the Defdt up, Whereupon he is Prayed Commit'd. Stokes vs Goggins Dedimus Awarded the Defdt to take the Deposition of Cornelius Decease, Giving 10 Days notice D be ressee. Kinzey Asse. vs Miller, Tho. Miller Jr & Wm Miller Spl Bl. Welch vs Hale, Jno Willis Spl. Bl. Slone vs Underwod, It is Ordered & Decreed that the s'd Underwood After hearing the Bill Read, that he shall Convey unto the Pltf the 224 Acres of Land therein Mentioned & that the Defdt have Nine Months to Convey the Same in fee Simple. Court is Adjourned till To-morrow 9 O'Clock. HUGH INNES.

PAGE SIXTY-SEVEN

November Sessions 1786—At a Court Continued & Held for Franklin County of Quarterly Sessions, on Wednesday the 9th day of November 1786. Present: Hugh Innes, Peter Saunders, Moses Greer, Swinfield Hill & Thomas Arthur, Gent. An In-junction is Granted Nathan Swanson on his Mot. to stay the Proceedings of a Jud. Obtained agst him by Thomas Black and With Usebus Hubbard his Security entered into Bond & Ac-knowledged the Same. Thorp vs Isaac Rentfro, David Morgan Spl. Bl. & Spl. Impl. Willson vs Isaac Rentfro . . . . . Same. Joel Chitwood is Allowed One Days Attendance as a Witness for Jas Dillion vs William Mead. John Griffith is Allowed One Days Attendance as a Witness for Tho. Arthur ads Harkrider. John Gipson the Same. Holloday vs Willson, Lewis Davis Spl. Bl. Johnson vs Doggett Cont'd at Defdts Costs. Martha Miller is Allowed 2 Days Attendance as a Witness for Johnson vs Doggett. Mary Hartwell the Same. Hook Assee vs A Jury Sworn. John Edwards is Allowed 2 days Attendance as a Witness Stephen Wood ads Jno Hook. Philip Raley, the Same. James Burns, the Same.

PAGE SIXTY-EIGHT

November Sessions 1786—Richardson vs Lockman Dism'd Agreed. Maviety vs Jones Adm'r. Jury Sworn Issue waved & Jud. Confessed for £19.14 & Costs. when Assets. Graham vs Danger. A Jury Sworn Verdict Ret for the Defdt, a New Tryal Granted the Pltf on Paying the Cost of the Day. John Bates is allowed 2 Days Attendance as a Witness for William Mavity vs Joneses Adm'rs. Robert Mavity is Allowed 3 Days for the same. Poteet vs Jones a Jury Sworn Verdict Ret for the Pltf & O. R'd. Saunders vs Weeks, a Jury Sworn Verdict ret for the Pltf for

£50. & O. R. Lewis Davis is Allowed 3 days Attendance as a Witness for Ralph Douger ads Graham. William Thompson is all'd the same Attendance for Graham vs Dangger. Absent Hugh Innis & Spencer Clack-Gent. Richardson Assee vs Edwards, Hugh Innis & Spencer Clack Spl. Bl. & Delivered the Defdt up—Richard Newton is Allowed 3 days Attendance & Once Coming and Returning 35 Miles as a Witness for Saunders vs Weeks. Present: Hugh Innes. Absent: Moses Greer. Thorp vs Greer Jud Conf'd accordg. to Spl Stay Exeor 2 mo & an Attorneys &c not to be Taxed. Weeks vs Saunders Security to be given for Costs at the next Court Or to be Dismissed, William Ferguson Sur'y for Costs. Lewis Davis is Allowed 2 days Attend as a Witness for William Crump v. Parrot.

PAGE SIXTY-NINE

November Sessions 1786—On the Mot. of George Hancock Gent. Attorney for Wm. Weeks for a New Tryal Peter Saunders vs Said Weeks, the Same is Reported w'th Costs. Saml. Hairston is allowed 1 Day Attend. as a Witness for Peter Saunders vs Weeks. Also 6 Days Attendance for Maviety vs Joneses Adm'rs. Court is Adjourned till Tomorrow 8 O'Clock. HUGH INNES. At a Court of Q. Sessions Continued & held for Franklin County on Thursday the 9th. of November 1786. Present: Hugh Innes, Thomas Arthur, Moses Greer, Spencer Clack & Peter Saunders, Gent. Parriss vs Hale. Thomas Prunty Spl. Bl. Prunty vs Jones Adm'rs A Jury Sworn, Verdict Ret'd For the Pltf, that there is no more than £900. Paid to the Plaintf. Also One hundred & Eighty, Also the Bal. to be Scaled, at 65 for On & O R'd. Stone vs Aday & Craghed, Jud Accordl to Sply & Costs with Stay of Exon until the Pltf shall file a Deed in the Clks Office for Conveyance of the Land in Dispute Between the Parties. Thorp vs Woodson A Jury Sworn to wit, Saml, Hairston, Jno, Terry David Barton, Joshua Willson, Lansford Hall, Usebus Stone, Thomas Jones Sr. Jno Hale, Thomas Black, William Henderson, William Miller and Rich'd Ballard. Verdict Ret: for the Pltf, for £8.1.9. & O. R'd. Teal vs Farley, Cont'd.

PAGE SEVENTY

November Sessions 1786—Thorp vs Tho. Miller Sr. Jud. Conf'd Accordl. to Sply & Costs. Weeks vs Saunders. absent

Peter Saunders A Jury Sworn to wit, Benjamin Cook, John Terry, David Barton, Joshua Willson, Lansford Hale, Thomas Jones, Sr, John Hale, William Henderson, William Miller, Richard Ballard, Usebus Stone & Thomas Black. Verdict Returned for the Defedt & O. R'd & Jud, According. Willson vs Rentfro. Cont'd. Samuel Hairston is Allowed 2 days Attendance as a Witness for 2 Days Attend as a Witness for Weeks vs Saunders. Woods vs Willis. A Jury Sworn, to wit, Danl. French, William Ferguson, William Maviety, Jas. Stokes, Robt. Perryman, John Livsey, Walter Aday, Rob. Mason, Sam'l Hairston, Jno. Fuson, Jno, Edwards & Lewis Bryant, Verdict Ret'd for the Pltf for £4.0.0 & non Suit & Costs Atta for Sellers Att'd Iss'd. Elizabeth Wattson is Allowed 4 Days Attendance as a Witness for Willis ads Woods. Mary Spangler is Allowed 6 Days Attendance as a Witness for Woods Agst. Willes. Jean Sellers is Allowed 6 Days for the Same. Greer. vs Webb. A Dedimus is Granted the Pltf. to take the Depo. of Wm. Anderson Giving 16 Days Notice. Walton vs Kelly, Cont'd. Same vs Same. Same. Price, vs Woodson, Jud. by Nonsum & Informatus & Costs. Same vs Same the Same.

PAGE SEVENTY-ONE

Ross & Co. vs Swansons Extrs. leave Granted to Amend Writ Parriss vs Hale leave is Granted the Pltf to take the Depo, of Alex' Thomas. Giving 10 Days notice. Court is Adjourned till Court in Course—HUGH INNES. At a Court held for Franklin County on Monday the 20th day of November 1786, for the Examination of Jonas Jordan, On Suspicion of Stealing A Sorrel Horse of the Value of £20, the Property of James Fulkinson, Also One Woms Saddle the Property of Charles Semmons. Present: Thomas Arthur, Jonathan Richeson, Swinfield Hill & Moses Greer, Gent. The Said Jonas Jordan being led to the Bar in Custody of Robert Woods Gent. Sheff of S'd County to whose Custody he had been Commited for the Crimes aforesaid & it being Demanded of the Said Prisoner whether he was Guilty of the fact wherewith he stands Charged Or not Guilty, Answered that he was in no Wise Guilty whereupon the Court Proceeded to examine Divers Witnesses as well in Behalf of the Common Wealth as of the Prisoner at the Bar. On Consideration Whereof the Court are of Opinion that the said Jonas Jordan is Guilty of the facts wherewith he stands Charged & that he Ought to receive a further Tryal before the Honble the Genl. Court on the Second Tuesday in December Next, therefore he is remanded into the Custody of the Sheriff Afores'd. Frederick Fulkinson & James Fulkinson & Elijah Dowell Came into Court & Acknowl'd themselves Indebted to the Commonwealth of Virginia in the Sum of £100 each to be levied on their Respective Goods & Chattles, Lands & Tenements On Condition they do not Appear before the Honble the Gen'l.

PAGE SEVENTY-TWO

The Genl. Court in the City of Richmond on the 2nd Tues-day in Decm. next in Behalf of the Common Wealth Against the Said Jonas Jordan who is Accused of Stealing A Sorrel Horse of the Value of £20 of James Fulkinson & a Womans Sadle the Property of Charles Simmons. T. ARTHUR.

Pages 73-74-75-76-77-78-79-80-81 are blank.

PAGE EIGHTY-TWO

November Rules 1786—Patteson vs King Parment & Issue. Demoss vs Key Al Caps. Hill vs Webb. Jud. Accordl. to Sply & Atta. Effects Released. Hackaly vs Willson. C. O. & Atta. Effects Released Lovell vs Swanson, Jud. Accordl. to Splly & Costs & Atta Effects Released. Martin vs Raley. W. E. & Ord. Condema of Atta. Effects Pincards vs Randal, Abates by Ret. Snuffer vs Bybe, Jud. Accordl. to Sp. & Atta Effects Released. Swanson vs Haynes Jud, Accordl to Sp. & Atta effects Released. Richardson vs Hubbard, N, Atta. Demoss &c Binnian &c vs Binnion & C. O. v Edwards Marcum vs Hartwell, Jud. Accorl. to Accot. Callaway & Co. vs Taylr Jud. Accordl. to Sp. & Atta effects Released. Same vs Richardson C. O. vs Defdt & Shf. Same vs Banks C. O. Mullender vs Bybee Atta. Martin vs Farley. Pl. Caps. Thorp vs Rentfro C. Order. Martin vs Cowlmen. Dism'd. Jones vs Webb, Impl. Com. Wealth vs Ellis N. P. Same vs Frame N. P. Same vs Kieth. N. P. Same vs Greer. Oyer. Same vs —————. Same vs Hill. Jud. Same vs Roberts, Jud. Ac-cordl. to Law. Same vs Mullins, Judg. Accorg. to Law. Same vs McCravey N. P.

PAGE EIGHTY-THREE

November Rules 1786—Com. Wealth vs Kelley N. P. Same
vs Callaway Oyer. Same vs Jno. Kelley Jud. Accordl. to Law.
Same vs Doggett. N. P. Same vs Chitwood N. P. Same vs Bates,
Oyer. Same vs Griffith. N. P. Same vs Terry N. P. Same vs
Edmondson Jud. Accordg. to Law. Same vs Hale. N. P. Same
vs Martha Vincent, N. P. Same vs Sarah Johnson. N. P. Same
vs John Gipson. N. P. Same vs Sarah Johnson, N. P. Same vs
James Bird. N. P. Early vs Pate &c Dis'd by Plfs Order. Cheet-
wood vs Coleman, Impl. Spl. Kinsey vs Miller, C. O. Holliday
vs Wilson C. O. Deft & Shf. Same vs Same. Cont. Callaway
& Rent vs Christian. C. O. Deft & Bl. Ross & Co. vs Swansons
Adm'r & C. O. Hent vs Bartee. Atta. Dudlsey vs Markum.
C. O. Jenkins vs Wynne &c Atta vs Wynne & 6. 0 vs the other.
Logan Assee vs Gordon, C. O. Rentfro vs Bates. C. O. Same vs
Doggett. C. O. Clay vs Wilson. AC. Thorp vs Greer. C. O.
Same vs Rentfro Cont:

PAGE EIGHTY-FOUR

November Rules 1786—Callaway Shf vs Guterys Exors Spl Im.
Same vs Same. Same. Callaway & Co. vs Booth, Jud. by Default.
Morgan vs Hodges. N. P. Cook Assee. vs Weaks, C. O. Wilson
vs Smith Exors, Spl Impl. Rentfro vs Rowland & C. O. vs Webb
& Bl. & A Capt Rowland. Lawrance vs Rentfro. C. O. Cook
vs Young N. P. Same vs Davis Wm. Davis Spl. Bl'd & Impl.
Same vs Realey & N. P. Same vs Parrott C. O. Same vs Same.
C. O. Same vs Perryman, C. O. Same vs Ulman, C. O. Doe vs
Roe Jno Hook Makes himself the Plt. & Chs. Vincent & James
Wright, came into Court & Made themselves Def't Leave Entry
& ouster Conf'd. Not Guilty & Issue. Ferguson vs Miller, C. O.
Stober vs Davis Patterson Spl. Bl. & Impl. Young vs Simmons.
Murphie & Co vs Hunt. A. C. Cheetwood vs Napier. Spl. De-
lancy vs Bates. Impl.

PAGE EIGHTY-FIVE

November Rules 1786—Delancy Q vs Bates D'd. Ogler vs
Turner. Dismiss'd. Jamison vs Gordon C. O. Calland vs Gorman
C. O. Thompson vs Greer, Spl. Impl. Farley vs Martin C. O. V
Df & Sh. Saunders vs Kelly. Cont'd. Same vs Rentfro C. O.

Flowers vs Rentfro Dismissed. Patteson vs Bird. Dism'd Agreed. Saunders vs Bybee Jud. Arthur vs Carter & Livsey C. O. Jones vs Jones Peter Saunders Spl. & Impl. Hoff vs Hale C. O. Parriss vs Hale Dismiss'd. Mead vs Rentfro. Cont'd.

PAGE EIGHTY-SIX

December 1786—At a Court held for Franklin County On Monday the 4th Day of December 1786. Present Peter Saunders, Thomas Arthur, Swinfield Hill, Robert Hairston & Moses Greer, Gent. The County of Franklin for the Year 1786 is made Dr. U Tob'o. To the Clerk for his Annuel Sallery................1248; To the States Attorney................Do................1248; To the Sheriff Do................1248; To the Surveyor of the County for Runing the Divid'g Line................1084; To Easter Rentfro, for Young Wolfs head............050 To Thomas Stanten for 1 Old & 4 Young Do................300; To John Rodgers for Serving as a Guard 14 Days Over John Barnett & Others................350; To Pierson Hale for Do 3 Days as a Guard over James Stokes................75; To Peter Saunder John Parker for Guardg. Barnett & Other 9 Days................225; To William Willson........4 Days Do............100; To Benja Hale................8 Days Do................200; To Thomas Prunty Assee of Charles Bradshaw 4 Days Do................150; To John Hale................7 Days Do................175; To Tho Prunty Assa of Berryman Shumate. 9 Days Do................225; To Peter Geerheart for Two Pair Hand Cuffs................50; To Alexander Watson for Guarl. the Prison over John Barnet & als 8 Days..........200; To Owen Ruble for Damages Done a horse & Sadle in Conveying Jno. Bernard to the P. Gaol................240; Carried forw'd 7286.

PAGE EIGHTY-SEVEN

December 1786—Br. Forward 7286; Elijah Warron for guarding William Dillingham 6 days................150; To Luke Thornton for the Same 7 Days................175; to Obediah Gravet Same 2 Days................50; To Thomas Warren Same 6 Days................150; To Daniel Brown for Visits & Medicines for Jno. Barnet a Wounded Prisoner................920; To George Ferguson for Guarding James Stokes 3 Days................75; To Walter Bernard Guardg. Jno Bernard 6 Days................150;To Hugh Woods for Keeping Wm. Dillingham 6 Days................50; To Jas. Callaway & Co. Assee of Thomas Prunty as & Account................864; To Thomas

Doggett Jr. Guardg. Bernard 11 Days................275; To William Wright for 9 Young Wolfs heads................450; To Edw'd Willson, Guardl. Jno. Bernard 6 Days................150; To James Greer Guardg Do................4 Do................100; To Jas Callaway & Co Asse of Robert Mason for Guarding Jno. Barnett 6 Days..........150; Tom David Atkins for Do 4 Days................100; To the Gaoler as & Account 2952 W. Tobo................2952; To Tho. Prunty, D Shf, for Conveying Jno Bernard to the Publick Gaol...........1000; To James Callaway & Co Asse of Janes Herd 7 Days as a Guard Over Jonas Jordan................175; To the Clerk as & Account.... ....3220; To Alex Rives for Damage done a Horse Remg. Ramsey................200; To Daniel Ross as Guard Over Weeks & Bernard 2 days................50; To Joshua Noals for Removg. Barnet from Colo Saunders................112; To Thomas Hale for Self & Horse Removg Barnet................33; To Robert Carter L P. Hand Cuffs................40; To Peter Saunders for Expences Allen G. Barnet & Weeks................50; To Owen Ruble 3 Days Guard Over Bernett & Weeks................75; Carried Over 1808.

PAGE EIGHTY-EIGHT

December 1786—Thomas & Sebret Crutcher Came into Court & Chose William Menefee Sr. their Guardian, whereupon the Said Wm. Menefee With James Callaway his Security Ent'd into Bond & Ack'd the Same According to Law. Hugh Woods Producing A Comin Appointing him a Lieut of the Militia for this County & Qualf'd Accordg to Law Swinf'd Hill, Thomas Hale & Jonathan Richeson Produ'd a Com'n. from his Excellency the Gov. Apptg. them Capts in the Militia of this County Whereupon they Qu'd According to Law. Samuel Haiston, Joshua Rentfro & Isaac Rentfro & Skelton Taylor the Same. Jubal Early Qual. as Lieutena. Thomas Hill, Lewis Davis & William Rentfro Qual'd as Ensigns. Court is Adjourned till Tomorrow 9 OClock. PETER SAUNDERS.

PAGE EIGHTY-NINE

December 1786—At a Court Continued & Held for Franklin County on Tuesday the 5th. Day of December 1786. Present Robert Harston, Swinf'd Hill, Moses Greer & John Dickenson, Gent. A Deed William Maviety to William Kennedy Ack'd & O. R'd Tax P'd. John Dickenson Esq. Sher of this County is

Appointed to Purchase Record Books for his Office & to be Repaid Out of the County Depositum. The Clerk of the Court is Appointed to furnish a Press for the Use of the County & to be Paid Out of the County Depositum. On the Motion of Francis Thor by Rich'd Veneble his Att A Jud is Granted him Against Joseph Miller & Saml Stout on Replevy Bond With Costs. Also the Same vs William Bell & Will Kelley the Same. Also George Snuffer vs William Bell & Wm. Kelley the Same (no Secury to be taken). Court is Adjourned till Court in Course.—T. ARTHUR.

PAGE NINETY

December Rules 1786—Demoss vs Key Plu Caps. Huckaby vs Willson Ret. Guilty w'th Leave & Issue. Martin vs Raley Cont'd. Richardson vs Hubbard N. Atta vs Garshee. Demoss Exetr &c vs Benian & Edwards C. O. Conf'd vs Edwards. Plee Caps Binion. Mullenden Assee vs Bybee, New Atta. Martin vs Farley Al Plee. Thorp vs Isaac Rentfro Payl & Issue. Jones vs Webb Gl. Issue. Com. Wealth vs Ellis. N. P. Same vs Frame. N. P. Same vs Keith. N. P. Same vs Greer Genl. Issue. Same vs Elij. McCravy N. P. Same vs Callaway Gl. Issue. Same vs Doggett N. P. Same vs Chitwood N. P. Same vs Bates Gl. Issue. Same vs Griffith N. P. Same vs Terry N. P. Same vs Eliza. Hale N. P. Same vs Martha Vincent N. P. Same vs Sarah Johnson N. P. Same vs Same N. P. Same vs Gipson N. P. Same vs Bird N. P. Kinzey vs Miller C. O. Conf'd. Haolladay vs Willson Co. O. Conf'd & W. E. Same vs Same Cont'd. Callaway & Trents vs Christian C. O. Conf'd. Ross & Co. vs Swanson Admrx. Same.

PAGE NINETY-ONE

Decem. Rules Continued. Hunt vs Bartee. Cont'd. Jenkins vs Wynne & Ramsay, Atta v Wyne. W. E. V. Ramsey. Logan Assee vs Gordan C. O. M. Rentfro vs Bates tax. C. O. Conf'd W. E. Same vs Doggett Same. Clay vs Willson Plee Caps. Thorp vs Greer Sr. C. O. Conf'd. Callaway vs Brooks & Guttereys Exetrs. Payl. & Issue. Same vs Same the Same. Morgan vs Hodges N. P. Jno. Rentfro vs Pyett N. P. Cook Assee vs Weeks C. O. Conf'd. Willson. vs Smith Exetr Non Asse & Issue. Rentfro vs Rowland & Webb C. O. Conf'd v Webb & P. Caps. V. Rowland. Lawrence vs Js. Rentfro. C. O. Conf'd. H. Cook vs Davis. Paymt & Issue. Same vs N. Parrott C. O. Conf'd. Same vs Same. Same. Same vs Perrymon. Same. Same vs T. Parrot Same. Holland vs Jones Cont'd. Ferguson vs Miller C. O. & W. E. Stover . . . Davis C. O. Conf'd & W. E. Cheetwood vs Napier Non Asse & Issue. Muchie & Co. vs Hunt Plee Caps. Delancy vs Bates Not Guilty w'th Leave & Issue. Same vs Same C. O. Conf'd & W. E. Jamison vs Gordon Same. Calland vs Gormon C. O. Conf'd Thompson vs Greer. Not Guilty w'th leave & Issue. Farley vs Martin C. O. Conf'd.

PAGE NINETY-TWO

December Rules cont'd. Saunders vs Kelley Jr. Cont'd. Same vs Jesse Rentfro C. O. Conf'd. Arthur vs Carter & Livsey C. O. Conf'd V Levsey & W. E. Rachel Jones vs Jones Gl Issue. Hoff vs Hale C. O. Conf'd & W. E. Hunter vs Stogdon Cont'd. Mead vs Rentfro, Cont'd. Young vs Weeks Cont'd. At A Court held for Franklin County on Monday the first day of January 1787. Present: Hugh Innis, Peter Saunders, Thomas Arthur, Robert Haiston, Moses Greer Jr., & Swinf'd Hill, Gent. Squires vs Craigheads Dism'd Pltfs Cost ch. Colo Mykepe Saml. Calland vs Gormon Dismiss'd Defdt. Hunter vs Stogdon a Dedamus Awarded the Defdt to Take the Depo. of Isaiah Walkins & John Willson, Gvg 10 Days Previous Notice. A Deed from McGrady to James Wray Proved by 3 Witnesses & O. R'd. A Deed from Will. Archer to Isham Choat Ack'd & O R'd. A Deed from Archelaus White to Jno Van Maple Proved by 2 Witnesses & O. C. Record. Paid & Tax.

PAGE NINETY-THREE

A Deed from Sam'l Randolph to Saml Letter & further Proved by one Witness & O. R'd. A Deed from Saml. Randolph to Danl. Jones, the Same. A New Commission from under the Seal of the Common Wealth to Hugh Martin & Others was Presented in Court Whereupon the Said Hugh Martin took the Oath of a Justice of the Peace for the County of Franklin & a Justice of Oyer & Tumener. Burwell Reives Presented a Commission from under the hand of his Excellency the Governor, Appointing him a Capt. of the Militia for this County & Qual.

Accordingly. Samuel Hairston, Joshua Noles, Owen Ruble & Thomas Hale, Or any Three of them, do View a Way for a Road from Saml. Garst to this Courthouse & make Report thereof to this Court. A Deed from Jacob Clower to John Jakes (Jacques) Ack'd & Anna the Wife being Privily Examined Relinguished her Dower & O. R'd. On the Mot. of Jas. Stokes vs Richardson & Martin By Rich'd Venable his Atto Jud. is Awarded the Pltf On Repley Bl. A Deed from Will Vincent to Geo. Robertson Proved by Two Witnesses & O. C. A Deed from Will Vincent to Ann Praddy further Proved by one Witness & O. R. Arthur v Martin, Jud. Confedd'd by Martin On Repley Bl & Costs. David Morgan is Appointed Liet, in Capt. Rentfros Compny of Militia in the Room of Geo. Turnbull who Refuses to Serve. Abram Absher is Appt'd Ensign to Said Compy. Robert Woods Gent Shiff Came into Court & entered into Bond in the Penalty of £1000 for the Collection of the County Levy with Jno Martin, Hugh Martin, Jno Woods & Robert Woods Jr. their Securitys & Ack'd the Same.

PAGE NINETY-FOUR

John Smith & William Ryan Qual. as Captain of the Militia for this County. George Asberry Quallif'd as a Deputy Sheriff for the Collection of his Old Arrears due in this County. Hook vs Griffiths Jud. Granted the Pltf on Replevy Bond & Costs. It is Ordered that the Shereff Collect the County Levy at 12/6 & Cert.

PAGE NINETY-FIVE

County Levy Bro. forw'd U Tob 233.82; To the Shereff for a Crill'd Court Over Robert Edmunds................200; James Mead ....200; Jonas Jordan................200; 23.982. Depositum for the Use of the County................2070. 26052. To the Shereff for Collecting 25982 U Tobo at 6 P Cent................1558; 27600. 27610. 1255 Tythes at 22 U Tobo Tythe........is................27610. Court is Adjourned till Court in Course.—HUGH INNES.

PAGE NINETY-SIX

At A Court held for Franklin County on Monday the 5th, Day of February 1787. Present: Peter Saunders, Thomas Arthur, Jonathan Richardson, Moses Greer and John Smith, Gent. Ferguson vs Stewart. Ref'd to Jonathan Richards & John Smith & in Case they Disagree to chuse an Umpire & His or their Determination to be the Jud. of this Court. An Inventory of the Estate of Henry Guttry Ret. & O. R'd. A Deed from Wm. Duease to James Webb Ack'd & O R'd. Also a Deed from Benja. Clardy to Jno. Hook Prov'd & R. R'd. Also William Swanson Sr. to Philimon Sutherland. Same. Also John Craighead to Peter Cragheads Orpin Ack & O. R'd. Also John Epperson to Rich'd Radford the Same. Also Jesse Law to Frances Bell the Same, Recordl. Paid & Tax. Also John Craighead to George Kee the Same. Also William Kee the Same. Also William Trent to John Sullvant. the Same. George Turnbull One of the Gent. named in the new Commission of the Peace, Came into Court & took the Oaths to the Common Wealth. Also as a Justice of the Peace, A Justice of Oyer & T'mer & a Justice in Chancery. Leave is Granted to Saml. Webster to Build a Water Grist Mill on Blackwater, he being Proprietor of the Land or Both Sides Said Stream.

PAGE NINETY-SEVEN

A Deed from John Thorp to Richard Thorp Prov'd & R. R'd. William Toney, Saml Henderson, Jacob Wimmer, & Jacob Miller, or any three of them, are App'd View a Way for a Road from the Hf Way Spring to Jacob Millers & make report thereof to the Court. A Deed from Francis Kerby to Harmon Cook further Prov'd & O. R'd. Also from Jonathan Pratt to John Craghead Proved by One Witness O. C. A Deed from Peter Gillam to Joel Chitwood Proved by 2 Witnesses & O. C. Also from William Trent to Smith Webb Ack'd & O R'd. Joshua Rentfro is Appointed Sur of the Road from the ford of B. Water at Theo Webbs to the ford of Pigg river At Robert Joneses & the List to be filed to be his Gang. Joel Walker is Appointed Surv of the road from the Ford of Pigg River at Robert Jonses to Ryans Cabbins & List to be filed to be his Gang. A Deed from John Kerby to Ashford Napier Prv'd by 1 Witness & O. C. David Barton, Thos. Jones, Joshua Rentfro & Jacob Prillamon, or any three of them, are Appointed View Bartons & Jonses Sper and Make Report to the Court W'ch is the best for a Road. William Rentfro Qualif'd as A Capt of the Militia for this County. David Barton, Luke Standefer & Jno. Divers Qual'd as Lieuts. Israel Standifer, Jno Taylor & Peter Holland as Ensigns.

PAGE NINETY-EIGHT

A Report of a View of a Road from Sam'l Drists to Franklin Courthouse Ret & O R'd. Bailley Carter is Appointed Sr. of the Road from Otter Creek near Gideon Smiths to the first Branch near the Pole Bridge. William Ferguson is Appointed Surv of the Road from the Branch Near the Pole Bridge to the X Roads. Luke Standifer from the X. Roads into the Road leading to I. Works. Capt. Hale With his Gang to Open a Road from the Road leading to the Iron Works to F. Courthouse. Edward Richards is appointed Sur. of the Road from the North fork of Chesnut Creek down to Pigg River Road & List fild to be his Gang. White vs Quizley. Dismiss'd. A Deed from Abel Edwards to Danl. Jett Proved by One Witness & O. C. A Report for the View of a Road from Chattin Doggets to Story Creek, Re & O. R. John Early is appointed Capt, of the Company of Light Infantry. Moses Greer Jr, is App'd Lieut to S'd Compy. John Hale. Ensign to S'd Compy. Jubal Early is App'd a Capt of the Militia in the room of Early who has excepted of a Capt's Commission in the Light Infantry. William Wright is Appointed Liuten. to S'd Compty William Charter is Appointed Ensign.

PAGE NINETY-NINE

William Chitwood vs Thomas Parker. Dismiss'd. Leave is Given John Dickinson Esq. to Build a Water Grist Mill on Pigg River, he being Proprietor on Both Sides said River. Hugh Innis has Leave to build a Water Grist Mill on Snow Creek to being Proritor of Both Sides Said Creek. Court is Adjourned till Court in Course. JONATHAN RICHESON. At A Court of Quarterly Sessions Begun & Held for Franklin County on Monday the 5th Day of March 1787. Present: Hugh Innis, Thomas Arthur, Swinfield Hill, John Smith, John Rentfro & John Dickenson, Gent. Delancy vs Bates W. E. set a Side & Genl. Issue. Same vs Same vs Same. The. Webb Spl. Bl. & Gl. Issue. Asberry vs Early Dism'd at Pltfs Costs. Trent vs Early. Same. Cook vs Ramsay, Jud. Confess'd Accordg. to Sply & Costs. James Callaway, Jub. Early vs Robert Napier. Asf'd Napier Spl. Bl. & Jud. Confee'd W'th Stay of Exeor 3 Months .V. Paid Tax According to Sply & Costs.

PAGE ONE HUNDRED

Samuel Hairston Foreman, Elisha Estes, Amos Richardson, Samuel Patteson, Joseph Price, Isaac Bates, Peter Geerhart, Joseph Davis, Owen Ruble, Henry Jones, James Turner, William Toney, John Crump, Amos Ellison, James Greer, John Harger & John Hunter, were Sworn as a Grand Jury of Inquest for the Body of this County, Whereupon they Withdrew to Consult on their Presentments. Clerk &c vs Hunts. George Asberry Spl. Bl. & Deliver him up & he is Pray'd Commited. Clardy vs Same. the Same Ab. H. Trent Spl. Bl. Graham vs Law, the Same the Same. Call Surving Parter of Field & Call vs Daniel, Jno. Cox Spl B. & Delivered him up, Pray'd Commited & the Plf Attorney Agreed the Sheriff shall not be Culpable till Tomorrow Evening. Early vs Moodys & Coffry, Jno. Cooper Spl. Bl. for Moody & Thos. Martin Spl. Bl. for Martin. Callaway & Early vs Bryant. Thos. Hale Spl. Bl & Delivered him up, whereupon he is Pray'd Commited & Jud Accordl. to Speialty & Costs. Richardson vs Parberry, Hugh Innis Spl. Bl. & Deliver him up where upon he is Pray'd Commited Wm. Paid Tax James Stewart is Exempted from the Paymt. of County levies for the future. Callaway & Early V Edwards, Wm. Nolin Spl. Bl. Same v Wm. Stewart Jas. Stewart Spl. Bl & Delivered the Defd up whereupon he is Prayed Commited.

PAGE ONE HUNDRED ONE

Hunt vs Clardy and Clardy vs Hunt Referees Discharged & Ord to be redocketed for Tryal. Watts vs Hambrick Jud. Confessed Stay Exeor till the first of May 1/6. Martin vs Parberry Ord. Plt give Security for Costs or the Suit to be Dismiss'd at Next Court Whereupon Robt. Williams Came into Court & entered himself Scrty for the Costs. The Grand Jury Came into Court & made Several Presentments whereupon Process is Ordered to be Issued. Livsey vs Anderson Jas. Mason, Saml Webb & John Edwards Spl Bl. Rich'd Robinson Came into Court & with John Camp his Security entered into recognizance in the Sum of £20 each Payable to the Parrish of Patrick on Condition that the said Robertson does not keep the S'd Parish Clear of the Maintenance of A Bastard Child begot by the S'd Robertson on the Body of Eliza Hale. Robert Hairston & Moses

Greer Gent, are Appointed Commiss'r of the Tax for the Present year, & the S'd Hairstons Bounds to be that Part of this County formerly Henry & the s'd Greer of that Part formerly Bedford. Doson vs Campbell, Jere Shrewsberry a Garshee being sworn Sayith he owes the Defd Nothing. John Murphy is Allowed One Days Attendance & One Comg. & Returning 30 Miles as a Witness for Hook vs Wood. Court is Adjourned till Tomorrow 10 O.Clock.—HUGH INNES.

PAGE ONE HUNDRED TWO

At a Court Cont'd & held for Franklin County the 6th Day of Mar. Present: Hugh Innes, Thomas Arthur, Moses Greer & John Smith, Gent. Cook vs Young Abates by Returns. James vs Haynes & Kirby James. Ferguson vs Stewart, Ord: fo Refence set Aside Judgt According to Spy & Co. Hall vs Pate the Plt failing to give Security for Cost Dism'd. Hunter vs Stockdon, Cont'd. Holliday vs Wilson, Cont'd. Holland vs Jones, Jud. accg. to Spy & Co. Mead vs Renfro. Cont. Smith vs Cooke Admr Ptfs, to Geo Sully for Costs at next Court to be Dism'd Wm. Ryan Sur'y for the Same. Stewart vs Haynes, Cont'd. Saunders vs Wm. Kelly Judg, Accg. to Spy & Co. Thorp vs Wm. Renfro Jud. Accg. to Spy & Co. Buferd vs Kelly Jud. for 30/ & Cost. Boothe Assee vs Burnes Jud. Accg. to Spy & Co. Conner vs Finny. Dism'd Plt Cost. Cheatwood vs Parker & als Cont'd. Calland vs Parberry Jud. Accg. to Spy & Costs. Finney vs Miller Jud. for Spy & Co. Daniel vs Hughes Jas. Callaway inters himself, a Party Dism'd w'th Costs. Jones vs Ashly, Jud. for £47 16 & Costs. Kimmon vs Bransham, Jud. for Costs. Morgan vs Hodges Exers Jud. Accg. w Spy & Co. Prunty vs Woodson, Judgt for £4.0.0 & Cost.

PAGE ONE HUNDRED THREE

March Court 1787—Richardson vs Estes, Cont. C for Plf. Saunders vs Thompson &c Jud. Accg. to Acct &c cost. Sloan vs Griffith Jud. £1.14.1 & Cost. Thompson vs Griffith Jud. for £2-13-4 & Cost. Trent vs Cheatwood Cont'd. Stewart vs Ramsey abates by Defts. Death. Woods vs Willis, Judgt. for £15.7½ & Costs. Cook vs Ramsey Jud. accg. to Spy. & Co. Same vs Peak & Lutterel Jud. accg to Spy & Co. Call vs Winn Jud. & for £1.2.5 & Co. Irvin vs Hickey Exrs. Judt for £2.3.1 & Co. Cannor vs Milles Jud. for £5 & Costs. Colo. James Callaway who was Sum'd as Garshee Bailey vs Mead Came into Court and Agrees that he has a Sufficiency in his hands of Specie to Satisfy the Pltfs. Jud. Agst. the Def. W'th Costs. Dillion vs Same. the same. Callaway & Early vs M. Larry. Thomas Sloan came into Court & Made himself a Party, Judgmt Confessed accordg to Sply & Cost with Stay of Excn 3 Months. Hook vs Wood, the former Jury discharged for Tryal. Present: Hugh Martin Gl Grayham vs Dongger. a Jury Sworn, to Wit, Edw'd Wilson, Isham Choat, Robt. Mason, Jno. Martin, Ambrose Raines, Thos. Miller, James Martin, John Arthur, Samuel Calland, John Sullivant, John Hook, & James Rentro. Verd. Ret. for the Ptf. Prunty v. Woodson, judgment for £5 and costs.

March Court 1787—The Court doth set & Rate the follow-Liquors, Diets, Lodging, Pasturage, Stablage & Provinder as follows, Viz: For good West India Rum per Gallon £0.10 shillings; Continental ditto & ditto 8 shillings; Peach Brandy pr. ditto 8 shillings; Whiskey pr. ditto 6 shillings; Wine pr. ditto 12 shillings; Strong Beer pr. Quart 1 shilling 6 pence; Cyder pr. ditto 6 pence; Dinner (if hot) 1 shilling 6 pence; breakfast (if hot) 1 shilling 3 pence; A Cold Meal 1 shilling; Lodging for each Person 6 shillings; Corn or Oats Pr Gallon 9 pence; Stablage & fodder Pr. Night 9 pence; & so proportionably for a Greater or less Quantity. John Murph is Allowed one Days attendance for Hook agt Wood, as Witness. Nathaniel Tate is also Allowed one days Attendance as a witness for the same & once Comg. Returng 25 Miles & 2 fireages at Keys. Edward Hancock is Allowed one days Attendance & Once comg & returng 28 Miles as Witness for Hook at the Suit of Hook. Parberry vs Stokes, Judgt. for £2.16.8 condem'd in the hands of John Ferguson & O. Cond'a.

PAGE ONE HUNDRED FIVE

March Court 1787—Callaway & Early vs Forsythe. Judmt for £15.6.9 & Costs & O. Condemn'a. John Waller is Allowed 2 Days Attendance & one Comg. & Returning 25 miles as a Witnes for Prunty agt Woodson. Jas. Ferguson vs Martin, Jacob Clower a Garn being Swo. Saith he has in hands, a Blue Cloth

Coat. One leather ditto of Copper culler & one Jacket of a Lead Cullor. Judgt accordg to Spy & O. Condemn'a. Stegall vs Jenkins, John Jenkins a Garn. being Sworn Saith he has Neither Cattle nor Tobacco in his hands belonging to the Defend. & Cont. Thomas Haile is Allowed two days Attendance as a Witness for Cannon agt. Willis. Robert Williams Gt. Deputy States Attorney is allowed 1200 lb Tobacco for Attendg 2 Call'd Courts one the Exam'n of Wm. Dillingham, 2 on Weeks 1 on Stokes & one on George Ramsey, for which he is to be paid out of the Depositum if there be as much in the Shfs. hands after deduct & the Insolvents, which he may Ret. Asberry vs Stokes & King, Cont. at Defts. Costs. Cheetwood vs Williams and Williams vs Cheetwood. Ref'd to James Callaway & Jona. Richardson, & in case they disagree that they Choose an Umpire, & his or their Aw'd to be the Judgt. of the Court. & the Parties Agree that the same shall be tried on the 2'd Day of the Court in May next.

PAGE ONE HUNDRED SIX

March Court 1787 Cont.—Young vs Weaks, Jas. Davis a Garnt. being Sworn saith he owes the Defend. £2.17 to be paid in a Store. Charles Simmons Another Garn. being Sworn saith he has in his Possession a Coarse Staye, Judgt, for £2 & 0. Conda. & Atta. vs Dillingham another Garnishee. Lewis Davis is Allowed two days Attendance as a Witness for Dangges ads Graham. William Davis two days for the same. William Hynes two days for the same. David Peak two days for the same. Arthur vs Carter & Livesey in Barr to the Judgt in Bedford Court, agt. Thomas Livesey & other. It appears to this Court that the Plt. hath Recovered Damages to the Amount of Thirty Pounds with Cost in the said Court of Bedford, It is therefore Ordered by the Court to Dism'd on the Plts Costs, Whereupon he Pray'd an Appeal to the 8th Day of the next Genl. Court & It is further Ordered that the Plt. give Security in the Clks Office before the Next Court. Callaway & Early vs Lewis Bryant, Thos. Hale & Wm. Menefee Spl. Bl. came into Court & made themselves Parties, Judgt Confess'd accorg to Sply & Costs. Stay Exon. 3 Months. Joseph Griffith is Allowed 2 days Attence as a Witness for Livsey & Carter ads Arthur. Peter Hoff 2 days for the same. Will. Hayns 2 days for the Same.

PAGE ONE HUNDRED SEVEN

March Court 1787, Cont.—On the Motion of Milley Thomas Judgt. is Granted her against John Levisey &c on a Replevy Bond. Callaway & Early vs Livesey Gent. Geo. Asberry & William Young Spl. Bl. & the C. O. set aside. Also Frances Thorp agt. Wm. Tony & the same on a Reply Bond. Also George Griffith agt. P. Sloane the same Cheetwood vs Napier a Deds awarded the Deft. to take the Depo. of Peter Gilliam. Givg the Plt. 10 Days Notice. Court is Adjourned till Tomorrow 8 OClock.—HUGH INNES.

Page 108 is blank.

PAGE ONE HUNDRED NINE

March Rules for 1787—Cay vs Wilson C. O. Callaway vs Davis & Hall, Trial Exon. Demoss vs Key Costs. Same vs Binion & Edwards C. O. Conf'd vs Edwards & Impl. as to Binion. Dickerson vs Perryman Cont. Ferguson vs Martin Cont. Hunt vs Bartee. Impl. Murphie & Co. vs Hunt C. O. Deft & Bl. Mullender vs Bybee Judgt Confess'd accordg. to Spyl. Ryan vs King. Cont'd for Aw'd. Farley vs Martin Judgt. Conf'd accordg. to Spy & Co. Richardson vs Hubbard Cont. Young vs Weaks Cont. Arthur vs Greer Spl. Impl. Same vs Same & Wife same Asberry vs Cluthley Atta. Same vs Puckett C. O. Armstrong vs Spangler C. O. Impl. Asberry vs Blankenship &c Same Hale vs Blankenship. Bennett vs Kelly C. O. in Custody. Bell vs Jenkins Cont. Callaway & Early vs Rentfro C. O. Sl. & Bl. Clay vs Wilson C. O. Deft. & Bl.

PAGE ONE HUNDRED TEN

March Rules 1787 Cont.—Callaway & Co. vs Ferguson A. C. Clutcher vs Parker &c dism'd Want Prosecution. Same vs Hancock Impl. Callaway & Early vs Forsythe Judt. for £15.6.9 & O. Conda. Same & Earley vs Stokes Cont. Cluthley vs Asberry &c Dis'd for Want Prosecution. Callaway & Early vs Earnest. Same vs Willis. Atta. J. Early vs Moody & others, Impl. Ferguson vs Sheredon, C. O. Dt. & Bl. G. Farguson vs Hickey C. P. Deft & Bl. Greer vs Rentfro dism'd. Griffith vs Scruggs dism'd. Greer vs Arthur Impl. M. Greer vs Spangler Cont'd for Bill. Hairston vs Meredith Abates by Ret. Harris vs Miller & C. O.

Deft. & Bl. Hill vs Roberson. dism'd. agreed. Demoss vs Key dism'd. Agreed Duvolt vs Stanton & A. C. Jones vs Webb not guilty w'th Leave & Issue. Jones asse. vs Sutherland C. O. Same vs Same Same. Keefer vs Hodges. Atta. Livesey vs Anderson. Impl. Martin vs Parberry C. O. in Custody. Quigley vs Miles & Wife C. O. Deft & Bl.

PAGE ONE HUNDRED ELEVEN

March Rules for 1787 Cont.—Ritter vs Prater dism'd Agreed Richerdson vs Brook dis'd Agreed D. Richardson vs Parberry C. O. in Custody Rentfro Assee vs Callaway Spl. Impl Read & Arthur A. C. Saunders vs Bryant C. O. agt D & Bl. Stegall vs Jenkins Cont Stenson vs Levsey C. O. & In Custody Scruggs vs Griffith. Dis'd Stokes vs Duease. Atta Trent vs Bandy. C. O. V Dt & Shf Taylor vs Chitwood C. Order. Simmons vs Weaks dism'd Rentfro vs Rowland & Webb C. O. V. Webb Al Caps vs Rowland White vs Quigley Dis'd. Willis vs Miller C. O. Deft & Bl. Wright vs Sempson. Dism'd No. Pros. Wickham vs Griffith. Atta. Wilson vs England. Iml. Same & Son vs Choat Abates by Ret. Cook vs Grayham. Atta. Same vs Peak &c. C. O. Same vs Condy. Atta. Same vs McLary. C. O. Same vs Bryant C. O. in Custody.

PAGE ONE HUNDRED TWELVE

March Rules for 1787: Cont.—Callaway & Early vs Fuson C. O. & Def & Bl. Same vs Livesay C. O. Same Same vs Edwards Oyer of the Bond Same vs Stewart. C. O. Same vs Graham. Atta Same vs Napier, Judgt accorg to Spy, stay Exen 3 Months Call vs Hickeys Exors, C. O. & the Com B. Released Same vs Short A. C. Same vs Daniel. ConWealth vs Bates Oyer Same vs Sundries N. P. Same vs the Surveyor of the Road from Bradshaw to the Road above Wattses.

PAGE ONE HUNDRED THIRTEEN

March Court 1787—At A Court held & Continued for Franklin County on the Seventh day of March 1787 Present Hugh Innes, Tho. Arthur, Moses Greer, & Hugh Martin Gent. Moody Assee vs Booths, Jud. Confess'd Accg to Spty & Costs. Demoss vs Benman & Edwards, Geo Asberry Spl B. & Gl Issue Wright vs Simpson dis'd Want of Pro. On the Mot. of Samuel Calland

Judgt. is granted him against Thomas Jamison &c. On a Replevy Bond Also the same vs James Tusly &c the same Penn vs Mead, James Callaway a Garnt, being Sworn saith he has in his hands a Sufficiency of Iron, Castings or Speeci to Satisfy the Plts. demand. Judgt. Accordg. to Spy & Conda. M. Rentfro vs Stephens, Wm. Griffith a Garnishee being Sworn saith he owes the Def. 40/. Jud. for £6 & 0 Conda. Young vs Same, William Wilson a Garnishee being Sworn saith he owes the Deft. Eight Barrells of Corn Payable Next fall, O Conda & Cont. Ferguson vs Hickey, John Cheetwood, Spl B. ___ Delivered her up, Whereupon she is prayed committed. Absent: Hugh Innis, Present: Thomas Arthur, Gent.

PAGE ONE HUNDRED FOURTEEN

March Court 1787—Cook asse vs Richardson. A Jury Sworn, to wit, Sam'l Hairston, William Rentfro, William Thompson, Joel Walker, Thomas Hail, John Johnson, James McVay, Isaac Rentfro, David Morgan, John Cheetwod, William McVay & John Martin Verd. Ret. for the Plt & O. R. Hoff vs Hale Dis'd Agreed. Trent vs Huckaby, Jud. Accorg. to Sply & Costs & O. C. & it is further Ordered that Geo. Hancock be Allowed 40/ Out of the Conden'd Effects by the Consent of Trent of the Defts. Estate, O. Conda. & Cont. for further Service. Ordered that Robert Woods Gent, Sheriff, do enter into Bond with Security at the next Court for the Collection of the Certificate Tax & to be Spa for that Purpose. Trent vs Vaughan. Atta. Eliz Haiden ComWealth vs Dillingham, cn the Motion of Ro. Williams Deputy States Attorney, it is Ordered that the Clerk of this Court, do Issue, Exon, agt. the Deft. for the Costs of the said Com.Wealth Agt him on Indictmt. Edward Choat is Allowed two Days attendance as a Witness for Carter & Levisy ads Thomas Arthur. Sansford Hall is Allowed 8/ for 4 Days keeping two Horses, the Property of John Huckaby, taken by an Attachmt, Wm. Trent agt. the said Huckaby On the Complaint of Aliannah Hill, Daughter of Thomas Hill, against Benjamin Haile for an Insult offered her on the Highway. It is Ordered that the said Hail be taken into Custody by the Shf of this County, until he gives Su'y for his appearance

PAGE ONE HUNDRED FIFTEEN

March Court 1787—before the Next Grand Jury, in the Penalty of Twenty five Pounds & each of his Su'ys in the sum of £12.10 & It is further Ordered that he be in Custody of said Shf untill he gives Sur'y for the same. Whereupon the said Haile came into Court & with William Menifee & William Kelly his Sur'y Ack'd themselves Severally indebted to the Com. Wealth of Virginia, that is to say the said Haile in the afores'd Sum of Twenty five & his Sur'ys in the Sum of £12.10 each, to be levied on their Respective Goods & Chattles, Lands & Tenements, On Condition the said Benja. Haile appear at the Next Grand Jury to be held for this County. Peggy Livesey is Allowed two days attendance as a Witness for Carter & Livesey ads of Thom. Arthur. Daniel Jett is Allowed 3 Days Attendance as Witness for Benjamin Cook agt. Daniel Richardson. William Thompson is allowed two days, Attendance as a Witness for Danggers ads Graham Fergson vs Hickey, Ro. Perryman, Thomas Roberts & John Kelly Spl. Bl. Call vs Daniel Judgt. Confessed Accorg to Spy & Co. & the Plts Attorney agree to discharge the Defendant out of Custody. Callaway & Early vs W. Stewart, James Stewart Sen. came into Court & made himself a Party, Judgt, Confess'd accordg to Spy stay Exon 4 Months The Court is Adj'd till Tomorrow 8 oClock—T. ARTHUR.

PAGE ONE HUNDRED SIXTEEN

March Court 1787—At a Court held and Continued for Franklin County. On the Eighth day of March 1787 Present: Thomas Arthur, Swinfield Hill, Moses Greer & John Rentfro, Gent. Absent: Swinfield Hill. Callaway & Early vs McDowell Cont. Cheetwood vs Napier. Samuel Calland is Allowed Three days attendance & one Comg & Retg 25 miles as a Witnnes for Cook agt Richardson. Thomas Doggett Produced a Commission from his Excellency the Governor appg him Lieut. of the Militia of this County, Whereupon he took the Usual Oaths for the Comtee also the Oath as a Lieut of the s'd Militia. Barton vs Livesey a Jury Sworn, to wit, Samuel Hariston, Obediah Richardsson, Booker Josith, Amos Richardson Robert Perryman, Samuel Calland, Samuel Patterson, Geo. Asberry, Smith Webb, Wm. Thompson, Jas. McVey & Eusebus Hubbard, Verdt. Ret. for the Defendt & O. R. Greer vs Webb, a Jury Sworn, to wit, James

Rentfro Wm. Davis, William Mavity, Thomas Haile, William Henderson, Joel Walker, George Farguson, Lewis Davis, William Farguson, Ambrose Rainses, Thomas Roberts & William Bell, Verd, Retd for the Plt. Whereupon the Deft Prayed an appeal to the 8th day of the next Genl. Court & that the Pll Deff have leave till next Court to give Suty for the Prosecution of the same Callaway vs Brooks, Cont'd at Defts Costs. Same vs Same of Same.

PAGE ONE HUNDRED SEVENTEEN

March Court 1787—William Mavity is Allowed four days attendance as a Witness for Livisay ads Barton Andrew Ferguson is also allow'd four Days for the Same & one Comg. & retg 21 Miles. Acquila Greer is Allowed four days for the same. William Dodd is Allowed four days attendance for Barton agt. Leviesey. William Griffith four days for the same. Joseph Griffith four days for Barton. On the motion of Thomas Hill, License is granted him to keep an Ord'ny at his House, adjoin'g the Land belong. to Lieut. James Callaway & at Rocky Mount & with Swinfield Hill his Su'y ent'd into Bond & Ack'd the same. Also License is granted James Callaway Gent. to keep an Ord'dy at this Courthouse who ent'd into Bond w'th Stephen Smith & Ack'd the same. William Anderson is Allowed four days attendance & once Comg. & retg. 120 Miles as a Witn's for Webb ads Greer Demoss Exor. &c vs Clardy & T. Markum, a Jury Sworn to Wit, James Rentfro, William Davis, Wm. Mavity, Thomas Haile, Lewis Davis, William Farguson, Ambrose Rains, Thomas Miller & William Bell. Verd. Ret. for the Plt. & O. R. Calland vs Kimmins & O. Conda with Costs. Cook vs Davis, Judgt, Accorg. to Spy. & Costs.

PAGE ONE HUNDRED EIGHTEEN

March Court 1787—Frisby & Elliot vs Rentfro, Jury Sworn, to wit, James Rentfro, William Davis, William Mavity, Thomas Haile, William Henderson, Joel Walker, Geo. Farguson, Lewis Davis, William Farguson, Ambrose Raines, Thomas Miller & William Bell. Verd't Ret'd for the Pl & O. R. Parris vs Haile, A Jury Sworn, to wit, James Rentfro, William Davis, William Mavity, Thomas Haile, William Henderson, Joel Walker, James Mc Vey, Lewis Davis, William Ferguson, Ambrose Rains, Thomas

Miller, & William Bell. Verd't Ret'd for the Plt & O. R. The Court is Adj'd till Court in Course—T. ARTHUR. At a Court held for Franklin County, On Wednesday the 14th. March 1787, for the Examination of John Howel Jones on Suspicion of Stealing A Dark Brown Mare the Property of William Laney. Present: Hugh Innes, Thomas Arthur, Moses Greer, Swinfield Hill. John Rentfro, Spencer Clack, Jonathan Richeson & Hugh Martin Gent. The Said John Howell Jones being led to the Bar in Custody of Robert Woods, Gent. Sheriff of Said County to whose Custody for the Crime Aforesaid he had been Commited, and it being Demanded of the Said Prisoner Whether he was Guilty of the Fact Wherewith he Stands Charged or Not Guilty, Answered that he was in no Wise Guilty.

PAGE ONE HUNDRED NINETEEN

Whereupon the Court Proceeded to examine Divers Witnesses as Well on behalf of the Common Wealth as the Prisoner at the Bar, on consideration whereof the Court are of Opinion that this Said Prisoner is Guilty of the fact wherewith he stands Charged And that he Ought to receive a further Tryal before the Honble the Genl. Court in the City of Richmond on the first day thereof Whereupon he is remanded into the Custody of the Sheriff Afors'd. William Laney, Elizabeth Laney & Thomas Tounsend Came into Court and Acknowledged themselves Severally Indebted to the Common Wealth of Virginia in the Sum of £100 Each to be levied On their Respective Goods & Chattles, Lands & Tenements on Condition they do not Appear before the Honble the Genl. Court in the City of Richmond on the first day thereof in April next on behalf of the Common Wealth Against John Howel Jones who is Accused of Stealing a Dark Brown Mare the Property of Wm Laney.— HUGH INNES.

PAGE ONE HUNDRED TWENTY

April Court 1787—At a Court held for Franklin County on Monday the Second Day of April 1787. Present: Hugh Innes, Peter Saunders, Spencer Clack, John Smith, George Turnbull, Gent. A Deed from Robert Boulton to Thos. Boulton Proved & O. R. Also John Keen to James Marcum Ack'd & O R'd. Also

Stephen Law to Jno. Keen Prov by Two Witness & O. C. Also Thomas Doggett to Jas. Callaway Proved & O. R'd. Also John Starkey to Robert Prisley Prov'd & O R'd. Also Thomas Poteet to Jno. Divers Prov'd & O R'd. Also Joseph Carter to Jno. Carter Prov'd & O. R'd Also Jonathan Pratt to Wm. Swanson Prov'd & O R'd. Also William Swanson Sr. to John Davis Prov'd & O. R'd. A Power of Attorney from Benoni Perryman to Jas. Mason Prov'd & O R'd. Paid. A Deed from John Starkey to Will Martin Prov'd & O R'd. Also Obadiah Gravit to Jno Thornton Ack'd & O. R'd. Also John Starkey to Jno. Clack Prov, & O. R'd. Also Charles Hutcheson to Paul Hutcheson Prov'd & O R'd. Also Moses Wray to Jacob Flora Prov'd by 2 Witness & C. C. Also Joseph Kerby to John Muse Prov'd O. R'd. Also Nathan Barnet to Same Ack'd & Ann the Wife being Privily Exam'd Ack'd her right of Dower & O. R'd.

PAGE ONE HUNDRED TWENTY-ONE

April Court 1787—A Deed Frederick Rives to Harmon Cook Prov'd & O R'd. Also Stephen Law to Jas. Stone Prov'd & O. R'd. Also James Slone to David Polley Ack'd & R. R'd. A Dedimus for the Relinguishmt for Mary, Wife of Wm. Swanson Sr. On a Deed to Philimon Southerland Ret. & O. R'd. A Deed Jonathan Pratt to Jno. Craighead further Proved by Two Wit' nesses & O. R'd. Also Minor Wilks to Jno. Wilks further Proved & O. R'd. Ambrose Wood is Exempted from the Payment of County Levey in Future. Also Abram Stober the Same. Court is Adjourne'd till Tomorrow 10 o'clock.—HUGH INNES. At a Court held & Continued for Franklin County on Tuesday the Third Day of April 1787. Present: Peter Saunders, Swinfield Hill, John Smith, Moses Greer & Jonathan Richeson, Gent. A Deed from James Parberry to Callaway & Early Prov'd & O. R'd Agreeable to an Act of Assembly the Court Proceeded to lay off the County in Districts for Electing Overseers of the Poor that the North of Blackwater River in this County, shall be one District for Electing Overseers of the Poor & that Moses Greer Gl. Superintend the said Election at Thomas Watts's on Satur' day the 28th of this Instant or in his Absence Jno. Smith. One other District the Road from Patrick Sloans ford on Black Water to Henry Line, Crossing Pigg River at Thos. Hill's that the

PAGE ONE HUNDRED TWENTY-TWO

April Court 1787—the Election for the said District be held at Capt. Rubells & that Peter Saunders Gl. & in his Absence John Rentfro Superintened the S'd Election of the other District for the East of the S'd Line to be held at John Dickinson, on the 27th Day of this Instant, & that Hugh Innis Superintend the said Election, or in his absence John Dickerson, to Superintend the Same. John Rentfro Gent. Ret, a Certificate from under his hand of the Qualification of Robert Hairston & Moses Greer Gent. Commissioners of the Taxable Property in this County & O. C. Swinfield Hill Gent. is Appointed to Settle w'th & Receive of the Dpty States Attorney for this County for all fines at Forfeitures by them Received for the use of the Com. Wealth, County & Parish & to Account for the Same with the Court. Agreeable to an Act of Assembly in that Case made & Provided, Licence is Granted to Daniel Brown & Co. to Keep a Retail Store for the Space of One Year. Thomas Hill the Same. William Kerby the Same. Samuel Hairston, the Same. Peter Saunders, the Same. Swinfield Hill is Appointed Surveyor of the Road from this Courthouse to Harwells Cabbins & the usual hands to be his Gang. A Deed from Hills Legatees to Walter Bernard Ac'd & O. C.

PAGE ONE HUNDRED TWENTY-THREE

April Court 1787—Theodrick Webb Came into Court and Entered into Bond w'th Thomas Watts his Security in the Penalty of Twenty Pounds, Curt. Money to Prosecute an Appeal Granted him this Court ads. M. Greer. William Davis is exempted from the Paymt of County Leveys for the future. Jacob Adkins, the Same. Jacob Prillaman, the Same. On the Motion of Thomas Watts, Jane, a Negro Slave of his Property is exempt from the Payt. of County Leveys in future Also on the Motion of Theodorick Webb, Melender & Peter, Two Negro Slaves of his Property is Exempt from the Payt. of County Leveys in future. John Booth is App'd Sur. of the Road from Radfords Ford to the fork of the Road below Asa Hollands & the List filed to be his Gang. Thomas Prunty is Appointed Sur. of the Road from Colo. Jas. Callaways Plantation on Blackwater to the fork of the Road above Cowls Cabbins & List fild to be his Gang. Court is Adjourned till Court in Course.—PETER SAUNDERS.

PAGE ONE HUNDRED TWENTY-FOUR

May Sessions 1787—At a Court of Quarterly Sessions held for Franklin County On Monday the 7th. May 1787. Present: Hugh Innes, Peter Saunders, Jonathan Richardson, & John Rentfro, Gent. Hancock vs R. Prunty, Jud for 55/6 & Costs. Harmon Cook vs Sally Smith, Jud. Accorg to Sply & Costs. Morgan vs Choves Extrs. Jud. Accordg. to Aw. & Costs, stays Exon till November Court next. Edwards vs Edmondson, Jud. Accordl, to Spy & Co. Armstrong vs Spangler Tho. Prunty Spl. B. & Thomas Armstrong Su'y for Costs. James Blair, Gt. Produced a License to Practice in this Court & the other inferior Courts in this State, Whereupon he took the Usual Oaths to the Com. Wealth & the Oath of an Attorney. On the Motion of William Walton, Judgt. is granted him agt. Kelly & others, on Replevy Bond. Same vs Same Same. Lyon vs Lyon, A Ded's aw'd the Plt to take the Depos. of Daniel Mahoon & Sally Mahoon, Mary & Robt Johns. Giv'g the Deft. 10 Days Notice. Johns vs Same a Deds. aw'd the Dtd to take the Depos of Mary Finney & Patty Johns & Daniel & Sally Mahoon Giv'g the Deft. 10 Days Notice.

PAGE ONE HUNDRED TWENTY-FIVE

May Session 1787—Webber vs Webster Judgt. Conf'd Accorg. to Sp'y & Costs, Stay Exon. three Months A Deed from Abner Cockram to Tho. Townshend Prov'd by 2 Witn's & O. C. Also Wm. Graves & Lewis Jenkins to the same Same Benjamin Cook, Foreman, Benjamin Greer, Alexander Ferguson, James Greer, William Swanson, Samuel Patterson, Robert Prunty, Amos Richardson, John Hunter, Joseph Lewis, Peter Young, William Mullins, Joseph Davis, Peter Geerheart, Stephen Stone & Robert Woods, were Sworn a Grand Jury of Inquest for the Body of this County, Whereupon they withdrew to Consult on Winff Jenkins. Young vs Stephens, Judgt for £4.0.0 & C Conda, of Atta effects Spearpoint vs Martin dism'd with Costs. License is granted John Hook to keep a Retail Store for the Space of One Year. Also Hugh Innes Gl. the same. Cuff vs Wade dism'd with Costs. On the Motion of Thomas Poteet Judmt is granted him agt Jones & Co their or a Replevy Bond. Abshire vs Flowers. Dism'd Agreed. Stintson vs Levisey, Jno, Cheetwood Spl. Bl. On the Motion of Peter Livesey, Bobbin, a Negro Man Slave, is exempted from the Paymt. County Levies for the future. Teal vs Farley, dism'd Agreed. Bryant vs Miller, Judgt. for £— & Costs. Blankinship vs Eurbanks, Judgt. for £2 & Costs

PAGE ONE HUNDRED TWENTY-SIX

May Court 1787—Benjamin Haile came into Court & with Thomas Prunty his security, acknowledged himself indebted to the Com Wealth in the sum of £10 & the said Prunty in the sum of £5 to be levied on their respective goods and chattels, lands & tenements on condition the said Haile shall make his appearance before this court in Aug. next to answer as Indictm. Exhibited ag. him by Alianner Hill, Daughter of Thomas Hill. Grayham vs Elliott dism'd. Bolton vs. Smith. Judg. accordg to Spy & Costs. Smith vs Cooks adm. Judg. for 27/ & Costs. Cook vs. Peck. Judge. Confessd, accordg to Spy & Costs. Lyon vs Lyon, Will Ryan & Hugh Woods Spl. Imp. Bail. Johns & ux. vs. Same. Same same. On the mot. of Will Crump, Judge. is granted him ag. Moses Greer. On a Replevy, as Secy for Parrott. Robert Woods, Gent. Shf. of this County came into Court & with John Dickerson, Hugh Martin, John Martin, Daniel Richardson & William Hunter his Secy entered into Bond & acknowl. the same for the True & faithful Collection of the Certificate Tax. License is granted John Martin to keep a retail store for one year. Callaway vs. Brookes & Guthreys Exors. a Jury sworn, to wit, Wm. Kelly, Jas. Lewis, Joseph Jones, George Levisey, William Mullins, Shores Price, Samuel Patterson, Wm. Stanley, Barttell Wade, David Jones, James Beavers & Peter Storm. Verd. retd. for the Deft. & new Tryal granted the Pf. on Payg Costs of the day.

PAGE ONE HUNDRED TWENTY-SEVEN

May Court 1787—Livesey vs Anderson. James Mason, John Edward & Samuel Webb Spl. Bl. & delivered him up. Whereupon his Prayd Commit. John Rentfro fur. bail. Boyce Eadson is allowed one days attendance & one comg & retg 40 Miles as a witness for Guthreys Exors. ads. Calloway. Galligoe &c vs Clark Saml. Patterson & Benj. Cook Spl. Bl & Spl. Impl. Same vs same. Same & Spl. Impl. Guffey vs Underwood, Anthony

Pate a Garn. being sworn saith he owes the Deft. the sum of
£40. when the said Underwood conveys to him a right in fee
simple to a certain tract of land he purchased of the Deft. The
Court is adj. till tomorrow 10 o'clock. HUGH INNES. At a
Court of Quarterly Sessions contd. & held for Franklin County
on the 8th day of May, 1787. Present: Hugh Innes, Peter Saunders, Jonathan Richardson & John Smith & Moses Greer, Gent.
Jubal Early produced a Commission from his Excellency the Governor appointg. him Capt. of the Militia of the Company in this
county William Miller Ensign whereupon, they took the usual
oaths to the Com Wealth of the oaths of a Capt. & Ensign of the
Militia. Present: Spencer Clack, Thos. Arthur.

PAGE ONE HUNDRED TWENTY-EIGHT

May Session 1787—On the Complt. of Joanah Wife of Phil-
lip Sheredon, agt William Griffith for an Insult on the Highway,
It is Ordered that the Sherif Take the said Griffith into Cus-
tody Until the said Griffith Gives Surity for his Good Behavior.
Sherewood vs Edwards, Judgt Confess'd for £6.0.8 & Costs
Graham vs Dongger Jury Sworn, to Witt, Caleb Tate, William
Walton, Samuel Cockran, John Cheetwood, Trails Nicholls, Wil-
liam Kelly, Robert Prunty, Isaac Bates, George Wright, Isaac
Rentfro, Will Counnaugh & Joseph Shores Price, Verd. Ret. for
the Deft & O. R. Lewis Davis is Allowed 2 days Atta. as a Wit-
ness for Dangger ads Graham William Davis the Same the Same
John Rodgers is Allowed 5 Days Attendance as a Witness for
Graham agt Dangger Hook vs Wood, A Jury Sworn, to wit, Wil-
liam Akers, Benja. Duvall, Thomas Jones, James McVey, David
Barton, Benjamin Greer, Skelton Taylor, Israel Standifer, John
Martin, John Hunter, James Huston & Jubal Early. Verd. Ret
for the Plt for the Sum of £70.12—5 & Costs. Philip Raley is
allowed On Days Atten'd as a Witness for Wood ads Hook.
James Burns the Same ads Same.

PAGE ONE HUNDRED TWENTY-NINE

May Session 1787—John Murphy is Allowed Two Days At-
tendance and One Coming & Ret. 30 Miles as a Witness for
Wood ads Hook. Nathl. Tate is Allowed One Days Attendance
& One Coming & Ret. 25 Miles As a Witness for Hook vs Wood.
John Edwards is Allowed Two Days Attendance as a Witness

for Wood ads Hook. Thomas Watts is Allowed One Days Attendance as a Witness for Wood ads Hook. On the Motion of Dan'l Richardson an Injunction is Granted him to stay the Proceedings of a Jud. Obtained by Benja. Cook assee of Joseph Cook vs him, Whereupon he with Hugh Innes Gt. his Su'y into Bond & Ack'd the same. Trent vs Cheetwood dis'd w'th Costs. William Ryan is allowed 9 Days Attend. as a Witness of Benja. Cook ads Smith. Abadrah Richardson. the Same. John Sullivant is Allowed 5 Days Attce as a Witness for Jno. Trent vs Jno. Chitwood. Cap. Issued. William Nolen is Allowed 3 Days for Jno. Chitwood Ads. Trent. James Mason is Allowed 4 Days for the Same. Cap Iss'd.

PAGE ONE HUNDRED THIRTY

May Session 1787—Hook vs Vincent & Wright On the Motion of the Plt. It is Ordered that the Shf. Summon 22 Truholders of this County, to Attend the Survey Juds to lay Off & Ascertain the Quantity of Land in the Dispute between the Plt. & Defts on a Writ of Equitmt & made Report thereof to the Court. ROBT. HAIRSTON. Brown assee vs Richards, Will. Kelly Sen, & Ambrose Rains. Spl B. & Imp. The Court is Adj'd tomorrow 10 OClock At a Court held of Quarterly Sessions Continued & Held for Franklin County On Wednesday 9th Day of May 1787. Present: Robert Hairston, Thomas Arthur, John Rentfro, Spencer Clack and Moses Greer. Callaway & Jubal Early vs Trembee, Jud & Accord & to Spy & Costs. Storm vs Hieth Same. Kelly vs Miller and Miller vs Miller Ref'd to Thomas Hale & Thomas Prunty & in case they disagree to choose an Umpire & his or their Awd to be the Judgt. of the Court. Rentfro vs Bates. dism'd. Thomas Arthur is Allowed 14 Days Attendance as a Witness for John Hook vs Stephen Wood.

PAGE ONE HUNDRED THIRTY-ONE

May Session 1787—Patterson vs King. a Jury Sworn, to wit, John Huston, William McCoy, Thomas Jones, Samuel Kierby, Rich'd Booth, William Rentfro, Chattin Doggett, John Spangler, David Guttery, Isaiah Wilson, Stephen Wood and Robert Holliday. Verd. Ret, for the Plt. & O. R. Miller vs Kelly Ref'd to Thomas Hale & Thomas Prunty & in case they disagree to Choose an Umpire & his or their Award to be the Judgt of the Court. Huckaby vs Hodges. Su'y to be given Next Court, or to be Disd. Stokes vs Goggins Cont. Perryman vs Rowland Exors. Judgt Accorg to Spy When assets. Patterson vs Hubbard. Hucoby vs Patterson Su'y to be given Next Ct. or to be Dism'd. Same vs Wilson Same. Jones vs Spangler, a Jury Sworn, to Wit, William McCoge, Samuel Kearby, Richard Booth, Chattin Doggitt, David Guttery, Isaiah Willis, Stephen Wood, Robert Holliday, Peter Gearhart, Benjamin Duvalt, William Eubanks & Thomas Doggett. Verdi. Ret for the Deft, with Costs. Same vs Same Cont. Martin Woody is Allowed 3 Days Attendance as a Witness for Callaway against Price. John Roberson 3 Days for the same. William Akers is allowed 10 Days Attendance for Wm. Miller against Wm. Kelly. James McVey is Allowed 7 Days for the Same.

PAGE ONE HUNDRED THIRTY-TWO

May Sessions 1787—Woods & * * * vs Coleman dis'd at Defts Costs. Mary Huff is Allowed Six Days Attendance as a Witness Jas. Jones Agt Spangler. Thomas Haile is Allowed Ten Days Attendance as a Witness for Daniel Spangler ads Tho. Jones. Lewis Bryant the Same. Thomas Miller 10 Dys. for the Same. John Spangler is Allowed 3 Days Attendance as a Witness for Thomas Jones agts Daniel Spangler. Callaway vs Peirce a Jury Sworn (to Wit) Theodorick Webb, John Kelly, Thomas Haile Thomas Miller, William Farguson, Thomas Watts, Joseph Ellis, David Baiton, Thos. James, John Campbell, Isaac Rentfro & William Cavenaugh. Verdt. Ret for the Pt. for £3.0.0 & Costs. William Eubanks is Allowed 6 Days Attendance as a Witness for Jno. Peice ads James Callaway. Johnson vs Doggett Cont. at Defts Costs. Martha Miller is Allowed 6 Days Attendance as a Witness for Johnson agt Doggett 3 Days to be Tax'd the Deft. Mary Harwell, the Same. Rachel Wright is Allowed 6 Days Attendance as a Witness for Will Kelly ads Wm. Miller. Thomas Prunty is allowed 10 Days Attendance as a Witness for Spangler ads Jones. Thorp vs M. Rentfro, Issue Waved & Judgt, Confessed Accorg & to Spy & Costs.

---

* * * Missing.

PAGE ONE HUNDRED THIRTY-THREE

May Session 1787—Walker vs Jones's Admr. Judgt. for £11.10.6. When Assets. Wilson vs Js. Rentfro, dism'd at Defts. Costs. Welch vs Kelly, Adm'd Cont. Griffith vs Kelly dism'd Agreed. Theat vs Booth, Cont. Callaway & Early vs McDowell. A Jury Sworn, to wit, Samuel Kearby, Mordecai Moseby, Robert Holliday, Peter Gearhart, Wm. Ferguson, Thomas Welch, Isaiah Willis, Benjamin Duvalt, Elisha Estes, David Guttery, Saml Patterson & Thomas Miller. Verd Ret for the Plt £2.16.9 & O. R. Jones vs Webb. A Jury Sworn, (to wit) Samuel Kearby, Mordecai Moseby, Robert Holliday, Patrick Sloane, Thos. Watts, Thomas Welch, Isaiah Willis, Wm. Cavenaugh, Elisha Keen, David Guttry, Samuel Patterson & John Johnson. Verd. Ret for the Plt. for 1/. & O. R. Prunty vs Jones. A Jury Sworn (to Wit) John Hunter, Richard Richards, Joel Chitwood, William Ferguson, Thomas Miller, John Booth, Peter Greeheart, Daniel Brown, William Thompson, James Huston & Stephen Wood. Verd. Ret for the Plt. for 12/ & Cost & O. R. Thorp vs Rentfro Judg. Confessed by the Deft. accordl. to Spy & the Deft. to have Leved it for the Costs. Thomas Haile is Allowed 10 Days attendance as a Witness for Prunty agt Jones. Obediah Richardson is Allowed 10 Days for the Same. William Rayan is Allowed 10 Days Attendance as a Witness for Patterson vs Hubbard.

PAGE ONE HUNDRED THIRTY-FOUR

May Sessions 1787—John Fuson is Allowed 6 Days Attendance as a Witness for * * * Jones agt. Webb. John Rentfro is Allowed 3 Days Attendance as a Witness for Webb ads Jones. Elizabeth Rentfro is Allowed 6 Days Attendance as a Witness for Mark Rentfro ads Thorp. John Rentfro Gent is App'd Surveyer of the Road from William Fargusons on Pigg River to the Top of the Mountain & a List filed be his Gang. Houston vs Livesay a Ded aw'd the Plt. to take the Dep of Jno. McCary & Eliza Kenney Giving the Deft 10 Days Notice. Call vs Short Jno. Cheetwood Spl. Bail & C. O. The Court is Adj'd till Tomorrow 8 o'Clock.—T. ARTHUR. At a Court of Quarterly Sessions Cont'd & held for Franklin County on the 10th. Day of May 1787. Present: Hugh Innes, Thomas Arthur, John Rentfro & Moses Greer & P. Saunders, Gent. On the Motion of Stephen

71

Smith Clerk of this Court, John Cox is Admited as a Depty. Clerk, Whereupon he took the Usual Oaths to the Common Wealth & Also the Oath of a Depty. Clerk.

PAGE ONE HUNDRED THIRTY-FIVE

May Sessions 1787—R. Jones vs. Tho. Jones. A Jury Sworn, to Wit, John Hunter, William Cavanaugh, Thomas Watt, Samuel Kearby, David Guttery, John Terry, Lewis Davis, Archibald Farley, Isaac Bates, John Jamison, Martin Binan & William Jamison. Verd. Ret. for the Dft. & O. R'd. Elizabeth Webb is Allowed One Days Attendance as a Witness for Thom. Jones ads R. Jones. Milley Anduson is Allowed Six days Attendance as a Witness for the Same ads Same. Anna Buckanan is Allowed 2 Days for the Same. John Hoff is allowed 5 Days for the Same. William McCoy is Allowed 4 Days Attendance as a Witness for Rach'l Jones vs Thos. Jones. Rachel Jones is Allowed 4 Days for the Same vs Same. Jameson vs Gadon, Cont'd at Defts Cost. Holliday vs Willson, Cont'd for award. Chitwood vs Coleman Cont'd. Obadiah Richardson is Allowed 5 Days Attendance as a Witness for John Chitwood agt, Ashford Napier. Delaney vs Bates, Cont'd at Pltfs Costs. Delancy vs Bates, Cont'd Same.

PAGE ONE HUNDRED THIRTY-SIX

May Sessions 1787—Thorp vs Rentfro. Ferguson vs Miller a Jury Sworn, to Wit, Obediah Richardson, John Hunter, John Haile, Henry Jones Peter Geerheart, Daniel Brown, Walter Bernard, Wm. Thompson, Martin Binnion, William Cavennough, Thomas Jones & William Greer. Verdi. Ret. for the Pltf, for £9.0.11 & O. R'd. Exor Ren'd & waved & Set for Augment Exon waved & Jud. Accdg. to Verd. Menefee vs Hale and Hale vs Menifee Dism'd Agreed. Asberry vs Stokes & King Cont'd Williams vs Chitwood and Chitwood vs Williams Cont'd for Award. Thorp vs Isaac Rentfro. Jud. Confess'd accordl to Splty & Costs. On the Motion of Thomas Jones for an Injunction to Stay the Proceedings at Common Law on a Jud. Obtain'd Against him by Thomas Poteet, the Same is Requested with Costs. Greer vs Webb, the Plt Agrees to Stay Exem. on a Former Jud. of this Court untill the first Day of Apl. next. John Hunter is Allowed 3 Days Attendance as a Witness for Isaac Bates ads Delancy.

* * * Missing.

Wattson vs Simpson, Jud. for £5 & Costs. Delancy vs Bates Referd to Colo. H. Innes & Colo. James Callaway & in Case they Disagree to chuse an Umpire & his or their Award to be Jud of the Court.

PAGE ONE HUNDRED THIRTY-SEVEN

May Session 1787—Willson vs Smith Exetrs, A Jury Sworn, to Wit, Samuel Kerby, Lewis Davis, John England, Thomas Watts, William Rentfro, Thos. * * *, John Terry, William McCoy, Saml. McCoy, William Cavnough, John Hale, & Chattin Doggett, Verd. Ret. for the Defts & O R'd. Welch vs Rae, A Jury Sworn, to wit, Saml Kerby, Lewis Davis, John England, Thomas Watts, William Rentfro, Thomas Plastun, John Terry, William McCoy, Sam'l. McCoy, William Cavenough, John Hale, & Chatten Doggett, Vert. Ret. for the Dft. & O. R'd. It is Ordered that the Shereff make his Returns in future Agreeable to Law. Mead vs Rentfro Cont'd Thomas Prunty is Allowed 6 Days Attendance as a Witness for Josiah Hale ads Welch. Webster vs Isaac Rentfro Jno. Ferguson Spl. Bl. & C. O. Quigley vs Miles Genl Issue. Arthur vs Levsey, It is Ordered by this Court that No Costs for the Witnesses Attendance to be Taxed in the Bill of Costs. Arthur vs Greer Greer vs Arthur Dism'd, Agreed. Brandon vs Jones & Rentfros Tho's Prunty Spl. Bl. & Imp. The Court is Adjourned till Court in Course.—HUGH INNES.

PAGE ONE HUNDRED THIRTY-EIGHT

June Court 1787—At a Court held for Franklin County On Monday the 4th Day of June 1787. Present: Hugh Innis, Thomas Arthur, Jonathan Richeson, Spencer Clack, Hugh Martin, Moses Greer & Geo. Turnbull Gent. A Deed from Archilaus White to Jno. Meapell further Prov'd & O. R'd. Also from Daniel French to Danl Laymon Prov'd & O. R'd. Rich'd Salsberry is Exempt from the Payt. of County Levis in future. A Deed from Danl. French Sr. to Stephen Peters Prov'd & O. R'd. James Turner is exempt from the Payt. of County Levies in future. A Deed from Danl French to Danl. Rudy Prov'd & O. R'd. Also from Ashford Napier to John Burgess Ack. & O R'd. Also from Joel Atkins & William Young to David Shockley Act. & Eliz the Wife of Wm. Young Religt &c. Also.

* * * Missing.

Elijah Jones to Isaac Lemmon Prov'd & O R'd. Also. Abraham Vanwindee to Benja. Cook Prov'd & O R'd. Also from Thos. Jones to Sam'l Underwood Ack'd & O. R'd. Also from Thos. Jones to John Hook Prov'd & O R'd. Also the Same to Wm. Martin, for the Same Land w'ch was Considered by the Court to be Subsiquint to Hooks Deed & also Considered to be Fraudulent & therefore Not to be admited to Record.

PAGE ONE HUNDRED THIRTY-NINE

June Court 1787—A Deed from William Young to Danl. Richardson Jr. Ack'd & O R'd. Also from Martin Binnion to Saml. Webb. Prov'd by 2 Witnessed & O. C. Also Joshua Brock to Ashford Napier Jr., Prov'd & O. R'd. Also Rich'd Bailey to John Arthur Prov'd by One Witness & O. C. Also Hills Extrs. to Walter Bernard Further Ack'd & O R'd. Thos. Arthur, John Rentfro Gent. are Allowed Eight Dollars, Each & Spencer Clack, Seven Dollars for their Survices as Commissioners who Attended the Survey in Running the Dividing Line between this & Henry County to be Levied at the Laying the Next County Levy. Thomas Prunty, Saml. Hairston, Jno. Dickenson, Wm. Ryan Rich'd Radford, Alex Ferguson, George Tumbull & Thomas Hale. Jas. Prunty took the usual Oaths to the Common Wealth & Also as Overseer of the Poor. David Jones is Appointed Surv. of the Road in Place of Bailey Carter. A Deed from Benja. Poteet to Jno. Divers Prov'd by 3 Witnesses & O. R'd. John Smith is App'd a Constable in Place of Bailey Carter. Joseph Trent is Exempt from the Payt. of County Levies in future. Present: Robert Hairston, Swinfield Hill, John Rentfro, & John Smith & John Dickenson Gent. Hugh Innes, Peter Saunders, & Thos. Arthur Gent. are Recom'd to his Excellency the Governor as Proper Persons to Serve as Shiff of this County for the Ensuing Year.

PAGE ONE HUNDRED FORTY

June Court 1787—A Deed Abel Edwards to Danl. Jett fur. Proved & O. R. Also from Edw'd Choat to Callaway & Earlys Prov'd & O R'd. Lyon vs Lyon, a Dedimus is Awarded the Pltf. to take the Deposition of Daniel Burnit. It is Ordered by the Court that the Hands of Thos. Prunty, Isaih Willis & His Gang,

Joel Walker & His Gang, David Jones & his Gang, do Work One Day Each on the Road of w'ch Jno. Rentfro Gen is Surv. The Report of a Road from the Hf. way Spring to the head of the North fork of Blackwater Ret. & O R'd & John Lisaney is Appointed Sur. of the Same & the List Filed to be his Gang W'ch he is to Keep in Repair Accordl. to Law. Daniel Richardson is Appointed Sur. of the Road from Wm. Jamisons to Chestnut Creek & the List fil'd to be his Gang. Jas. Williams is Appointed Surv. of the Old Road from the Muddy fork of Chestnut Down by John Birds to the fork of the Road to Henry Courthouse & the List filed to be his Gang w'ch he is to Clear Out & Keep in Repair accordl. to Law. (List not fild). James Rentfro is App'd Sur. of the Road in the Place of Thos. Prunty. Geo. Ferguson is Appointed Surv. of the Road in Place of Thos. Hale. Ordered that Perryman Webb, Austin Choat Rich'd Glover, Thos. Chandler, William Chandler, & Smith Webbs and Make Tythe are to be add to Edw'd Choats List of hands. Order'd that Danl. Brown, Rich'd N, Venable, Thos. Crutcher, Pratt Hughes, Ambrose Goff and Jno. Cox, are to be add to Moses Greers List of hands.

PAGE ONE HUNDRED FORTY-ONE

June Court 1787—A Deed from Lewis Jenkins to John P. Anderson Prov'd by 2 W's & O. R'd. John Law Produced Comm. from his Excellency the Governor apptg him Lieut of the Militia in this County, Whereupon he took the Usual Oaths to the Com. Wealth & the oath of a Lieut of the Militia of this County. Hugh Innis Gent. is Appointed to Import for the use of this County Weights and measure of the Proper Standard and that a Sufficiency of Tobacco to Levied for him at the Laying of the next County Levy to satisfy & pay him for the Same. The Court is Adjourned till Court in Course.—HUGH INNES. At a Court held for Franklin County on Monday the Second Day of July 1787. Present: Hugh Innes, Thomas Arthur, Jonathan Richardson, John Rentfro, Spencer Clack, Gent. Sheridan v Hill. Dism'd. It is Ordered that Jesse Thompson an Orphan Child be bound to Robert Boulton. Also Jas. Stephen a Bastard Child Bound to Jas. Prunty. Also James Butler to Jno. Turner. Also Isles Cooper Hoff to Thos. Prunty. Also Elish Jones to Geo. Slaton.

PAGE ONE HUNDRED FORTY-TWO

July Court 1787—Ordered that the Overseers of the Poor do Bind Out Also Rebecca Thompson to James Greer. A Deed from Graves & Jenkins to Towsend further Proved & O. R'd. Same from Cockron & Jenkins to Same further Prov'd O &. R'd. Also from Jno. Scrugs to Wm. Griffith Prov'd & O R'd. A Bill of Sale from Chattin Pollard to Wm. Pollard ack. & O. R'd. The last Will & Testament of Thomas Smith Produced in Court, Proved by one Witness & O. C. Cook vs Jamison. Jud. Rep Bond vs Thos. Jamison. An Injunction Granted Jas. Dillion to Stay the Process of a Jud. Obtaind vs him by Littleberry Stewart, who with Robert Napier, Joel Chitwood & Sam'l Dillon ent. into Bond & Ack'd the Same. An Injunction is Granted Robert Holliday to Stay the Proceedings of a Jud. Obtained Agst. him by Sam'l Calland who with Wm. Eubanks & Marin Duvall Ent.'d into Bond & Ack'd the Same. Walton vs Js. Rentfro & Wm. Milla (Miller) Jud. on Rep Bond. Asbury vs Pucket, John Hook Spl. Bl. & Impl.

PAGE ONE HUNDRED FORTY-THREE

July Court 1787—It is Ordered that the following Persons be Summoned to next Court to Show Cause why they failed Giving in a List of Their Taxes Property, Viz. Saml. Keith, Nathaniel Law, George Haynes, Parmenas Haynes, William Stewart, Jno. Stewart. William Dillingham, Sr., Wm. Dillingham, Jr., Joshua Dillingham, John Loyd & George Robertson. William Dodd is Appointed Surv. of the Road from the B. Water Road Crossing B. Water at Pat Stones & from there to the Grassyhill Road W'ch he is to keep in Repair accordl. to Law & the List filed to be his Gang. Ordered that the Clerk of this Court do Certyfy to the Governor & Council that Mary Troup. widow of Jacob Troup Dec'd, an Inhabitant of the County of Henry (Now Franklin) & who Died in the Service of the Militia at York is in Indigent Circumstances having 3 Small Children. A Deed from Robert Hills Exetrs & Legatees to Jas. Callaway by Swinfield Hill, Walter Bernard & Bartlet Wade Ack'd & O. R. Frisley & Elliot vs Rentfro. Jud. Confess'd Agreeable to Seifa & Costs. Arthur Graham is Appointed Surv. of the Road in the place of William Thompson. Cook vs Richardson leave is Awarded the Deft. to take the Depos. of Witnesses.

PAGE ONE HUNDRED FORTY-FOUR

July Court 1787—William Toney Appeared Agreeable to his Recogce & Sundry Witness being Sworn & Examined as well in Behalf of the Comm. Wealth As the Said Toney, It is the Opinion of the Court that he the S'd Will. Toney should appear before Next Grand Jury Whereupon he Came into Court with Thos. Arthur & James McVay & Severally Acknowledged themselves Indebted to the Common Wealth of Virginia that is to Say the Said Toney in the Sum of £20 & the Said Arthur & McVey in the Sum of £10 Each to be Levied on their Respective Goods & Chattles Land & Tenaments on Condition he does not Appear before the Court on the First Monday in Augt. Next. William Ryan D. S. Came into Court & Quallifyed to his Collection Agreeable to Law W'ch is Ordered to be Certf'd. William Cowden is Appointed Surv. of the Road from the X-Road by Saml. Sullevants to the Old Road by Harwells Cabbins the Way Israel Standifer & John Law Marked it & the List filed to be his Gang w'ch he is to keep in Repair Agreeable to Law. James Rentfro Qualif'd as an Ensign of the Militia of this County. William Greer is Appointed Surveyor of the Road from Witchers Road at the Pittsylva. Line towards Franklin Courthouse, Extend-ing to the Cross Road by Saml Sullivants the Way 1st Was Marked by Israil Standifer to Jno. Law & the List fild to be his Gang W'ch he is to Keep in Repair &c.

PAGE ONE HUNDRED FORTY-FIVE

Hugh Woods D. S. Came into Court & Qualified to his Colectns Agreeable to Law w'ch is Ordered to be Certifyed. Thomas Prunty John D. S. Came into Court & Qual'd to their Collections Agreeable to Law, W'ch Ordered to be Certifyed. On the Motion of Robert Williams, Gent. D. States Attorney for this County, Jonathan Richardson A Justice of the Peace for the S'd County who had been Represented to the Court as a Person who had Declared himself Against the Payment of the Publick Taxes. On Consideration whereof & after examining Divers Witnesses the Court are of Opinion that the said Rich-ardson was rather Intoxicated & Expressed great Concern for what he had Said, Therefore in the Oponion of the Court he stands Excused & that the Same be Certifyed to his Excelly the

Governor. George Lamb Appeared Agreeable to his Recognizance
& Divers Witnesses being Sworn as well on behalf of the Common
Wealth as of the Prisoner at the Bar, on Consideration whereof
of the Court are of Opinion that he is Guilty of the fact whereof
he stands Charged, & that he Ought to receive a further Tryal
before the Honble the Genl. Court on the first day thereof,
Whereupon he threw himself on the Mercy of the Court & It is
Ordered that he receive 10 lashes on his Bare Back.

PAGE ONE HUNDRED FORTY-SIX

July Court 1787—Information being given the Court by the
D. States Attorney that John Chitwood had opposed the Sheriff
of this County in the Collection of the Publick Taxes, and for
Declaring himself Determined not to pay his Own Taxes, & Also
for resisting the Sheriff & Continuing to Stand in Opposition
and also far saying he Ought to go to Gaol, but that the Court
nor all their friends Could not Carry him there, It is therefore
Ordered by the Court that he be find Ten Pounds & to be imprisoned till he Pays the Same & then to Give 2 Securities for
his Good behaviour the S'd Chitwood in the Sum of £20 & his
Securities in the Sum of £10 each. Whereupon the said Chitwood W'th Thomas Arthur & Isaac Rentfro his Securities Came
into Court and severally Ack'd themselves Indebted to the Com.
Wealth of Virginia in the Sum of £10, that is to say the S'd
Chitwood in the Sum of £20 & the S'd Arthur & Rentfro in the
sum of Ten Pounds each to be Levied on their Respective Goods
& Chattels Lands & Tenaments on Condition the S'd Chitwood
does not behave himself in an Orderly Manner to All the Officers
of this County for a Twelve Months & a Day. The Court is
Adjourned Till Court in Course.—HUGH INNES.

PAGE ONE HUNDRED FORTY-SEVEN

August Court 1787—At a Court of Quarterly Sessions Be-
gun & Held for Franklin County On Monday the Sixth Day of
Aug. 1787. Present: Hugh Innes, Jonathan Richardson, Moses
Greer & Hugh Martin, Gent. Pate vs Wright, James Wright
Spl. B. & Spl. Impl. Greer vs Wright, William Rentfro Spl. Bl.
& Delivered him up whereupon the Deft. is Prayed. Same vs
Same. in Custody. Callaway & Co. vs Webb Spl. B. Wm. Rent-
fro Spl. Bl. & Saml Simmons vs Hudgins, Peter Wood Spl. Bl.

& Spl Im. Gallaway & Co vs O Tarby, Judgt, Conf'd accordg to Sply & Costs, Stay exon. till 1st Day of Oct. Next. Same vs Jno. Markum. Same. Thomas Hail, foreman, Robert Prunty, John Wilkes, Wm Swanson, Wm. Haynes, Elisha Estes, Samuel Bird, Owen Ruble, Daniel Ross, David Barton, Peter Geerheart, Peter Young, Edmund Levisey, Benjamin Cook, Elisha Estes, Sen, Skelton Taylor, Benjamin Griffith & John Clybourn, Who were Sworn as a Grand Jury of Inquest for the Body of this County. Whereupon they withdrew to Consuit on their presentments. Frens vs Anderson, Wm Ryan Spl. B. & Jud by defaul Hook vs Cockran, Saml. Cockran Spl. Bl. & Spl. Iml. Tax. The Grand Jury Returned into Court whereupon they made Several Presentments & Process Ord. & Issued.

PAGE ONE HUNDRED FORTY-EIGHT

Callaway & Co. vs N. Adey. Judgmt, Confessed Accorl. to Spy & Costs, Stay Exen. Untill Novem. Court Not. Replevey. Same vs H. Lavine Same. Ferris vs Anderson. Jud. Conf'd Stay Execu. till Novem. Court & Costs. Gallasos &c vs Edwards, Ro. Perryman & Jas. Turley Sp. Bl. Graham & Co vs O. Farguson, Thomas Simmons Spl. Bl. & Delivered the Deft. Up & Prayed Committed. Hook vs Same Same. Same vs Simmons, Geo & Thomas Simmons Spl. Bl. Same vs Jones dism'd. Harkrider vs Morgan dis'd. Hook vs Jones Elisha Bowls a Garshee, being Sworn Sayith he has in his hands One Reel, 1 Qt. Bottle & a Drawing Knife of the Defts Property. Wm. Martin and other Garishee Says he hath in hands 2 Chears & a Plow Hoe. Also Stephen Holland and Other Garshee Says he Owes the Def. nothing. Judgt for £39.13. out of which is to be deducted the neat proceeds of the Sale of a Tract of Land originally sold at Sheriff Sale for £30.10s, but liable to a Discount of whatever the Claim of Richard Bandy can be Purchased for who has the apparent Title to a Part of the Sail Land or in case the said Hook and Bandy cannot agree on the Compound for the Land a Suit in Chancery to be instituted for the decision of the Title & Sum to be Discounted & Ord. Conda.

PAGE ONE HUNDRED FORTY-NINE

August Court 1787—Flowers vs J. Jones, Thomas Jones Spl. B. & Spl. Impl. Callaway & Early vs Austin & Boyd. Judgt. Confessed.

Accordl to Spy & Co. Stay Exon. till Novemr. Court. Christopher vs Jones. Judgt. for £3.10.7 & O Conda. Atta effect. Callaway & Co. vs Cockran, Saml Cockran Spl. B. Judgt. Confessed Accorgly to Spy. Stay Exon. till November Next. Hill vs Evans, Judmt for £12. Agreeabel to the Scale for Sept. 1788, With Int, till Paid & O Conda. Callaway & Co. vs S. Thompson, Moses Greer & Thomas Thompson Spl. Bl. Mary McVey is Allowed 5 Days Attendance as a Witness for William Miller Agt. William Kelley. Dickerson vs Keen. Samuel Patterson Spl. Bl. Cook vs Simpson. Judgmt for £77.10.4 & O. Conda. On the Motion of Jasper Houser by his Atta Judgt is Granted him agt Thos. Jamerson & his Su'rs on a Replevy Bond. Hook vs Jones an Atta brought up, & it is Ordered that an apple Mill, A parcel of Flax, Some old Casks, a Keg of Vinegar, and the Mulatto Wench & one Child, be sold to satisfy the Said Judg't. Same for the benefit of Nathan Turner Judgmt for £30 with Interest from the 25th Day of December 1785. & Cost & O Conda. Subject to their Hook vs Jones.

PAGE ONE HUNDRED FIFTY

August Court 1787—J. Callaway & J. Early vs Geo. Livesay, Thos. Doggett. Same vs John Livesey Spl. Bl. Howard vs Anderson Wm. Ryan Spl. Bl. Jud. Conf'd According to Spl & Cost W'th Stay. Js. Rentfro vs W. Mead (an Atta) Judmt for £30. Jas. Callaway a Garn' being Sworn Saith he Owes the Deft. £10. has Specie & Castings, Barr Iron & Steel Sufficient to Satisfy the Pltfs Demand & Costs. Grayham vs Graves, Peyton Smith Spl. Bl. Scott vs Miller Dism'd. It appearing to this Court, that about 8 Or 9 Days that Mavey Jones, Wife of Thomas Jones Condenily forced from Thomas Prunty, Deputy Shf. for this County, a Replevy Bond, Danl. Spangler agt the said Thomas Jones. The Court are of Opinion that a Judgmt, may Pass, when the said Bond Expires. Also John Farguson Motion agt. the same. Parker vs Whitworth. Same. A Deed from Jno. Grimmit to Jas. Gallaway & Early, Ack'd O. R. David Beheler Having Carved the Peace agt. Zachariah Davis & John Griffin, It is ordered that the said Davis & Griffin give Su'y for their Good, Behaviour. Whereupon the said Davis & Griffin came into with Zachariah Davis & Edward Shoat their Securitys came into Court & Ack'd themselves Severally indebted to the Com. Wealth of Virginia, that is to say the said Davis & Griffin in the Su. of £10. each & each of his.

PAGE ONE HUNDRED FIFTY-ONE

August Court 1787—Securities in the Sum of £— each to be Levied on their Respective Goods & Chattles Lands & Tene- ments. On Condition they be not of Good Behavior One Year & A Day & Especially towards David Behler. Willson vs Jones Dism'd. The Court is Adj'd till Tomorrow 9 o'clock.—HUGH INNES. At a Court held & Continued for Franklin County on Tuesday the Seventh Day of August 1787. Present: Hugh Innis, Robert Hairston, Peter Suanders, Swinfield Hill, Moses Greer, Gent. Johnson vs Doggett. A Jury Sworn, to wit, Joel Estes, John Wiles, James Turley, James Cannon, Obediah Richardson, Samuel Bird, Thomas Jones, William Menifee, Martin Binnion, Thomas Jones, William Menifee & William Thompson. Jury not agreed on Verdict. Doggett vs Johnson, A Jury Sworn, to Wit. Joel Estes, John Wilkes, James Turley, James Cannon, Obediah Richardson, Samuel Bird, William Cowden, William Ferguson, Martin Binnion, Thomas Jones, William Menifee & William Thompson. Jury not agreed in Verdict. Martin Assee vs Par- berry, A Jury Sworn. Verdict Ret. for the Plf. for Damages & O Rd. Martin Assee vs Parberry. A Jury Sworn. Verdit Ret. for the Plf. for Damages & O. Re.

PAGE ONE HUNDRED FIFTY-TWO

August Court 1787—On a Mot. for Injunt. Jones vs Souther- land Ref'd to Peter Saunders Esq. & William Crump, & in case they disagree to Choose an Umpire & to stay Exon until the Referees Make Report to the Court & C. On the Complaint of Peter Saunders Gent. Against Thomas Arthur Gent. On Sus- picion as being Immecable of the Com. Wealth & on the Exami- nation Divers Witnesses the Court are of opinion that the said Ar- thur is not Guilty of the said Complaint. On the Complaint of Robert Williams Gent. States Atto. for this County by Informa- tion, That Thomas Arthur Gent. had Refused the Payment of Taxes & resisted Government & Endeavored to Excite the People Against the Same, On the Examination of Sundry Witnesses As Well on behalf of the Com. Wealth as the Said Thomas Arthur.

It appeared to this Court that the Information is Groundless &
the Said Thomas Arthur Stands Acquited. On the Motion of
John Kelly to Stay the Proceedings of a Jud. at Com Law w'ch
Will Walton Obtained agst. him the Same is regected with Costs.
Callaway & Co. vs Ellison, Amos Spl. Bl. Jud. Confessed w'th
Stay of Excon One month. Huckaby vs Patteson Dismissed for
want of Su'y for Costs. Same vs Willsen Dismissed for want of
Su'y for Costs. Same vs Holliday Dismissed for want of Su'y for
Costs. William Dillingham Sr. is Released from his fine for not
Giving in his Taxable Property.

Across the second paragraph of this page are four large
XXXXs which are said to mean that the entry was expunged
and the complaint against Thomas Arthur reopened.

PAGE ONE HUNDRED FIFTY-THREE

August Court 1787—Holley vs Cockram. A Jury Sworn, to
Wit, Samuel Kerby, Lewis Davis, Robert Holliday, James Rich-
ardson, John Early, Jno. Guttery, Alexander Sutherland, George
Ferguson, James Prunty, Moses Wray, Obediah H. Trent, & Danl.
Spangler. Ret. for the Plft for £18.0.0 w'th Int. Agreeable to
Sply. & Costs. Sheridan vs Hill. Dismiss'd Agreed. Stober vs
Davis Refered to William Ryan & Robert Woods & in Case they
Disagree to Chuse an Umpire & his or their Determination to
be the Jud. of this Court. Present: Swinfield Hill Gent. Hancock
vs Clardy. Jud. Confessd for £1.15.10. Stay of Exeon. 3 Months.
William Stewart & John Stewart Released from their fines for
not Giving in their Taxable Property. Samuel Cockram is Allowed
4 Days Attend'ce as a Witness for Wm. Cockram at the Suit of
Wm. Holly. John Cockram 3 Days for the Same. Hill vs Early
for £12-10- & Cont'd for Garshees. Mary Hartwell is Allowed
One Days Atta. as a Witness for Jno. Johnson vs Tho. Doggett.
Martha Miller a Days for the Same. Jno. Rentfro vs Jesse Rentfro. Cont. Philip Miller is Bound to Jno. Chitwood. Nancy
Frame & Chrisly Frame is Bound to Chrisn. C. Long. Henry Ines
to Jas. Slone. Court is Adjourned till Tomorrow. 9 OClock.

PAGE ONE HUNDRED FIFTY-FOUR

August Court 1787—At a Court held & Cont'd for Franklin
County on Wednesday the 9th Day of August 1787. Present:

Hugh Innes, Thomas Arthur, Swinfield Hill, John Rentfro, Peter Saunders & John Smith, Gent. Chitwood vs Parker &c dism'd. Mead vs Rentfro. Cont. at Plfs Costs. O. Richardson vs Estes, Judgmt. for £4.0.0 & Costs. Holliday vs Willson. Cont. for Plt. Hunter vs Stogden Cont.'d for Aw'd. Stewart vs Haynes. Cont. Dickerson vs Perryman Cont. Stegall vs Jinkins Cona Cont. Richardson vs Hubbard Judgt. for Costs. McGuffy vs Underwood. Cont. Gallaway & Earlys vs Earnest. Cont. Same vs Stokes, Cont. Com Wealth vs Surv. of the Road from Turnbulls to Griffiths Creek (T. M.) Jud. Agreeable to Law. Same vs Elisha Estes Jud. Same vs Jno. Chitwood, Jud. Same vs Sur. of Road from Wm. Jamisons to Chestnut Creek (Dk).

PAGE ONE HUNDRED FIFTY-FIVE

August Court 1787—Graham vs Malin. Harris vs Hodges. Jud. Accg. to Sply & Costs. Tittle vs Haile Same. Moore vs Wade Same. Prunty vs Brown. Jud. for £55.6 & Costs. Parker vs Whitworth. Judgt. Accordl. to Note & Co. Barton vs Livesey (In Edjectmt.) Dism'd. Callaway & Early vs Hailes Judgt. Accy to Spy & Cost. Same & Co. vs Webb. Jud. Accg. to Sply & Co. Same vs Blain, Jud. Accordg. to Spy & Co. Lyne vs Gee. Same. Hook vs Martin. Same Aug. to Acct & Costs. Radford vs Wright dism'd at Deft. Costs. Saunders vs Millers, Judgt. Accg. to Spy & Co. Wm. Ashurst vs Abshire. Judgt. Accy to Spy & Co. Staples vs Gordon Judgt. Accg to Spy & Co. Trent vs Demoss, Jud. for £3. & Costs. Brown & Co. vs Vest. Judgt. Accorg. to Spy & Co. Callaway & Early vs Christian. Same. Brown vs Jones, Judgt, Conf'd Accordl. to Acco's. Thorp vs Greer. dism'd. Same vs Wm. Thompson Jud. Accg to Spy & Cost. Same vs Spangler. Dism'd. Same vs Wm. Doggett. Judgt. Accordg. to Note & Co. Same vs T. Thompson dism'd at Defts Cost. Same vs Terry Judgt. accorg to Spy & costs Dismed.

PAGE ONE HUNDRED FIFTY-SIX

August Court 1787—Thorp vs Johnson & wife dism'd. Same vs Conner. Dism'd. Mason vs Mullins. Judg. agreed. Johnson vs Greer Judgt. accg. to Acc't & Co. Richardson vs Plaster Judg. accordg. to Spy & Co. Holliday vs Christian Cont'd. Binnion vs Divine, Jud. for £3.10 & Costs. Cook vs Menis. Judgt. Accordg to Spy & Co. Daniel Brown & Co. vs Gibson, Judgt, for

£19.15-3 & O. Conda. of Atta. Effects. Willis vs Miller on a Replevy Miller vs Willis (Action) Ref'd to Daniel Spangler, Wm. Akers, Robert Jones, & Moses Rentfro & their Award to be the Judgment of this Court. Johnson vs Doggett and Doggett vs Johnson. The Jurys Sworn Yesterday not Agreeing & being Call'd today & they not Appearing they are therefore disch'd. Jas. Callaway (Garshee) William vs Mead, Judgt for £17.19.5 & O. Conda & subject to Smith & Rentfro Jud & Cont'd for Garshees. Obediah Henry Trent is Allowed 2 Days Attendance one Com'g & Return'g 28 Miles as a Witness for Asberry against Puckett. Asberry vs Puckett Ref'd to Ob. H. Trent & John Hook & in case they disagree to Chose an Umpire.

PAGE ONE HUNDRED FIFTY-SEVEN

August Court 1787—Hook vs Jones. Richard Bandy A Garn. being Sworn saith he Owes the Defent. Nothing. Com. Wealth vs Morgan. Jud. Accordg to Law. Same vs Charter. Same. Same vs Turnbull. Same. Same vs M. Greer, oyer. Same vs Prunty. Dism'd. Same vs Wood a Judgt. Same vs Abshire. Same. Samuel Letterell is Allowed 3 Days attendance as A Witness for Ole Richardson against Joel Estes. Callaway vs Brooks & Guttery Exors. a Jury Sworn, to wit, Robert Prunty, James Greer, Arthur Edwards, Jacob Booth, George Farguson, John Livesey, Thomas Jones, Danl. Glaspy, John Harris, John Wilkes, Stenor Duvall & Israel Standifer. Verd. ret. for the Def. & O. R. Swinfield Hill Gent is recommended to his Excellency the Goven. as A Proper Person to Act as Coroner for this County. Asberry vs Puckett. Aw'd Ret'd for the Plt, for £2.10.3 & O. R. Certif'd. Rich'd Compton is Allowed 2 Days Attendance as a Witness for Asberry against Puckett. Wm. Martin one day for the same. Peter Wood. One for the same. James Radford is allowed 3 Days Attendance as a Witness for Guthry Exors ads Wm. Callaway & One Comg. & Ret'g.

PAGE ONE HUNDRED FIFTY-EIGHT

August Court 1787—Thomas Lumpkin is allowed 3 Days at-tendance one coming & Retg. 40 miles as a Witn. for Callaway against Gutrys Exors. Holliday vs Bartee. Lewis Davis Spl. Bl. Never Obs cond'd G. Issue. Hunt vs Clardy &c. A Jury Sworn, to Wit, William Walton, Joshua Rentfro, Samuel Kearby, John

Early, Luke Standifer, John Chitwood, Oran Farlon, Thomas Toney, Fraggle Nicholas, Robert Mason, John Jameson & Thomas Cragg, Verd. Ret'd for the Bl. & O. R. Callaway & J. Early vs John Terry. Moses Greer came into Court & made himself a Deft. & Judgt. Con'd Accordl. to a Costs. Stay Exon. Till Oct. Court. Same vs Thos. Greer Same. Clardy vs Hunt, a Jury Sw'n, to Wit, William Walton, Joshua Rentfro, Samuel Kearby, John Early, Luke Standifer, John Chitwood, Archibald Foster, Thomas Terry, Frayl Nichols, Robert Mason, John Jameson, & Thomas Craig. Verd. Ret. for Defend. & O. R. Hook vs Ferguson and Graham & Co. Same. Will Martin & George Simmons & further Spl. Bail. A Deed William Trent to John James Ack'd the Wife Rlng'd & O. R.

PAGE ONE HUNDRED FIFTY-NINE

August Court 1787—Thomas Watts is Allowed 7 Days Attendance as a Witns for Thomas Hunt agt. Benja. Clardy. David Guttery is Allowed 7 days for the same. Samuel Langden is Allowed 2 Days Attce as a Witness for Tho. Doggett ads Johnson & One Coming & Ret. 45 Miles. Early vs Moodys &c. A Jury Sworn, to Wit, Joshua Rentfro. Samuel Kearby, John Chitwood, Ashford Napier, Luke Standifer, Jas. Greer, Samuel Boyd, Robert Perryman, Robert Mason, Thomas Craig, William Cavanaugh, & John Guttery. Verd. Re'd for the Def. & O. R. Thomas Moody is Allowed 3 Days Attend'ce as a Witness for Moody ads Early. Asberry vs Stokes &c Refr'd to Swinfield Hill & Moses Greer & In Case they Disagree to Chuse an Umpire & his or their Award to be the Jud. of the Court. Thomas Jones is Appt'd Guardian to Thos. Ramsey, Jas. & Wm. Ramsay, On his Giving Suty. at Next Court. Boyce Eidson is Allowed 4 Days Attendance & One Comg. & Ret. 45 Miles as a Witness for Guttrys Exon ads Callaway. Isles Cooper is Allowed 2 Days Attend'c as a Witness for Jno. Early Agst. Moodys. Thos. Booth is Allowed 6 Days Atte. as a Witness for Hunt vs Clardy. Trent vs Rob. Wood Gen. Shff. Jud for the Amt. of a Jud Trent vs Huckaby & Costs. Hook vs Rentfro and Bell vs Same. Jno. Rentfro Spl Bl & Spl Impl.

PAGE ONE HUNDRED SIXTY

George Simmons is Allowed 3 Days Attendance as a Witness for Jno. Early vs Moodays &c. John Wilks & Jas. Prunty are Allowed 3 Days attce Cash as A Witness for Ro. Prunty vs Brown. Court is Adjourned till Tomorrow 7. O Ck.—HUGH IN- NES. At a Court of Quarterly Sessions held & Continued for Franklin County on Thursday 9th Day of August 1787. Present: Hugh Innis, Thomas Arthur, Peter Saunders, Moses Greer, John Smith, Jno Rentfro & Swinfield Hill, Gent. Brandon vs Rentfrow &c. Thos Arthur Gent. Sur'y for Costs. George Asberry is Al- lowed 3 Days Attendance as a Witness for Ob. Trent vs Tho. Demoss. Hill vs Duval. Jud. Confessed to Stay Exeon till X Mass. Peter Sanders Genl Absent. Jno. Rentfro Present. Saunders Assee vs Miller Jud. for £2.0.0. with Int afr 7th Day of Decem. 1784 & Costs. Early vs Saunders. Dism'd w'th Costs.

PAGE ONE HUNDRED SIXTY-ONE

August Court 1787—Armstrong vs Spangler, a Jury Sworn, to Wit, Thomas Hale, Wm. Cavenaugh, George Asberry, Daniel Ward, James Buford, John Guttery, John Ferguson, Nathaniel Ofett, Samuel Webb, Philman Hairston, David Hughes & Rob- ert Perryman. A Jury Man with Drawn & it is Ord. that the Pltf. pay the Costs of the Court. Davison vs Stephanson Dism'd. John Ferguson is Allowed 3 Days Attendance as a Witness for Gutterys Extrs ads Callaway & One Coming & Ret. 58 Miles. Mary Spangler is Allowed 2 Days Attendance as a Witness for Danl. Spangler ads Armstrong. Cook vs Benja. Cook & Perryman Jud. is Granted the Plf. on Rep. Bond vs Both & the Exeon. to be Credited for £3.10.0 w'ch Sum is Enjoined whereupon the Said Perryman Came into Court & W'th John Braden his Security Ent'd into Bond & Acknowledged the Same. J. Callaway & J. Early vs Jno. Edwards, a Jury Sworn, to wit. Sam'l Kerly, Wm. Thompson, William Ferguson, Lewis Davis, Sam'l Webb, John Spangler, James Mason, Robert Johns, Wm. Cavanaugh, Thomas Miller, Thomas Hale & John Harris. Verd. Ret. for the Pltf. & O R'd. Thomas Prunty, Wm. Ryan, Jno. Ferguson, and Hugh Woods Produced before the Court a List of their Several Collec- tions Sence their Last Returns & Qualify'd to the Same Agreeable to Law.

PAGE ONE HUNDRED SIXTY-ONE B

August Court 1787—Rentfro Assee vs Callaway. A Jury Sworn, to Wit. Samuel Kerby, Wm. Thompson, Wm. Ferguson, Lewis Davis, Saml. Webb, John Spangler, James Mason, Robert Johns, William Cavanaugh, Thomas Miller, Thomas Hale & John Harris. A Juror withdrawn & Cont'd. Marcum vs Martin Jud. for £4.7.1 & Costs. Ferguson vs Sheridan, A Jury Sworn, to Wit, Thos. Hale, Sam' Kerby, Shardlow Whiteman, Joshua Rentfro, Thomas Miller, Jas. Wright, William Thompson, William Cavenaugh, John Harris, Robert Johns, Samuel Webb & Robert Perryman. Verd. for the Def. & O. R'd. Sam'l Derest is Allowed 3 Days Attend'ce for Farguson vs Sheridan. James Kennon is Allow'd 3 Days for the Same. J. Callaway & J. Early vs Jesse Rentfro. A Jury Sworn, to wit, Daniel Ward, Robert Napier, Smith Webb, James Mason, Thos. Marcum, Jas. Kennon, Lewis Davis, Plum. Hairston, Wm. Standley, Thomas Demoss, Stephen Wood & Wm. Buckannan. Verdict Ret. for the Plf. £20.12.2. Damages & O. R'd. Callaway & Co. vs Ferguson Dism'd. Thomas Evans is Allowed One Days Attendance as a Witness for J. Callaway & J. Early vs Jesse Rentfro. William Buckanan is Allowed 3 Days Attendance as a Witness for Wm. Ferguson vs Philip Sheredan. William Wright is Allowed 3 days attendance as a Witness for Sheredan ads Farguson. Absent: Hugh Innis, Thos. Arthur & Moses Greer, Gent.

PAGE ONE HUNDRED SIXTY-TWO

August Court 1787—Gillaspy vs Asberry. Thos. Arthur Spl. Bl. W. E. Set a Side of Issue, & a Jury Sworn, to Wit, Andrew Armstrong, William Ferguson, Daniel French, Jr., Mark Rentfro, John England, Ralph Bogle, William Ingram, Joshua Starkey, Martin Wooddy, John Jamison, Joseph Webb & Edward Lyon & Verd. Ref'd for Costs & O. R'd. It Appearing to this Court that Geo. Asberry & Danl. Gillaspy was Drunk at Last March Term, they are Ordered to be fined Accordg. to Law & Costs. Hugh Innis Gent. Produced a Commission from the Lieut. Governor of Virginia Appointing him Sheriff of this County Whereupon he took the Oath to the Com. Wealth as Also the Oath of a Sheriff & With James Callaway, Thomas Arthur & Moses Greer his Securitys Enter'd into Bond Accordg. to Law & Ack'd the Same. Callaway & J. Early vs Thos. Livesey, Gent. Judgt, Conf'd Accordg. to Spy & Costs Stay Exon. 2 Months. William Crowe is Allowed 2 Days attendance & One Cong. & Retg. 55 Miles as a Witnes for Levisey ads Huston. On the Motion of Hugh Innis Gent. Sheriff, William Ryan, Thomas Prunty & Hugh Woods are Admitted his Deputy Shfs. whereupon they took the Oath to the Com. Wealth & also the Oath of Depy. Shf. Francis Kellor is Allowed 3 Days Attendance as a Witness for Willam Faruson vs Phillip Sheridan. On the Motion of Stephen Smith, Clerk of this Court, Judg. is Granted him against Robert Woods late Shf of this Court for 4468 Pounds of Tobacco, Levied for the Said Smith

PAGE ONE HUNDRED SIXTY-THREE

September Court 1787—as Clerk of the said Court in the County Proost for the Year 1786. Wood vs Smith Refer'd to Hugh Innis & Swinfield Hill, Gent. & in Case they Disagree to Chuse an umpire & his or their Award to be the Jud. of the Court. Leave is Granted the Def. to take the Depo. of David Brazen on Giving 10 Days Prevs. Notice. Hugh Innis Gent. Sheriff of this County, Objects to the Sufficiency of the Gaol. Jones vs Spangler, Referd to Peter Saunder & Thomas Hale & Saml. Hairston & their Award to be the Jud. of the Court. The Court is Adjourned till Court in Course.—PETER SAUNDERS. At a Court held for Franklin County on Monday the 3rd Day of September 1787. Present: Peter Saunders, Thomas Arthur, Moses Greer & George Turnbull, Gent. Jones vs Sutherland. Award Ret'd for the Pltf, for £8.1.1½ & O R'd. It is Orderd by the Court that Thos. Arthur & Moses Greer Appointed to Regulate the hands who work on the Road from the head of Maggotty to Blackwater.

PAGE ONE HUNDRED SIXTY-FOUR

September Court 1787—A Deed from Geo. Haynes to Barnabas Arthur Ack'd & Lucy Ann the Wife being Privily Ex'd Reling'd &c. A Deed from David Shockly to Robert Boulton Proved by One Witness & O. C. Also from Hampton Wade to Antho. Pate Prov'd by Witness & O. C. Also from David Polley to James Brummit Ack'd & O. R. Also from Walter Aday to Jno. Craighead Ack Mary the Wife Relinguish'd &c. Also from

Wm. Jenkins to Willson Douglass Proved & O R'd. Also from Thomas Potter & Frederick Rives to Harmon Cook Ack & Susannah the Wife of Potter being Privily Exam'd Relinguish & O. R. Also from Thos. Hukenson to Wm. Long & Wm. Huckenson Ack'd & Mary the Wife bing Prively Ex'd Reling'd &c. Mary Boulton Came into Court & Volentarily Relinguished her Dower in a Tract of Land Sold to Lodowick Tuggle by her Dec'd Husband & the Same is Ord. to be Recorded. A Deed from Wm. Hutcherson to Philip Hutchenson Ack'd & O. R'd. Also from Peter Blankenship to Jno. Stewart Proved & O. R'd. Also from Josiah Maxcey to Mathew Agee Proved & O. R'd. Also Peter Blankenship to Jno. Jones Proved by 2 Witness & O. C.

PAGE ONE HUNDRED SIXTY-FIVE

September Court 1787—A Deed from Richard Bailey to Jno Jones Proved & O R'd. Also from William Stegall to Wm. Bohanon Prov'd by 2 Witnesses & O. C. On the Motion of Benja. Clardy, an Injunc. is Granted him to Stay the Proceedgs of a Jud. Obtained Agst. him by Thos. Hunt, whereupon he Entered into Bond W'th Richard Booth his Security in the Sum of Twenty Pounds & Ack'd Same. A Deed from William Bohanan to Edgcomb Guilliams Ack'd & Judith the Wife being Privily Examined Relinguish &c. Articles of Agreement Between Sam'l Hairston, Thomas Livsay & John Bobdy, was Ack'd by the s'd Hairston and Livsay & O R'd. A Deed from John Roberts to John Johnson Proved & O. R'd. Moses Hudgins, Chas. Semmons, Wm. Simmons, & Jas. Roe are Appointed to View a Way for a Road from Bratchers ford on Stanton River to Danl. Frenches & Make Report &C. An Inventory of the Estate of Jesse Kerby dec'd was Produ'd in Court by the Executors & the Same Was Order'd to be Recorded. Thomas Douglass Came into Court & took the Oath to the Com. Wealth, and Entered into Bond W'th Frederick Rives & Saml. Patteson his Securitys in the Sum of £500 for the Performances of his Duty in the Solemnization of Matrimony. A Deed from Jno. Heard to Hezekiah Farmer Ack'd & O R'd.

PAGE ONE HUNDRED SIXTY-SIX

September Court 1787—A Deed from William Weeks to Wm. Mavity further Prov'd & O. R'd. Mary Boulton Came into Court and W'th Thomas Boulton & Robert Boulton her Securtys.

Entered into Bond in Penalty of £500 for the Faithful Performances of her Duty as Admrx of the Estate of Robert Boulton
Dec'd & Fred. Rives, Wm. Graves, Frank Graves & Wm. Greer
are Appointed to Appraise the S'd Eatate. It is Ordered that the
Overseers of the Poor do Bind Sarah Miller to Jacob Prillaman
Sr. Agreeable to Law. Also Peter Miller to Jacob Prillaman Jr.
Also Jno. Blankenship to Thos. Parker. Also Jno. Blankenship
to Joseph Hambrick. On the Motion of George Asberry to remit
the Costs of a Suit Awarded Jere. Puckett at his Suit, the Same
is agreed with costs. Trent vs Hardin. Thos. Parker Spl. Bl.
George Turnbull, Gent. is Appointed a Captain of the Militia
of this County in the Place of Capt. Isaac Rentfro who is Re-
moved. Joseph Webb is Appointed Constable for this County
in the Room of Wm. Canaday who Qualified Accorg. to Law.
On the Motion of Joshua Starkey, it is Ordered that his Negro
Man Bristol be Levy free in future. James Kenneday is Appointed
Surv. of the Road from Shooting Creek to Ottar Creek in the
Room of Jno. Peek & the usual hands to be his Gang. It is Or-
dered by the Court that Eliza Butler be bound to Jno. Bryan
Agreeable to Law.

PAGE ONE HUNDRED SIXTY-SEVEN

September Court 1787—John Ferguson D. L. Came unto
Court & Qualif'd to his Collcn. Accordg to Law. On the Motion
of James Callaway & Co. A Jud. is Granted him Against John
Hook & John Hook on Rep. Bond. Finney vs Miller the Same.
Cook vs Ramsey & Jones the Same. Wm. Ryan, Thos. Prunty
and Hugh Woods Came into Court & Qualifyed to them Several
Collections accordl to Law. Smith Webb is Appointed Sur. of
the Road in the Room of Edw's Choat & the usual hands to be
his Gang. It is Ordered that Jno. Woody w'th all Rosses Male
Tythes on that Plantation be Added to Capt. Hills List of hands.
William Griffith is Allowed 4 Days Attce as A Witness for
Thos. Jones vs Spangler. Court is Adjourned till Court in
Course.—PETER SAUNDERS.

PAGE ONE HUNDRED SIXTY-EIGHT

October Court 1787—At a Court held for Franklin County
on Monday the first Day of October 1787. Present: Jonathan
Richardson, John Smith, Moses Greer, George Turnbull & Jno.

Rentfro, Gent. An Inventory of the Estate of Robert Boulton was Produced in Court & the Same was Ordered to be Recorded. Miller vs Willis Award Ret. & O. R. A Deed from Turner Rich- ardson to Rich'd Richardson Proved & O. R. Also the same to Thomas Martin Proved & O. R. Also Arthur Cooper to Thomas Martin Proved & O. Rd. Also Thomas Martin to John Early. Ack'd & O. R. Also from Jesse Hall to Wm. Clay Proved & O. R. Also Richard McClary to John Slone Ack'd & Mary the Wife being Privily Ex'd Reling'd & O. R. Also Jno. Edwards to Jubal Early Ack'd & Ruth the Wife being Privily Ex'd Reling'd & O. R. Also from John Kandy to John Slaughter Ack'd & Eliza the Wife being Privily Ex'd Reling'd & O. R. Also from Daniel Stewart to Evan Price Ack. & Amy the Wife being Privily Exam'd Reling'd & O. R. Also Wm. Young to Lodowick Tygle Ack'd & O. R. Also The same to Nathaniel Law the same. Also David Shockley to Robert Boulton Ack'd & O. R. Also Rich'd Edmundson to Isham Farguson Ack'd & O. R. Also Leonard Tenant to Amoss Richardson P'd & O. R. Also from John Willis to Thomas Miller Ack'd & Pheby the Wife being Privily Exam'd Reling'd & O. R.

PAGE ONE HUNDRED SIXTY-NINE

October Court 1787—A Deed from Rich'd Venable to Jas. Prunty Ack'd & Mary & O. R'd. Dukeson Ext. vs Keen. Dism'd at Defdts Cost. Jubal Early, Tom Moody, John Cooper, & Thos. Martin or any three of them are App'd to View a Way for A Road from the Mouth of Prater Run on Staunton River to the Blk. Water Road where Early's Road Crosses the Same & Make Report thereof to this Court. A Deed from Thos. Miller & Elizabeth his Wife, Jno. Willis & Phoebe his Wife to Chas. Menis Proved as to Willes & Phoebe the Wife being Privily Ex'd Reling'd & O. C. A Deed from Thos. Miller & Eliza. his Wife, John Willis & Phebe his Wife to Seicily & Catherin Minnix Proved as to Willis & his Wife being Privily Exam'd reling'd & O. C. Also Hugh Innes to John Bird. Ack'd & O. R. Hook vs Frith Judgt: Conf'd for £10.9.8½ & Int. from this date & Costs. Thomas Hale is Allowed One hundred & 75 Tobo: for Arm- strong Hails Attce as a Guard Over Jno. Barnett, w'ch is Ordered to be P'd Out of the County Depositum, If Sufficent. Thomas Jones is App'd Guardian to Thos. Jas. & Wm. Ramsey & with

Daniel Jones, Wm. Jameson & Eusebus Hubbard his Securities ent'd into Bond & Ack'd the same. Jas. Greer vs Dodson Jubal Early Spl. Bl. On the Motion of Francis Thorp by his attorney Judgt. is Granted him against Daniel French & On a Replevy Bond with Costs. Joel Estes is app'd Survey of the Road from Beards Cabbins into the Pigg River Road to Dan'l Richardsons Mill the List filed to be his Gang.

PAGE ONE HUNDRED SEVENTY

October Court 1787—Benjamin Griffith is Appointed Survey'r of the Road in the Room of Thomas Arthur Gt. & his list to be his Gang. Moses Ray is Exempted from the Paymt. of County Levie in the future. On the Motion of Thomas Arthur Gt., Leave is Granted him to build a Water Grist Mill on Little Creek he being Owner on both sides thereof. Richardson vs Cook a Dedims Awarded the Plt. to him the Depo. of Spencer Clack. An Injunction is Granted John Booth to stay the Proceedings of a Judment Obtained against him in this Court by James Callaway & Co. & with John Hook & George Hancock his surety ent'd into Bond & Ack'd the Same. A Deed from Richard Baily to Jas. Hambrick Proved by 1 Wit. & O. C. A Dedimus for the Privy Exam'n of Elizabeth the Wife of David Kearby on a Deed to Ashford Napier Re'd & O. R. A Deed from W. Stegall to William Bohannan further Proved & O. R. Hunter vs Stogdon Dismiss'd. The Last Will & Testament of Elisha Lyon was Produced in Court. Proved by 2 Witness & O R'd. A Deed from James Rogers to Wm. Ryan Ack'd & O. R. Also Jas. Hail to Jacob Prillimon Prov'd by 2 Witnesses. John Stewart is Allowed 4 Days Attce. as a Witness for Eliz'a Hudson ads Trent—JOHN SMITH.

PAGE ONE HUNDRED SEVENTY-ONE

October Court 1787—William Ryan, John Ferguson and Hugh Woods Came into Court & Qualifyed to there Collection wch is Ordered to be Certify'd. On the Mo. of Hugh Innis Gent, Sheriff of this Cty, Nathan Ryan is Admited to Act as D. S. whereupon he took the Usual Oaths to the Com. Wealth as Also the Oath of a D. S. On the Mot. of Ashford Napier to have Obadiah Richardson Attce Dock'd as a Witness for Jno. Chitwood vs S'd Napier, the Same is Rejected w'th Costs. Leave is Granted Wm. Toney to Take the Depo. of Thomas Arthur in a Suit Depend'g between s'd Toney & Henderson. William Austin having Craved the Peace agst. Joseph Webb the S'd Webb w'th Edward Lyon & John Price his Securitys Came into Court and Ack'd themselves Severally Indeb'd to the Com. Wealth, that is to say the S'd Webb in the Sum of £20 & each of his Securitys in the Sum of Ten Pounds Each, to be Levied on their Respective Goods & Chattles, Land & Tenaments On Condition the Said Webb does not Act w'th Good behavior for One Year & a Day, Especially toward the S'd Austin. The Court is Adjn'd till Court in Course.

PAGE ONE HUNDRED SEVENTY-TWO

November Court 1787—At a Court of Quarterly Sessions held for Franklin County On Monday the 3rd Day of November 1787. Present: Peter Saunder, Jonathan Richeson, Moses Greer, George Turnbull, Hugh Martin & John Smith, Gent. Callaway & Early vs Ernest Dismiss'd. Brown & Co. vs Geo. Kelly Dismissed. Early vs Bradshaw Dismiss'd. Hook vs Same, Same. Chastin vs Ferguson Same. A Deed Henry Rogers to Hugh Innes Ack'd & Elizabeth the Wife Reling'd her Dower & O. R. Also Acquilla & Wm. Greer to Richard Beaseley Ack'd, Elizabeth & Jean their Wives Reling'd their Dower & O. R. Also Jeremiah Puckett to Job Meador Proved & O. R. Also Daniel Farley to George Turnbull Ack'd & O. R'd. On the Motion of Joshua Rentfro, It is Ordered that Rachel Jones Ex'r of Isaac Jones, dec'd, be Summond'd to Appear at the Next Court to Give Court Su'y for their Exorship. A Dedimas for the Relinguishmt of Mary the Wife of John Heard, on a Deed from him to Hezekiah Farmer Ret'd & O. R. A Deed from Wm. Warren to Joseph Broady. Ack'd & O. R.

PAGE ONE HUNDRED SEVENTY-THREE

November Court 1787—Craig vs Simmons, Jud. Confess'd Accorl to Spy & Costs. A Deed Luke Thornton to Walter Dent Ack'd & O. R. J. Callaway & Early vs Clower C. O. set A Side & David Beheler Spl. B. & Impl. A Deed David Kearby to John Woodall P'd by 2 W. & O. C. Edward vs Turleys John Wilkes Spl. Bl. & Delivered him up & Pray'd into Custody. Whereupon Hugh Innes Gent ent'd himself farther Spl. Bail. Gilliam vs

Cheetwood. Ashford Napier Spl. Bail Judgt Confess'd Accordg to Spy & Costs. The Last Will & Testament of Daniel Spangler dec'd was Exhibited in Court by Mary Spangler the Executrix therein Mentioned, who Affirmed accord & to Law & with John Noftsinger his Security entered into Bond & Ack'd the same. JOSHUA RENTFRO. Jas Shores Price, Shadrick Woodson & Isaac Bates or any three of them are Appointed to Appraise the said Estate. Richardson vs Cook. Sam'l Patterson Spl. Bl. & Spl. Impl. Clardy vs Hunt (on Injun) the Arguments of the Parties heard by their Councell & the same is disolve w'th Costs. John Hook & John Bozwell, who Purchased the Plts Land from Clardy & John Hook & Reling'd all Claim as to Mrs. Hunts Dower in this Land in disp. Read vs Teal Thomas Watts Spl. Bl. Paymt & Issue. Evans vs Cook on the Mot. of the Deft. C. O. Conf'd Sit a Side & Jno. Woodall Spl. Bl. Payt. & Issue. Prunty vs Davis & Doughten. Wm. Davis Spl. Bl. Payt & Issue. Underwood vs Slone. William Slone. Spl. Bl. Paymt. & Issue.

PAGE ONE HUNDRED SEVENTY-FOUR

November Court 1787—Amos Richardson being Sum'd to Attend as a Grand Jury Man, & being Call'd & not appearg is find accordg to Law. Benjamin Cook, foreman, David Clarkson, Elisha Estes, Henry Page White, Robert Prunty, Samuel Hairston, Peter Holland, Thomas Jones Jr., David Barton, Daniel Ross, Henry Jones, Padrick Woodson, Amoss Richardson, John Hunter, John Turner & Richard Edmundson, Were Sworn a Grand Jury of Inquest for the Body of this County, Whereupon they withdrew to Consult on their presentments. Baldwin Rowland behaving Contemptiously to the Court is fined Ten Pounds Current Money & Its Ordered that be be in Custody of Shf untill he pay the Same with Costs & It is further ordered that the Shf. Put him in the Stocks & there Remain One Cour W'th Costs. Thorp vs Doggett, Judgt. on Replevy Bond With Costs. Trent vs Jones, John Hook a Garnishee being Sworn Sayith he hath no Property in his hands Of the Defts & the same is Cont'd. William Henderson is Allowed 9 Days attendance as a Witness from Wm. Miller agt. Wm. Kelly. Mary Henderson is Allowed 10 Days for the same. Isbell McClure is Allowed 10 Days for The Same. Brown & Co. vs Mills. Judgt confess'd accorg to Spy &

Cost. Stay Exon till January Court next. Callaway & Co. vs Napier. Judgt. Confessed accord to Spy & Costs. stay Exon 3 Months.

November Court 1787—Demsey Assee vs. Jno. Kelley. Will Bill Sp. Bl. The Grand Jury Return'd into Court, & made Several presentments Whereupon Process is Ordered to Issue. Brown & Co. vs E. Choat. Saml. Patterson Spl. Bl. Same vs Willis (Isaiah) Thomas Prunty Spl. Bl. Callaway & Co. vs Farley Danl Farley Spl. Bl. Monah vs Estes. dism'd. Haile vs Craighead. a Deds. Awd. the Plt. to take the Dep'os of Richard & Philemon Edmundson, Giving the Defendant 10 Days Notice. Gallaspy &c vs Edwards. Jas. Turly Spl. Bl. & Delivered him up whereupon he is Pray'd Commited. Trent vs Bandy C. O. & W E set aside by Consent of Parties W'ch was Taken on the Rules & Ord. to be Redockited Jno. Booth Sp. Bl. Payt. & Issue. J Callaway & J Early vs Thos. Miller Jr. John Fuson & William Toney. Sp. Bl. Paymt. & Issue. The Court is adj'd till Tomorrow 8 oClock.— PETER SAUNDERS.

November Court 1787—At a Court of Quarterly Sessions Continued & held for Franklin County on Tuesday the 6th of November 1787. Present: Peter Saunders, Jonathan Richardson, John Smith, Hugh Martin, Moses Greer, Gent. Armstrong vs Spangler, Abates by the Death of the Deft. Murry Assee vs Brown. Peter Saunders Spl. Bl. & Impl. William Crow is Allowed two days Attendance & one comg. & Returning 55 Miles as a Witness for Livesey ads Huston. Stober vs Davis, A Jury Sworn, to Wit, Thomas Crump, Lawrence McGeorge, Thomas Lumpkin, Jubal Early, Richard Radford, Wm. Thompson, John Sullivan, Thomas Jones, Jr., Thomas Doggett, Jr., David Barton, Robert Johns & William Henderson. Verd. Ret. for the Ptf for £7.2.9 & O R'd. & the Def. by his Atto. Motioned for a New Tryal & the Same is Rejected w'th Costs. It is the Opinion of the Court that the Attorneys are not Chargable w'th a Tax on their Appearances on Motion for Injunctions or Judgment Obtained by Sinks at Com. Law before the Law took plan for Imposing a Tax on Attorneys of One Tenth of their Legal fees.

On the Motion of Antho. Pate, Rich'd Radford &c for an In-jun't to stay the Proceeds for a Ju'd Obt'd Agst them as Security for Geo. Asberry to Obadith H. Trent, the Same is Granted on their Giving Suty. this Court. William Christopher is Allowed One Days Attee. as a Witness for Trent vs Jones.

PAGE ONE HUNDRED SEVENTY-SEVEN

November Court 1787—Kinsey vs Ramsey, Hercules Ogle, a Garshee being Sworn saith he Owes the Def. Nothing. Saml Patteson on Other Garishee & Dis'd. Huston vs Livesey Dism'd. Plt. not fur. Pros. Armstrong vs Spangler abates by Def's Death. Thos. Jones vs Same, Same. Holden McGee is Allowed five days Attendance as a Witness Stober agt. Jona. Davis. Jeremiah Stober is Allowed 2 days for the same. Irvin Asse vs Anduson, Jno. P. Anderson Spl. B. & Jud. by Defdnt. Tate vs Young Dism'd at Defts Costs. Callaway & Co. vs Same, the Same. Brown Asee vs Richards, Judt & Confes'd accg to Spy & Cost Stay Exo. till February Court and the Pltf agrees to admit any Receipts by way of Discount which the Defndt. Shall Produce authenticated previous to the Paiment of the Tobacco. Patteson vs Hubbard, a Jury Sworn, to Wit, James Cannon, Moses Rentfro, Saml Kerby, Wm. Christopher, Rich'd. Edmonson, Wm. Walton, Thos. Camp, Sam'l Thompson, Thos. Hale, Jno. Smith, Wm. Henderson & John Sullivant. Verdit. Ret. for the Plt. £14.10. & Costs & on the Motion of George Hancock, cl. for the Def. a New Tryal Granted him on Paying Costs of the day.

PAGE ONE HUNDRED SEVENTY-EIGHT

November Court 1787—On the Motion of Sarah Grymes Jud. is Granted her Agst Robert Woods, Gent. Late Sheriff of this for £8.4.0 on an Execution Said Grymes vs Thos. Arthur & Cost. Brown & Co. vs Joseph Hambrick, Jud. Confess'd w'th Stay of Exon 3 Months Accorg. to Spy. & Costs. Nowel vs Booth, Rich'd Radford Spl Bl. & Jud. Confess'd Stay Exeon till Apl. Court. J. Callaway & J. Early vs McLary & his Security, Jud. Agreeable Rep. Bond & Costs. Delancy vs Bates On the Mot. of the Pltf. by Rich'd Venable his Atto. It is Ord. that the Same be Reinstated & Set for Tryal. Richardson vs Cook. Leave is Granted the Def. to take the Depo. of David Willis, on Giving

10 Days Previous Notice. Lyon vs Lyon, A Jury Sworn, to wit, John Hook, William Walton, Wm. Thompson, Wm. Swanson, Sam'l Kearby, John Smith, James Bearford, Ashford Napier, Anthony Pate, Thomas Haile, John Harris & Joel Cheetwood. Verd. Ret'd Not Agreed.

PAGE ONE HUNDRED SEVENTY-NINE

November Court 1787—George Griffith is Allowed Six Days Att'ce as a Witness for Thomas Miller, Sr., Agst. John Willis. Pate vs McGrady C. O. Conf'd vs Defts & Shff. It is Ordered by the Court that the first Tuesday in Each month Shall be the Rule day. It is Ordered by the Court that 250 Pd Tobacco be Deducted Out of the Jud. Spangler ads Jones. Robert Napier is Allowed 5 Days Attce as a Witness for M Lyon ads Lyon. Stephen Wood is Allow'd 2 days Atta. as a Witness Edw'd Lyon vs Lyon. Nancy Wood is Allow'd 4 Days for the Same. Agness Marcum is 6 Days for the Same. Frances Smith is Allow'd 4 for the Same. Joshua Starkey is Allow'd 2 Days Same. Alex. Ross is Allow'd 6 Days for Edw'd Lyon. The Court is Adjourn'd till Tomorrow 10 oClock.—ROBERT HAIRSTON.

PAGE ONE HUNDRED EIGHTY

November Court 1787—At a Court of Quarterly Sessions held & Continued for Franklin County On Wednesday the & Day of November 1787. Present: Peter Saunders, Robert Hairston, Jonathan Richardson, Moses Greer, George Turnbull & Hugh Martin, Gent. Bryant vs Thos. Miller, Jud. Agreeable to Rep. Bl. & Costs. Ferguson vs McVey, Sur'y for Miller Jud. Agreeable to Rep. Bl. & Costs. Bates vs Delancey & McVey, Jud. Agreeable to Rep. Bonds & Costs. John Chitwood vs Ashford Napier, Jud. Conf'd for £3 & Costs. Johns & wife vs Lyon. A Jury Sworn, to Wit, Humphrey Edmondson, Amos Richardson, Abraham Jones, David Barton, Moses Rentfro, Wm. Wright, John England, William Mavity, Samuel Henderson, George Livsey, Thomas Watts, & Jacob Oldakers. Verdict Ret. for the Deft. & O. R'd. Griffith vs Chitwood, On the Motion of the Pltf. by his Atto. Leave is Granted to Amend Writ. Agreement between Stephen Wood & Thomas Hill Prov'd & O. R. I. Callaway &

Early vs S. Cockran, Rob. Wm. & Joel Chitwood Bl. & Spl. Impl. Lyon vs Lyon The Jury Sworn Yesterday & Being Called & Not Appearing the Same is Discharged.

PAGE ONE HUNDRED EIGHTY-ONE

November Court 1787—Stogdon vs Garmon Jud. Accg. to Spy & Costs. B Savers vs Peeks. the Same. Clutcher vs Hancock, a Jury Sworn, to wit, John Hook, Wm. Walton, Sam'l Pattison, Saml Kerby, Thos. Hale, Antho. Pate, Israel Standifer, John Harris, Edward Willson, James McVey, John Johnson and Stephen Wood. Verd. Ret. for the Def. & O. R'd. Nancy Woods is Allowed One Days Attce as a Witness for Johns & ux. vs Lyon. Stephen Harris is Allowed 3 Days & One Coming & Ret. 80 Miles as a Witness for Robert Johns & Wife Agst Lyon. Augustin Knight is Allowed 3 Days & Comg. & Ret. 80 miles as A Witness for Lyon ads Johns & Wife. Thomas Johns is Allowed 3 Days for the Same. Stephen Wood is Allowed 1 Days Attce. as a Witness for Johns vs Lyon. G. Griffith vs Joel Chitwood, dism'd at the Defts Costs.

PAGE ONE HUNDRED EIGHTY-TWO

November Court 1787—On the Motion of Benja. Cook to Desolve an Inj'n of a Jud. Obtained by him Agst Daniel Richardson—On reading the Bill, & Depo's & hearing the Arguments of Councell on both Sides, It is Considered by the Court that the S'd Inj'n be not Desolved but that the Jud. at Com. Law be Perpetually Enjoyned, whereupon the Deft. Prayed an Appeal to the Eighth Day of the next Genl. Court on Giving Bond w'th Security Accorg to Law w'ch is Granted him & w'th Saml Patterson his Security Ent'd into Bond Accordg. to Law & Ack'd the Same. The Court is Adjourn'd till Tomorrow 8 oClock. JOHN SMITH. At a Court of Quarterly Sessions held and Continued for Franklin County on Thursday the Eight Day of November 1787. Present: John Smith, Swinfield Hill, Moses Greer & George Turnbull, Gent. Stewart vs Harris, Cont'd. Meador vs Rentfro, Cont'd. Holliday vs Willson, Cont'd. Ryan vs King, Dismiss'd. Callaway & Early vs Stokes, Dis'd. Dikenson vs Perryman, Cont'd. Stegall vs Jenkins, Cont'd. Hill vs Early, Cont'd.

Rentfro vs Rentfro, Cont'd. Brown & Co. vs Gipson Jud. for £19.15.3 & Atta. Effects Condinde. Same vs Js. Miller Jud. Same vs Norcutt Jud. Same vs Teal Jud.

PAGE ONE HUNDRED EIGHTY-THREE

November Court 1787—Robinson asse vs Bybe Jud. Thorp vs Walton Cont'd. Cowden vs Harris Jud. Accorg. to Acct' Costs. Craig Assee. vs Semmons Jud. Hancock vs Norcott Jud. Thorp vs Thompson Jud. Toney vs Lures Dis'd Ptf. not Further them Pross. Harris vs Sebret Jud. for £7. & O Ca. Atta Effects & Cost. Dillon vs Stewart (on an Inj'd) on hearing the Arguments of Counsel on both sides the (Leave is Granted the Deft. to Amend his Answer at his own Costs). the same is Dissolved w'th Costs. Wm. Bartee is Allowed 7 Days Attendance & One Comg. & Ret. 40 Miles as a Witness for Stokes Agst Goggins. J. Callaway & J Early vs Tobias Miller Dis'd. Logan vs Gordon Jud. is Granted him agst the Def on Rep Bond & Costs J. Callaway vs Price. Jud. is Granted him Against the Deft & Joel Chitwood One of his Securitys on Rep Bond & Costs. James Radford is Allowed is Allowed 4 Days Attce & Onee Comg & Ret 44 Miles as a Witness for Gutterys Exors. Jno. Ferguson is Allowed 4 Days Attce as a Witness & one Comg. & Ret. 58 Miles for the Same.

PAGE ONE HUNDRED EIGHTY-FOUR

November Court 1787—On the Mo. of Danl. Brown Jud. is Granted him agst. Robert Woods Gent. late Shff for Nine hundred & twenty Pounds of Tobacco Levyed for the S'd Brown in the County Levy & Costs. On the Motion of Stephen Smith Clerk of this Court, Jud. is Granted him for Thirty One Thousand three hundred & Ninety Six Pounds of Tobacco against Robert Woods Gent. Sheriff for Ticketts Put into his hands a Pr. Receipt & it is Ordered that all Just Credits be Allowed and that Ten Days Begin the Parties to Settle before Exeon Shall Issue & Costs. John Hale is Allowed Six Days Atta. as a Witness for Anderson ads Livsay. Lewis Davis is Allowed 5 Days Att'ce as a Witness for Willson vs England. James Cannon is Allowed 2 Days Attce as a Witness for Toney vs McLueres. William Ryan is Allowed 1 Days Attce for Patterson vs Hubbard.

William Godsey is Allowed 4 Days Atta as a Witness for Austin vs Webb, Elisha Blankenship the Same. Chattin Doggett is Allowed 4 Days Attce. for Thorp vs Walker. Com. Wealth vs Toney leave is Granted to Take the Depo's of Wm. Miller On giving reasonable Notice. Wm. Miller is Allowed 4 Days Attce as a Witness for Com. Wealth vs Toney. Dolley French is Allowed 5 Days for Toney ads C. Wealth. Rebecca Scruggs is Allowed 4 Days for Toney vs M. Lucas. Edw'd Willson is Allowed 4 Days for Christian ads Holliday.

PAGE ONE HUNDRED EIGHTY-FIVE

December Court 1787—Welch vs Kelly Admrs vs leave is Given the Ptf. to take the Depo's of Jno. Rentfro, Michl. Dunn, Jno. Hale they being About to move to the State of N. Carolina, On giving 10 Days Notice. James Napier is Allowed 4 Days Att'ce as a Witness for Austin vs Webb. Com. Wealth vs Toney Ded's awarded the Def. to take the Depo of Tho. Doggett On giving Legal Notice. The Court is Adjourn'd till Court in Course.—JOHN SMITH. At a Court held for Franklin County on Monday the 3rd of Decem. 1787. Present: Jonaathan Richeson, John Smith, John Dickinson and George Tunbull, Gent. A Deed from Walter Aday to Thomas Preston. A Deed Benja. Smith from Wm. Maviety Ack'd & O. R'd. Also George Medley from James Parker Ack'd & O. R. Also Power of Attorny from Smith to Wilks Prov'd & O. R. Field & Call vs Parriott & Richardson Judg. injoined as to Richardson. A Deed from John Wilks to Isaiah Turner Ack'd & O. R. Also Saml. & Joan Gamble to William Write P'd & O R. John Jamison App'd Surv of the Road in the Room of Wm. Cowden & the List filed be his Gang. W. Bernard vs Kelly Dism'd.

PAGE ONE HUNDRED EIGHTY-SIX

December Court 1787—On the Motion of John Divers leave is Granted him to Build a Water Grist Mill on Gills Creek be being Proprietor of the Land on both sides. As further Inventory of the Estate of Robert Boulton returned & O. R. Thomas Demoss is allowed 7 Days Attendance as a Witness for Lyon at the Suit of Lyon. Mary Brown Came into Court & Volentiarly Relinquished her Right of Dower in & to a Certain Tract of Land convey'd by the John Brown dec'd to Rich'd Radford & O. R. Zack'h Jones & John Langdon are Exempted from Paying the County Levy for the future. A Deed from Rich'd Ballard to Jere. Saulberry prov'd & O. R. Elizebeth the wife of Thos. Miller came into Court & Volentiarily Relinguish'd her Right of Dower In a Tract of land Conveyed to Sicily & Catharine Minnix The Same to Chastin Minnix the same. Callaway & I. Early vs Fuson &c Judgt Accg to Repy Bond & Costs. John Turner is App'd Surveyor of the Road in the Place of Micajah Stone. A Deed from Abraham Penn to Luke Standifer Pv'd & O. R. Webb vs Austin, William Boid Sp. Bl. & Spl. Impl. Jas. Callaway, Jas. Hunt & Sam. Thompson is App'd to View a way for a Road from Terry Glade up Black Water to Joshua Rentfro's & Make the Report thereof. Spangler Ex's vs Jones Jud. Accordings to Repy Bond.

PAGE ONE HUNDRED EIGHTY-SEVEN

December Court 1787—Rich'd Farley attend 12 days as a Witness for Jno. Chitwood agt. Robert Williams. A Deed James Mc Vey to William Menifee Ack'd & O. R. James Akin is exempted from Paying the Parrish & County Leavey for the Future. The County of Franklin for the Year 1787 is made Debtor lb Tob'o: To the Clerk for his Annual Sallerye 1248; To Daniel Brown ap of Clack for Attending the Surveyor in Runing the Dividing Line 336; To the Deputy States Attorney his Annual salary 1248; To the Sherif for the same 1248; To William Burdett 4 Young Wolfs heads 200; To John Law 1 old Wolfs head 100; To Benjamin Cook for a County Seal 192; To Thomas Crutcher for Guarding Ben. Hensley 4 days 100; To Brown & Callaway as P. Acc't 212; To Hugh Innis Gent. for Attending Call Court for Examination of B. Hensley 200; Amount Carried forw'd 5144. David Morgin is recommended to his Excellency the Governor as a Proper person to act as Capt. of the Militia in Place of George Turnbull who refused to Act. Abraham Abshire is App'd Lieut. of the s'd Company & Will: Write is app'd Ensign for the same Shadrack Woodson is appinted Surv'y of the Road in the Place of S. Price & his List be his Gang. The Court is Adjourned Till Court in Course.—PETER SAUNDERS.

PAGE ONE HUNDRED EIGHTY-EIGHT

December Court 1787—At a Court held for Franklin County On Monday the 3rd of December 1787 for the Examination of Benjamin Hensley on Suspicion of Feloniously Stealin a Great Coat & Other Goods the Property of Oliver Orr. Present: Peter Saunders, Jonathan Richeson, John Smith, Moses Greer, John Dickinson And George Turnbull, Gent. The S'd Benjamin Hensley waving his Priviledge & being let to the Bar in the Custody of Hugh Innis Gent. Sheriff of Said County to whose Custody for the Crime Aforsaid he had been Commited, and it being Demanded of the said Prisoner whether he is Guilty of the fact wherewith he Stands Charged, Answere'd that he is in no Wise Guilty, Whereupon the Court Proceeded to Examine Divers Witnesses as Well on Behalf of the Common Wealth as of the Prisoner at the Bar. On consideration whereof the Court are of Opinian that the said Benjamin Hensley is Guilty of the fact wherewith he Stands Charged And that he Ought to receive a further Tryal before the Honble the Genl Court on the Second Tuesday in this Month therefore his in Remanded into the Custody of the Sheriff Aforesaid. Olliver Orr and Daniel Ross Came into Court and Acknowledged them Selves Severally Indebted to the Common Wealth of Virginia in the Sum of £100 each to be levyed on their Respective Goods & Chattles Lands & Tenaments on Condition they do not Appear before the Honble the Genl. Court in the City of Richmond On the 2nd. Tuesday in the Present Month as Witnesses in behalf of the Com. Wealth agst. Benja. Hensley.

PAGE ONE HUNDRED EIGHTY-NINE

January Court 1788—The Deposition of Oliver Orr of Lawful Age being first Sworn the Truth to say on behalf of the Common Wealth Against Benjamin Hensley who Stands Charged w'th feloniously Stealing a Great Coat & Other Goods the Property of S'd Orr Deposeth & Saith That Sometime in the Month of June Last his house was Broak Open & Robbed of a Great Coat & Other Goods which Great Coat this Deponent found in the Possession of the s'd Benja. Hensley on the 28th. of November Last. The Deposition of Daniel Ross of Lawful Age being first Sworn the Truth to Say on behalf of the Common Wealth Against Benja. Hensley who Stands Charged w'th feloniously Stealing a

Great Coat & Other Goods the Property of Oliver Orr. Deposeth & Saith that he was in Company with Oliver Orr when the S'd Great Coat was found in his Posession & the Said Oliver Orr Claimed the Coat as his Property and Enquired of the S'd Prisoner how he Came by it, who said he Won it at Cards of a person unknown to him.—JONATHAN RICHESON. At a Court held for Franklin County on Monday the 7th Day of January 1788. Present: Peter Saunders, Jonathan Richison, John Smith, Swinfield Hill & Moses Greer, Gent. A Deed Napier from Kerby further Proved & O. R. Also Spencer Clack to O. Hunt, Proved by 2 Wits & O. C. Also John Heard from Ste. Heard same P'd Tax & Rec'd. Also Joel Starkey from Joshua Starkey Ack'd & O. R.

PAGE ONE HUNDRED NINETY

January Court 1788—A Deed from Walter Aday to Joel Starkey Ack'd & Mary the wife being Exam'd Reling & O. R. Also a Deed from Walter Aday to Jno. Craghead the same. Ordered that Francis Hale Orphan of Rich'd Hale Deceased be Bound to James Burns till he comes to Age by Consent of his Mother Ex'd. A Deed from Walter Aday to Jere Saulsberry Ack'd & Mary the wife being Privily Ex'd Relinguish her right of Dower & O. R. Swinfield Hill Gent. Produced a Commission from his Excellency the Governor Appointing him Coroner for this County whereup he took the Oath to the Commonwealth also the Oath as Coroner. Hale vs Craghead Rich'd Booth. Sp B & Spl. Impl. John Thomspn is Exemp'd from the Payment of County & Parrish Levy. for the future. A Power of Atto. from James Cowden to S. Patterson Prv'd by 1 Wits. & O. R. On the motion of Ann Choice Sur a Negro Wench Sarah is Exemp'd from the Pay of County & Parrish Levy for Future. On the Motion of James Steptoe Clerk of Bedford County Judgt is Granted him agst. Robert Wood Gent Late Sheriff of Franklin County for Thirty Seven Pound fifteen Shilling & Six Pence for Clerk's fees for the Year of 1786 & Costs.

PAGE ONE HUNDRED NINETY-ONE

On the Motion of John Cox By his Atto. Judgt is Granted him agst Robert Wood Gent. Late Sheriff of Franklin County, for fifty one Pound Nineteen Shilling & P. for Clerks fees for the year 1785 & Costs. The Court is Adjourned till Court in

Course.—PETER SAUNDERS. At a Court held for Franklin County on Monday the 4 Day of Feby 1788. Present: Peter Saunders, Swinfield Hill, Moses Greer, John Smith, John Rentfro and George Turnbull, Esqrs. A Deed of Trust from Anthony Pate to Jubal & John Early Ack'd O. R. Also a Deed from Thomas Miller to Rob. Henry Ack'd & O. R. A Deed from Thomas Miller to Charles Minnix. Ack. as to Miller & O. C. And to Catherine & Cecily Minnix same. On the Motion of Rob. Hairston, Gent, his Negro Wench Lucy is Exempted from the Payment of the County Lefy. A Deed from Isaac Rentfro to Luke Webster Ack'd & O. R. A Deed Menifee from McVeay Mary the wife being Privily Examined as the Law Directs Reling her Right of Dower & O. R.

PAGE ONE HUNDRED NINETY-TWO

February Court 1788—A Deed William Wright to Christopher Ruble Ack. & O. R. Also William Rentfro to William Akers Ack'd & O. R. Also a Deed from Robert Donald Atta In fact for Jas. & Rob. Donald & Co. to John Hook Prov'd & O. R. A Deed from Peter Hairston to James Robertson Prov'd by Two Witns Who made Oaths they saw Stephen Lyon or 3 Wit Atteste the same & O. R. Also a Deed from Jas. Robertson to Andrew Polson Ack'd & O. R. A Deed from William Rentfro Sen to Nathl. Simmons Ack'd & O. R. Also a Deed from James Lewis to Lodewick Sheaster Ack'd & Mary the wife Relin'd &c O. R. On the Motion of Theodorick Webb. Jud. is Granted him agst Michael Rowland for £14.3.1 & Costs as Security for said Rowland to John Rentfro. Moses Greer is appointed Capt. of the Militia for this County in the Place of William Rentfro who hath Resign'd. Joshua Brock is appointed Surv'r of the Road from the County line above Jeffersons Crossing of Snow Creek at the s'd Brocks Mill to Beards Cabbins in Pigg River Road & the list filed be his Gang. Ordered that John Bishop be Exc'd from Payment of the County Levy.

PAGE ONE HUNDRED NINETY-THREE

February Court 1788—A Deed from Danl Richardson Rob. Shearwood Proved & O. R. Peter Wood Jesse Meadow, Jere Puckett & James Meadow or any three of them are appointed to view a way for a Road ford Up the River Settlement by Woods

Mill into the Road Leading to Brachers Pond & make Report thereo to the Court. John Craghead, Rich'd Booth, Rich'd Compton & Phillip Rasley or any three of them are app'd to View a Road from Hales Ford on Stanton River a Cross the County South, to Cross Black Water near John Cragheads & to lead into the Road that Goes by Black Place at the mouth of Snow Creek & make Report thereof. Josiah Hodges is ap'd Surv'y of the Road from Chesnut Creek to the Top of the Hill at Grimmits Folley & the List filed be his Gang. A Deed from J. Dillion to Jesse Dillion Proved & O. R. On the Motion of Skelton Taylor agst. Chitwood &c for a Jud. on Repy Bond the same rejected with Costs. It is ordered by the Court that Jeremiah Halcom & Ann Short be Summond to appear before the Court in April Next to Shew cause why their Children

PAGE ONE HUNDRED NINETY-FOUR

February Court 1788—may not be Bound out. A Deed from Hills Legatees to James Callawy Ack'd by Thos. Jones & David Barton, Thos. Hill. James Chrisly is app'd Cust. in the Place of John Fuson Com. Wealth vs Asberry Dis'd with Costs he having Pay'd 5. James Martin appearing to his Recogm't taken before Justice Martin on Suspicion of Stealing & Killing Two hogs the Property of Joshua Dillingham, whereupon the Court Proceeded to Examine Divers Witn. as well on behalf of the Commonwealth as the said James Martin, on Consideration whereof the Court are of the Opinion that the said Martin is not Guilty of the fact wherewith he stands Charged, therefore he is Discharged. John Bird is Ap'd Suv'r of the Road in the Place of James McWilliams. Ordered that the Road be Continued from the Top of Barton Spur to Capt. Saml. Hairston's Place and the list filed be his Gang While he Lives & Joseph Davis Ap'd Overseer for the same. Thorp vs Rentfro. David Morgan Spl. Bl. Delivered him up & prayed Commitment.

PAGE ONE HUNDRED NINETY-FIVE

February Court 1788—Charles Lumdson is app'd in the Room of Isham Blankenship. Information being given the Court by Swinfield Hill, Gent. that John Gipson, a Justice of the Peace for this County, hath Removed himself Out of the County, but on Passing & Repassing through the County Continues to Act as

Such. The Court are therefore of Opinion that from the Illegal Practices of the said Gipson, he should be Expelled from his Office & that the Clerk Certify the same to the Executive. Mary Lyon came into Court & Renounce Benifitt of Elisha Lyon's Will, her Husband Deceased, & Prayd the Benefitt of the Law, where-upon it is ordered by the Court that John Smith John Smith Hook, Jonathan Richardson, & Gwinn Dudley, or any three them, pay the third part of the s'd Lyons Estate to the said Widow agreeable to Law. Mary Troup the Widow of Jacob Troup dec'd who Died in the Army in the year 1781 is Recommend to Executive as a poor object of concern with 3 Small Children. The Court is adj. till tomorrow 8 oClock.—PETER SAUNDERS.

PAGE ONE HUNDRED NINETY-SIX

February Court 1788—At a Court Continued & held for Franklin County On Tuesday the 5th of Feb. 1788. Present: Robert Hairston, Peter Saunders, Thos. Arthur, Moses Greer, Jonathan Richardson, Swinfield Hill & John Dickerson, Gent. Benjamin Cook is Appointed Surv of the Road that Goes to Franklin Courthouse by William Jamison's Coming Past the Place where the Old Meeting House Stood to the Pigg River Road & the List filed to be his Gang w'ch is to Keep in Repair &c. Owen Hunt is Appointed Sur'v of the Road that Goes to Henry Court-house to William Jamison's & the List filed to be his Gang &c. Amos Richardson is Appointed Sur'r of the Road from Capt. Ryans to the Road leading to Henry Courthouse to the Henry Lyne & the List filed to be his Gang &c. Robert Prunty is Ap-pointed Sur'r of the Road from Capt. Ryans to the Pittsylv'a Line & the List filed to be his Gang &c. William Jamison is Appt'd Surv'r of the Road from his house to Chestnut Creek & the List to be his Gang &c. Absent: Robert Hairston & Moses Greer. Robert Hairston, Gent, is Allow'd £21 as a Commissioner for this County. Moses Greer, Gent, is allow'd £18 for same. The Adm'rs of Henry Guttrey Are Ordered to Appear at next Court to Give Counter Security for their Administration On the Mot. of Jno. Hook.

PAGE ONE HUNDRED NINETY-SEVEN

February Court 1788—Franklin Court is made Debtor, 18 Tob. Brought forward, 51.44. To Thomas Townson for 1 old wolf head, 1.00. To William Hunter for one Wolfs head, 1.00. To William Dowten 4 Day attendance as a Guard Over Weeks & Barnard, 1.00. To Thos. Hill for the Use of a Horse for conveyg Jordan to the P. Gaol, 2.00. To the Gaoler for P. Acct. 1.87. To the Clerk for Attending a Call Court for the Ex'n of John H. Jones, 2.00. The same for George Lamb, 2.00. The Same for Ben Handey, 2.00. The same for Pheley Hensley, 2.00. To the Clerk for Attending Commissioners, 12.80. To Nathan Ryan DS for the Conveyance of B. Hensley, 10.00. To Wm. Ryan D. S. for the Damage of a Horse for Conveying the same to the Publick Gaol, 1.60. To John Ferguson for the Conveyance of John H. Jones to the P. Goal, 10.00. To Ditto 5 Dicks found Stokes, 40. To George Ferguson for a Horse & Conveying John H. Jones, 2.00. To Thos. Prunty for 19 Insolvents at 22 each, 4.18. To William Ryan for 25 Do at 22 each, 5.50. To a Deposition in the hands of the County Collecting, 33.93. To the Sheriff Six P. Ct. for Collecting, 9.48. To 1305 Tythes at 12.18 Tobo. P. Bale 15660.

PAGE ONE HUNDRED NINETY-EIGHT

February 1788—Thos. Arthur & Swinfield Hill, Gent, On Appt'd the necessary Repairs of the Gaol to the Lowest Bidder Thos. Hale, Davis Barton, Thos. Jones, Jun., Frederick Rives, John Woods, Alexander Ferguson, Thomas Watts, Skelton Taylor, are appointed as Valuers of Property & as Judges of Security for This County. John Ferguson Qualified to his Collection Sence his last Return & O. R. Ordered Thos. Arthur, Moses Greer & Jonath. Richardson are appointed to Attend the Surveyor in adding as much to Prison Bounds as will increase it 10 acres. Hugh Innes is App'd to Settle W'th the Sale ———— for the Depo. of Last year. The Court is Adj'd till Court in Course—PETER SAUNDERS.

PAGE ONE HUNDRED NINETY-NINE

March Court 1788—At a Court of Quarterly Sessions begun & Held at Franklin Courthouse on Monday the 3rd Day of March 1788. Present: Peter Saunders, Moses Greer, George Turnbull, John Rentfro, Jonathan Richardson & John Smith, Gent. A Deed from John Harris to Wm. McCoy Pro'd by 2 Wits. & O. C. Also from Isaac Rentfro to William Walton pd & Mary the wife being Privily Examined as the Law Directs Relingued her Right of Dower & Ordered to be Recorded. James Callaway & Jubal Early vs Danl French Thos. Arthur Spl. Bl. Saunders vs Poteet Edw'd Choat Spl Bl. A Deed from Grayam & Wife Ack'd as theirs, & Wife to Long Ack'd as to Arthur & Proved as to Grayham & O. R. The Court is Adj'd till tomorrow 8 oClock.— PETER SAUNDERS.

PAGE TWO HUNDRED

March Court 1788—At a Court of Quarterly Sessions Cont'd & held at Franklin Courthouse on Tuesday the 4th Day of March 1788. Present: Peter Saunders, Swinfield Hill, John Rentfro & Moses Greer, Gent. Callaway & Early vs Wattson. Geo. Ferguson Spl. Bail. Ordered that it be Certified to the Governor & Coucil that Hugh Innis, Gent. Sheriff for this County, failing to Give Surety for the Collection of the Taxes & that a New appointment be made. I Callaway & Trent vs Wright James Wray Spl Bl. & Set aside & Issue. I Callaway & Co vs A. Farley Judg. Conf'd according to Spl. & Costs Stay Exon 3 Months. Thomas Hale, David Barton & the Thos. Jones Came into Court & quallified as Commissioners of the Exon. Law & Valuers & Judgt of Property. Cook vs Jameson Judgment according to Spl. & Costs. Cook Assee vs Bransum same. Daniel Brown & Co. vs William Thompson Judg for £4.19.8. Rich'd N. Venable a Garshee being Sworn sayeth that he is indebted to the Deft £2.15.6 & O. Condin'd. On the motion Philmon Greer leave is Granted him to Take the Depos. of John Cook, Mary Cook, William Green, Rhody Skelton & Maryann Greer, Giving Legal notice.

PAGE TWO HUNDRED ONE

March Court 1788—On the Motion of Marlin Binnion Judgt. is Granted him On a Reply Bond vs Danl. Divine & Wm. Chitwood According to Spy & Costs. Harmon Cook vs John Kierby Judgt. According to Spily & Costs. A Dedimus for the Relinguishment of Mrs. Richardson to Davis, Rob Sherewood Returned & O. R. Present: Thos. Arthur, Gent. On the Motion of Robert Woods, Gent, late Sheriff vs John Ferguson &c DS for Judgt & the same was ordered to be Rejected with Costs. Absent: Peter Saunders. A Power of Attorney from Ste. Cantrell to Joshua Cantrell & Proved & O. R. Absent: John Rentfro. Callaway & Earlys vs John Rentfro. Peter Saunders Spl. Bl. Sherewood vs Richardson Rob Williams Dism'd at the Pltf. Costs. Present: John Dickerson. Keen vs Grimmett Spl. Impl. Early vs Toney Judgt accd to Spl & Costs. Early vs Kelly the Same. Same vs Thos. Slone the Same. Cook vs Greer Rule to Spl Bail. It is the Opinion of the Court that Mrs. P. Guthery be Discharged out of the Custody of the Sheriff on Atta. vs her as Adm'x of Henry Guthery dec'd for Wits. Attendance at the Suit of Callaway which was ordered by John Hook Assee of James Buford & Eidson Ord. that he P'd & Costs &c.

PAGE TWO HUNDRED TWO

March Court 1788—On the Mot. of Jno. Hook Rich'd Booth It is ordered that in case P. Guthery the Widow of Henry Guthery dec'd fail Giving County Security for her Admr at the Next Court to be held for this County that then she be Ruled Deliver up the said Estate to John Hook for this Indemnification. Thorp vs Rentfro Sec'y for Mark Rentfro. Judgt. On Repy. Bond Accorg to Sply & Costs. I Callaway & Early vs Choat Ref'd to all matters in dispute between the s'd Parties on Ref'd to Colo. Innis, Colo. Saunders & Swinfield Hill, Gent. & their aw'd to be the Judgt. of the Court. Saunders vs Miller & Jas. Rentfro on Rep. Bond Judg acc'g to Spy & Costs. Williams asse vs Patterson William Ryan Spl. Bl. Dogett ads Johnson Ded. aw'd to Take the Depo's of Saml. Langdon, Ducker Toney, John Hartwell & Jas. Webb. Samuel Patterson is allow'd 1 days Attendance as a Wits for James Cowden vs William Harris. Sam'l Thompson vs Wm. Kerbey. Dism'd. Prunty vs Jones & Judgt. On Repy Bond accorg to Spy & Costs Patterson vs Hubbard, James Prunty Spy B. never Absconded. Buford vs John & Wm. Kelley. Judgt on Rep Bond & Issue Accg to Spl & Costs. Wm. Boyd vs Wm & Thos. Miller Jun. Judgt. according to Spt & Costs.

PAGE TWO HUNDRED THREE

March Court 1788—Thorp vs Isaac Rentfro & Bail Judg. for £5.19.3 & Costs. Danl. Brown & Co. vs Theodorick Webb Judg & for £14.8.3 & Costs. William Bartee is Allowed Two day Attendance coming & going 40 miles as a Wits. Stokes vs Goggins.

Hook vs Ferguson a Jury sworn to Wit. David Barton, James McVey, Saml. Miles, Jas Greer, William Eubanks, Thos. Hale, Wm. Bartee, I. Standifer, T. Livesey, Stinner Devall, William Walton & Walton Guild. Verdict Returned for the Pltf. & O. R. Walter Gill vs Thos. Levisey a Jury sworn, to Witt, Thos. Fitz-rimmons, David Barton, Thos. Hale, Jas. McVey, James Greer, Israel Standifer, Saml Miles, Robert Perryman, William Eubanks, Jesse Spurlock, Elisha Blankenship & John Smith. Verdict Re-turned for the Pltf £90.18.3 & Costs & O. R. A Deed from Daniel Richardson to Champion Napier Ack'd & O. R. Tax & Costs. Hook vs Cockram a Jury sworn, to Wit, Thomas Fitz-simmons, David Barton, Thos. Hale, Jas. McVey, Jas. Greer, Is-rael Standefer, Samuel Miles, Robt. Perryman, Wm. Graves, Elisha Blankenship, John Smith & Jesse Spurlock. Verdict Ret'd & O. R.

PAGE TWO HUNDRED FOUR

March Court 1788—On the Motion of Thos. Jones by His Attorney an Injunction is Granted him for staying the Proceed-ing of a Judg. Obtained in Common Law vs him by Thomas Prunty & it is ordered that he Give Bond & Secuty in the Clks Office before next Court. Hook vs Webb. A Jury Sworn & Withdrawn. J Callaway & Co vs Webb, a Jury Sworn, to Witt, Thomas Fitzsimmons, David Barton, Thos. Hale, James McVey, Jas Greer, Israel Standifer, Sam'l Miles, Robert Perryman, Elisha Blankinship, John Smith, Jesse Sperlock and William Graves. Verdict Returned & O. R. The Court is Adj'd till Tomorrow Eight OClock—PETER SAUNDERS. At a Court of Quarterly Sessions Continued & held for Franklin County the 5th. day of March 1788. Present: Peter Saunders, Jonathan Richardson, John Rentfro & John Dickerson, Esqrs. An Order is Granted Thomas Booth a Prisoner of this County for the Sum of Six Pounds Agreeable to Law. Edmunsen Assee vs R. Napier, Chas. Napier Spl. Bl. & Spl. Impl. Thomas Jones vs William Ferguson Dism'd. Same vs Same, the same. Present: Thos. Arthur. Hook asse of Callaway vs Webb. Cont'd. A Power of Attorney from Daniel Richardson to James Garret Ack'd & O. R.

PAGE TWO HUNDRED FIVE

March Court 1788—5th Day, Cont'd. Michael Grayham & Co vs Obediah Ferguson a Jury Sworn, to Wit, John Hook, Thos. Hale, Obh. Richardson, John Hale, Alex. Ferguson, John Ferguson, Isaac Bates, William Maviety, Jas. McVey, Daniel Barton, Thomas Jones & Robert Perryman. Verdict Returned for the Pltf & O. R. Present: John Smith Gent. Callaway & Earley vs John Livsey Plea ward & Judgt Confesed According to Spey & Costs. Galligo & Co vs Arthur Edwards, A Jury sworn, to Witt, John Hook, Thomas Hale, Obediah Richardson, John Hale, Alexander Ferguson, John Fergsuon, Isaac Bates, William Maviety, James McVey, David Barton, Thomas Jones & Robert Perryman, Verdict Returned for the Pltf & O. R. Present. Geo. Turnbull, Archibald Graham vs William Graves a Jury sworn, to Wit, John Hook, Thomas Hale, Obediah H. Trent, John Hale, Alexander Ferguson, John Ferguson, Isaac Bates, William Maviety, James McVey, David Barton, Thomas Jones & Robert Perryman. Verdict Returned for the Pltf & O. R. Moody vs Earley dismid. Same vs the same. Obediah Richardson is allowed 1 day attendance as a Witnesses for Danl. Richardson ads Sherwood. Underwood vs Slone Rule to give Security for Costs at the Next Court. Leave is Granted William Maviety vs Dedimus to Take Depos. of John Bates ags Jones Admr.

PAGE TWO HUNDRED SIX

March Court 1788—Peter Read vs Adam Teal. A Jury Sworn, To Wit, John Hook, Thomas Hale, Obediah H. Trent, John Hale, Alex. Ferguson, John Ferguson, Isaac Bates, William Meaviety, James McVey, David Barton, Thomas Jones & Robert Perryman. A Verdict Returned for the Pltf. & O. R. Callaway & Co. vs Samuel Thompson. A Jury Sworn, to Wit, John Hook, Thos. Hale, Obh. H. Trent, John Hale, Alexander Ferguson, John Ferguson, Skelton Taylor, William Meaveity, James McVey, David Barton, Thos. Jones & Robt. Perryman. Verdict Returned for the Pltf. & O. R. Absent: Peter Saunders, Gent. Peak vs Graves. Judgt. Conf'd accg to Spl. & Costs of £6.7.4. Assessed Jan. 30 1788. Hook vs Rentfro Jury sworn, to Wit, James Stone, Thos. Hale, Obh. H. Trent, Joel Walker, Alexander Ferguson. John Ferguson, Skelton Taylor, William Meaviety, James McVey, David

Barton, Thomas Jones & Robert Perryman. Jury withdrawn & Judgt. Conf'd by consent of Parties for £7.11.4 Hugh Innes Gent. Sheriff Came into Court & Enter'd Into Bond w'th Sur'y for the Collection of the Revenue Tax & the Same is Ordered to be Re-corded. Same for the Collection of Officers fees the Same. On the Mot. Of Hugh Innes, Gent, Shereff of this County, Wm. Swanson is Admited his Deputy who Qualif'd accordg to Law Dogitt vs Johnson and Johnson vs Dogett all matters in Dispute Beteen the Parties are Ref'd to Wm. Walton, Saml. Langdon, Joshua Rentfro & Sam'l Kerby, or any 3 of them, & their Judgt to be the Judgt. of Court.

PAGE TWO HUNDRED SEVEN

March Court 1788—On the Mot. of Jonathan Davis ads Jacob Stober a New Tryal is Granted him. Greer vs Webb. Jud. on Replevy Bond accg to Spy & Costs whereupon the Def'd pray'r an appeal to the 8th Day of the Genl Court whereupon he entered into Bond & with Su'y &c. Obediah H. Trent vs John Booth. A Jury sworn, to Wit, James McVey, John Haile, David Barton, Joshua Rentfro, Geo Ferguson, William Meaviety, Peter Finney, James Stone Thos. Hail, Thomas Demoss & Robert Perryman. Verdict Retu'd for the Pltf £11.11.6. Damages & O. R. Alex Ferguson, Skelton Taylor & Thomas Watts, came into Court & quallified as Commissioners of the Exors Law & Values & Juds. of Property. Hugh Innes, Gent, Sheriff, came into Court & en-tered into Bond with Sece'y for the Collection of the County Levy & O. R. Greer vs Doson. A Jury sworn, to Wit, James McVey, John Hale, David Barton, Joel Walker, Joshua Rentfro, George Farguson, William Walton, Samule Kerbey, James Slone, Thos Hale, John Arthur & Anthony Pate. Verdict Returned for the Pltf. & O. R. Charles Sperlock is allowed 1 day attend-ance & one coming & returning 40 Miles as a Wits. for Flowers agst Jones. Jesse Spurlock is allow'd 3 days & coming & ret'ng. 36 miles for same.

PAGE TWO HUNDRED EIGHT

March Court 1788—At a Court held for Franklin County on the 5th. day of March 1788, for the Examination of Edw'd Lyon on the Suspicion of Stealing a Negro fellow named Sip, the Property of Mary Lyon. Present: Thomas Arthur, Jno. Smith,

Jonathan Richardson, John Dickerson & George Turnbull, Gent. The said Edw'd Lyon was led to the Bar in Custody of Hugh Innes, Gent, Sheriff of the said County, to whose Custody for the Cause aforesaid he was Committed, & Waved his Priviledges & it being Demanded of the said Prisioner whether he was Guilty of the fact wherewith he stands Charged, on which he claimed the Priviledge of the Law as to his Tryal, & again wav'd his Priviledge, Whereupon Robert Williams, Gent, Deputy States Attorney, objected to his Tryal & the Court

PAGE TWO HUNDRED NINE

March Court 1788—Determined to Proceed. The Witnesses for the ComWealth not appearing, the Prisoner af'd stands acquitted & is Discharged accorgingly.—T. ARTHUR. Arthur Robertson vs Edw'd Lyon John Chitwood Spl. Bail Judgt. Conf'd accrding to Spy & Costs stay Exon. 3 months. William Christopher is allow'd 2 Day as a Wits. Trent vs Jones. Benja. Christopher 3 days for the same. John Bates is allowed 2 days Attendance as a Witness for Wm. Maviety agst Jones Admr's. Thos. Demoss allow'd 2 days attendance as a Wits. for Mary Lyon ads Edw'd Lyon. Leave is Granted Saml. Webb a Ded's to Take the Depos. of William Stewart & Jas. Ramsey giving legal notice. Prunty ads Jones, the same for Obh. Richardson. Flowers vs Jones Referred to Capt. Thos. Hale, David Barton, Rich'd Copland, Jesse Spurlock, Wm. Spurlock & Thos. Edwards, & in case they disagree, they are to chuse Thos. Goodson, Sen., as an Umpire & their aw'd take the Judgt. of the the Court. Jackson vs Frith, Geo. Asberry, Danl. French & Dav'd Guttery Spl. Bl.

PAGE TWO HUNDRED TEN

March Court 1788—Isaac Bates is allw'd one Day Attendance as a Witt. for Theodorick Webb Agst. Hook. The Court is adj'd till tomorrow 8 o'Clock.—PETER SAUNDERS. At a Court of Quarterly Session Continued & held for Franklin Court on Thursday the 6th. Day of March 1788. Present: Thomas Arthur, Jonathan Richardson, Moses Greer & George Turnbull, Gent. John Hook is Allowed 3 Days Attendce as a Witness for Hudgins ads Simmons. Harmon Cook vs William & Lewis Davis, Judgt. on Repy Bond accorg to Spy & Costs, & the Costs of the Witt attendance. James Dyer is allowed 1 day attendance & One Coming & Going 27 Miles to Prove a notice for Cook vs Davis's. I Callaway & Co. vs M. Rentfro. Joshua Rentfro Spl. Bl. & Ord. Ca. Set aside. Brown & Co. vs William Rentfro, same. Harmon Cook vs Ambrose Warren Judgt accg. Spy & Costs. Same vs same. same. Same vs Holdin McGhee. Judg. accg Spy & Costs.

PAGE TWO HUNDRED ELEVEN

March Court 1788—Vest vs Vest disd. at the Pltf Costs. Sally Vest is allow'd 4 days attendance as a Wits. for Rich'd Vest ads J. Vest. Mead vs Rentfro. dism'd at the Pltf Costs. Holliday vs Wilson Cont'd. Thorp vs Gipson. Cont'd. Hancock An atta. vs Webb Austin Choat, Wm Thompson & William Harris Spl Bl. Woods vs Asbury. Judgt. for £2.3.2 as P. Acc't & Costs. Lewis vs Hales's Cont'd. Hill vs Harrison Judgt. according to Spy & Costs. Brown & Co vs William Woods Judgt. accg Spy & Costs. Hancock vs Webb. Cont'd. Johns vs Keen Cont'd. McGeorge vs P. Gee Cont'd. Thos McGeorge vs John Bybee Judgt. accg to Spy & Costs. Thos. Miller vs Jas. Danl. Brown Cont'd. Wilson vs England a Ded's aw'd the Plf. to the Depos of George Moore, Sarah Moore & Lucy Moore. Kerby vs Jones, Judgt. accg to Spy & Costs. Cook vs Buckral Judgt. for 40/ & Costs.

PAGE TWO HUNDRED TWELVE

March Court 1788—Blankenship vs Perdue Cont'd. Comwealth vs Raner Bell, Judgt accg to Law. Same vs Lucy Webb, Same. Same vs George Lamb, same. Same vs Milly Young, same. Same vs Jas. Hale, same. Same vs William Thorp, Same. Same vs Wm. Thompson, same. Same vs William Griffith, same. Same vs William Rentfro, same. Prunty assee. vs Davis & Douton a Jury sworn, to Wit, Joshua Rentfro, Thos. Jones, Guy Smith, Isaac Bates, Robert Perryman, Edward Choat, Saml. Anglan, John Hale, Joseph Webb, Anslin Choat, Thos. Miller & James Conner. Verdict & retu'd for the Pltf & O. R. Mathurs vs Livsey, William Young & George Levsey Spl Bl. & Spl. Impl. Saml Langdon is allow'd 3 days attendance & one coming & Returg, 50 Miles, as a Wits for Doggit ads Johnson. Joseph Webb is allow'd 6 days Attendance as a Wits for the same at the Suit of the same. Delany vs Bates, Cont'd at the Pltfs Costs. Callaway & Early vs Thos. Miller. Ux Plead wav'd & Judgt, conf'd accg to Spy & Costs Stay Exon. 2 Mo.

PAGE TWO HUNDRED THIRTEEN

March Court—Moses Greer is allow'd 2 days attendance as a Wits. for Hudgin at the Suit of Simmons. William Ryan is allow'd a day's attendance as a Witness for Richard ads Sherwood. It is ordered by the Court that the Ovs'r of the Poor do Bind out Sarah Miller, Orphan of John Miller Dec'd, to George Medley, Also Peter Miller orphan of the said John Miller to Baley Carter. Thomas Watts is allowed 7 days attendance as a Wits. for Trent vs Jones. Same for 6 days attendance for Bott vs Chitwood. Thos. Doggett, Sen, is allow'd 3 days for Walton at the suit of Thorp. Lewis Davis is allow'd 2 days Atten'ce as a Wits. for Wilson vs England. William Godsey is allowed four days as a Wits. for Austin vs Webb. Thomas Prunty, William Ryan and Hugh Woods came into Court & Proved their Several Collections accg to Law. Ordered that Mary Lyan be Summoned to Next Court to Take upon herself the Admin. of the Estate of Elisha Lyon, dec'd.

PAGE TWO HUNDRED FOURTEEN

April Court 1788—The Court is Adj'd till Court in Course.— T. ARTHUR. At a Court held for Franklin County on Thursday the 13 day of March 1788, for the Examination of Edw'd Lyon on Suspicion of Stealing a Negro Man Slave by the name of Cip, the Property of Mary Lyon. Present: Thos. Arthur, Jonathan Richardson, Mose Greer, George Turnbull, Swinfield Hill & Hugh Martin, Gent. The said Edw'd Lyon was led to the Bar in Custody of Hugh Innis, Gent, Sheriff of the said County to whose Custody for cause aforesaid he was Committed & no Prosecutor appearing on the Behalf of the Commonwealth the said Prisoner afores'd is Discharged out of Custody.—T. ARTHUR. At a Court held for Franklin County on Monday the 30th Day of April 1788. Present: Peter Saunders, Jonathan Richardson, Moses Greer & George Turnbull, Gent. Samuel McCoy is App'd Constable in the Room of Jas. Christian who Quallifyed accorg to Law. It is Ordered by the Court that Hugh Innis, John Dickinson, Charles Pincard & Joel Estes, or any Three of them, being first Sworn do value & say of the Estate of the late John Pinkard Dec'd Agreeable to the Said Decedents Will. Absent Peter Saunders.

PAGE TWO HUNDRED FIFTEEN

April Court 1788—A Deed Peter Saunders from Robert Jones Ack'd & Martha the wife being Privily Examined, re-linguished her Right of Dower & O. R. A Power of Atto. from Benja. Potter to Peyton Smith Prov'd & O. R. A Deed from John Grimmit & Wm. Clay to Wm. Hall Prov'd & O. R. Also a Deed Samuel Dillion from Ste. Heard Frov'd by 2 Wits. & O. R. Also John Sandford to John Sneed Pro'd by 2 Wits & O. C. Also Hugh Innis from Spencer Clack Prov'd &' O. R. Also Isaac Dyer from Spencer Clack & Wife Prov'd & O. R. Also Arthur Ed-wards & Wife to Sarah Turley Ack'd & O. R. Also Charles Pinkard from Danl. Richardson Pro'd by 2 Wits & O. R. Hook vs Guthery Thomas Charter & John Cooper Spl. Bl. A Deed from John Turley to Isaac Dyer Prov'd & O. R. Charles Lums-den is app'd Sur'y of the Road from the head of the Maple Swamp to Dillons old mill & the list filed to be his Gang. James Burns is app'd Sur'y from the head of Maple Swamp to John Leviseys & the list filed be his Gang.

PAGE TWO HUNDRED SIXTEEN

April Court 1788—John Arthur Came into Court & made Oath that he was Taxed with 76 Acres of Land which was not his Property & it is ordered that the same be Certifyd to the Solicitor. A Deed John Pane from Turner Richardson proved & O. R. Callaway & Co. & Early vs French, Stay Exon. till June by the Consent of the Attos. On the Mot. of Hugh Innis Gent the Shf. of this County John Hale is admitted his Deputy Shf. he Quallified Accorg to Law. A Deed Harmon Cook from Wm. Vinson, Ack'd & O. R. The Court is Adj'd till to Morrow 8 O'Clock.—PETER SAUNDERS. At a Court Cont'd & held for Franklin County on Tuesday the 8th Day of April 1788. Present: Robert Hairston, Thomas Arthur, Jonathan Richardson & Moses Greer, Gent. Rich'd Edwardson is allow'd 3 Days Attce as a Wits for Ste. Wood vs John Smith.

PAGE TWO HUNDRED SEVENTEEN

April Court 1788—Nathan Ryan is appointed Guardian for John Pinckard, Orphan of John Pinckard Dec'd, & it is ordered that he Give Security at next Court. Penelope Guthery, Adm'x

116

of Henry Guthery Dec'd, who was Summond to appear at this Court to Give Counter Security for her Admin for the said Decedents Estate, & the s'd Penelope Guthery failing to give Such Security, it is ordered by the Court that John Hook & Rich'd Booth, her Securitys, Take Possession on the s'd Decedents Estate agreeable to the Inventory. It is ordered by the Court that the Exrs Mentioned in the Will of Elisha Lyon Dec'd, be Summon'd to the Next Court to be held for this County, to Give Security of their Exorship. On the Motion of Peter Saunders Leave is Granted him to Keep a Retail Store. Samuel Hairston, the Same. Ferguson vs McGradey, William Wright A Garshee being Sworn Saith the Def. has his bond for £74 & V2 Barrel of Corn, Out of W'ch is to be Deducted the Value of 2 Women's Sadles & Bridles, Twenty Pounds of the Above Bond is Payable in a Mare of a Bay Colour, formerly belong. to Geo. Wright, and the Balance to be Paid Next October Twelve Month in horse flesh to be Valued After the same Rate. Jas. Wray, another Garshee, says he Owes the Def. £73-15.6, £28.15.6 of w'ch now Due in Cash & £20. All above to be Credited Against another Pay w'ch he Owes the Def. pble the 25th. Dec. Next for £25.

PAGE TWO HUNDRED EIGHTEEN

April Court 1788—Wood vs Smith Award Ret. & O. R'd for £0.18.5 for the Pltfs. William Ryan is App'd Guardian for Churfott Pinckard, an orphan of John Pinckard Dec'd, & it is ordered that he Give Security at next Court. Samuel Patterson is appointed Guardian for Thomas & Jane Pinckard, Orphans of John Pinckard Dec'd, & it is ordered that he Give Security at next Court. On the Mot. of Absalom Bransom an Injunction is Granted him to stay the Proceedings of a Judgment Obtained agst him by Harmon Cook Asse. the same is Granted him, whereupon he entered into Bond with Robert Holliday his Security who Acknowledged the same According to Law. Farler vs Dillon Jesse Dillon Spl. Bl. Pleas fil'd & issue. Daniel Brown & Callaway is Permitted to keep a Retail Store. Also leave is Granted him to Keep a Tavern in Rocky Mount. Hancock vs Webb. Judgt for £1.10 & Costs. Leave is Granted John Hook to keep a Retail Store. A Deed from Thomas Arthur to Grayham Ack'd & O. R. Leave is Granted Thomas Hill to Keep Tavern. On the Motion of Joel Chitwood to stay the Proceedings of a Judgment Obtained

117

agst him by Danl. Brown & Co. the same is Granted him When up he entered into Bond with John Chitwood his Security & the same was Ack'd Accordg. to Law.

PAGE TWO HUNDRED NINETEEN

April Court 1788—McGeorge vs P. Gee Judgt is Granted him for £2.11 with Costs. It is Ordered by the Court that the Clerk Certify to the Solicitor that James Martin Came into Court & made Oath that he is Charged with Two Hundred Acres of Land w'ch is not his Property. Also a Negro under 16 Years old. It is ordered that the first Saturday in May next, the Elections for the Overseer of the Poor are to be held for the North & the Upper District & Colo. Arthur is App'd to Superintend to Election in the North District & Peter Saunders Gent, the Upper District, & the Third Saturday in May Next for an Election for Lower District & Colo. Hugh Innis is to Superintend the Same. It is Ordered that the Shf. Give Publick notice of the said Elections the Election for the North District to be held at G. Turnbulls, the Upper District at O. Rubles, the South District at J. Dickinsons. Hugh Woods came into Court & Qualified to his Collection since his last return & the same was ordered to be Certified. Hugh Woods Came into Court & Qualified to a list of Insolvents in his District & the same was ordered to be Certified. It is ordered by the Court that the Prices by which Taverns Keepers in this County sold Liquors Last year are Cont'd for the Present Year. Jacob Mullindon vs Bybee Dism'd Agreed.

PAGE TWO HUNDRED TWENTY

May Court 1788—John Ferguson came into Court & Qualified to his Collection sence his last Return & the same was ordered to be Certified. The Court is adj'd till Court in Course.— ROBT. HAIRSTON. At a Court of Quarterly Session held for Franklin County on Monday the 5th Day of May 1788. Present: Peter Saunders, Jonathan Richardson, John Rentfro, Moses Greer & John Dickerson, Gent. A Deed from Laughlin McGrady to Wm. Write Pro'd 2 Wits & O. C. On the motion of Swinfield Hill, Gent. Judgt is granted him agst George Spotts on Reply Bond Security for Nath'l Evins & Costs. A Deed from William Bohannon to James Young Prov'd & O. R. Also William Bohannon to Henry Bohanon, same. Skelton Taylor vs John Chitwood, Judgt. on Repy Bond & cost Cr. By £8.8 paid the 24th. of March 1788. I Callaway & Co. vs Parley Hatcher, William Swanson, Spl. & Bl. & Spl. Jun. Taylor vs Woodcock Israel Standifer Spl. Bl. & Spl. Impl. Stewart vs Napier &c David Hughes Spl. Bl.

PAGE TWO HUNDRED TWENTY-ONE

May Court 1788—Patrick Napier vs Bybee, Shadrick Wood-son Spl Bl. & Delivered the Deft. up whereupon the Def. Conf'd Judgt. Accg to Spl & Costs, Stay Exon. till November Next. Jackson vs Frith Conditional order set & Side & Paymt & Issue. Leave is granted Thomas Prunty D. S. to amend his returning Writ Greer vs Dodson & Charter. Brown & Co. vs Dillion William Rayan Spl. Bl. & Spl. Impl Austin vs Webb and Webb vs Austin Referred to Swinfield Hill & John Smith &, in case they do not agree, to Chuse an Umpire & their aw'd to be the Judgt of the Court. Miller vs Spencer Judgt. Conf'd & for 30/ & Costs. A Power of Atto from William Bohannon to Rich'd Standley Prov'd & O. R. Sanders vs S. Hill Sec'y for Miller & Rentfro Judgt is Granted him on Repy Bond & Costs. Livesay vs Davis Isham Hall a Garnishee being Sworn sayith he owes the Def. Nothing & Cont'd for Guarshees. Harmon Cook vs P. Greer Rich'd Edmondson & Nathan Sellers Spl. B. & Sp. Impl. A Dedimus for the Relinguishment of Dower, Cloe the Wife of Wm. Rentfro, Rent'd & O. R. It is ordered by the Court that Owen Ruble, Leonard Geerhart & Battom Estes be fined 400 Tobo. according to Law for not Attending as Grand Jurymen.

PAGE TWO HUNDRED TWENTY-TWO

May Court 1788—It is ordered by the Court that Hugh Innis, Gent, Shf. be fined According to Law for not Summong a Grand Jury as the Law Directs & Costs. Binnion vs Dillon Jesse Dillion Spl. Bl. Callaway & Co. vs Fitzsimmons, Thomas Prunty Spl. Bl. Farley vs Dillion Jesse Dillion Spl. Bl. At a Court held for the Examination of Dreusiller Huff Charged with feloniously taking from John Rentfro & Wife 2 Handkerchiefs of the Value of 1 Shilling Sterling. Present: Thos. Arthur, John Dickerson, Jonathan Smith, & George Turnbull, Esqr's. And the said Drewsiller Huff being led to the Bar in Custody of Hugh Innis, Gent. late Sherif for the said County, to whose Custody for the Crime aforesaid she was Committed & it being Demanded of the said Prisoner whither she was Guilty or not Guilty of the fact wherewith she stand Charged, Answered that she is in no wise Guilty, whereupon the Court proceeded to examine Divers Witness as well on Behalf of the Commonwealth as the Prisoner at the Bar, Whereupon it is the Opinion of the Court that she is Guilty of the fact wherewith she stands Charged & that she ought to be Examined before the Grand Jury in August next, Whereupon the s'd Huff w'th Mary Stout & Thomas Prunty her Su'ry Entered in Recognizance in the Sum of £10. each to be Levied on their respective Good & Chattles on condition the s'd Drewsiller Huff doth not appear before the Court on the first Monday in August next.

PAGE TWO HUNDRED TWENTY-THREE

May Court 1788—It is Ordered that David Hughes be put in the Stocks for an Insult offered to the Court & there remain one half hour & Pay Costs. Abigill Rentfro, Sarah Walker & James Christy Acknowledged themselves severally indebted to the Commonwealth of Virginia in sum of £20. to be levied on their Respective Goods & Chattles Lands & Tenaments, in case they do not appear at August Court next as Witnesses ComWealth vs Drewsiller Huff. Wallis & Campbell vs Dugless Joel Estis Spl. Bl. & Spl. Im. Ferguson vs Jones Judgt. According to Spy & Costs. Present: Geo. Turnbull. Absent: John Dickerson Greer vs Charles & Dodson Judg. Conf'd by Charter according to Spl. & Costs. John Dickerson Exrs. vs William Graves Judgt. accg to the Spl. & Costs. The Court is Adj'd till tomorrow 8 oClock. Robt. Hairston At a Court of Quarterly Sessions Cont'd & Held for Franklin County on Tuesday the 6th. May 1788. Present: Robert Hairston, Peter Saunders, Thomas Arthur, & John Dickerson, Gent. Calland vs Swanson Dism'd agreed.

PAGE TWO HUNDRED TWENTY-FOUR

May Court 1788—On the Motion of Moses Hudgins a Dedimus is granted him to take the Depo. of John Bratcher as a Witness for Hudgins ads Simmons. Hopkins vs Rentfro, Thomas Arthur a Guarnishee being sworn sayith he hath a Sword blade of the Def. in his Possession, also a Tract of Land, which is to be sold & half the Money arising from the said sale is to be applyed

120

to the said Rentfro's use which are be to Condem'd & applyed to the payment of the Debt Complained of accorg to Spk & Costs & ordered Condemnation. Hunt vs Young Dism'd agreed. Beasley vs Davis the Def. having stood out all Process of Contempt, on the motion of the Pltf it is ordered & Decreed, that 456 Acres of Land, lying on Owens Creek, sold by the Def. to a Certain James Walker by Deed bearing date the 17th. of November 1783, which was not been Prov'd nor Recorded according to Law, Be henceforth Vested in the s'd Beasley his Heirs or Assigns & that the Pltf. Recover his Costs about his suit in that Behalf expended. Patterson vs Hubbard Cont'd. Stober vs Davis. Cont. for aw'd. Williams vs Stewart & Chitwood Cont. foaw'd. Chitwood vs Williams, Same. Same vs Same, Same. Miller vs Kelly, Rule be given Sut'y for Costs at Next Court and be Dism'd.

PAGE TWO HUNDRED TWENTY-FIVE

May Court 1788—John Kelly vs Miller Con'd for Aw'd. William Miller vs John Kelly, Asberry vs Stoakes Ordered that the Referees proceed exparte in Case the Parties do not Attend. Martha Miller is allow'd 5 Days Attendance as a Witness for John Johnson vs Thomas Doggett. Edw'd. Lyon vs Mary Lyon Dism'd. Ordered that John Chitwood & Ashford Napier be Summon to Shew Cause why they should not be fined for preventing the Attendance of Mary Lyon in the Prosecution of the Commonwealth vs Edw'd Lyon. Present: S. Hill, Gent, on the Mot. of John Hook agst Hugh Innes, high Sheriff for Judgt. on two atta. agst. Guthry admx. the same is Rejected w'th Costs. But the Court considers that the Said Penelope Guthrie is Still liable to payment of the Witnesses attendance, & that She was discharged by a former Order of Court in consequence of a Clerical error in Sending the attachmt. in the name of the Asse. instead of the principal. John Dickerson, Esq. Return'd an Addition plott of the Prison bounds & O. R. Penelope Guthrie is Pursuance of a former order of this Court requiring her to give John Hook Counter Security for the administration of her Dec'd husband Estate, brought Stephen Goggins who entered into Bond for that Purpose, with the approbation of the Court and it is Ordered that the Cost of accruing

121

PAGE TWO HUNDRED TWENTY-SIX

May Court 1788—by virtue of the Said Hook Pursuing this moade for his indemnification be paid by the Said Penelope. I. Callaway & Co vs Fitzsimmans Judgt. Conf'd accordg. to Specy. & Costs & stay Exon. till ordered by the Pltf. On the Mot. of William Harrison a Jud. is Granted him to stay the Proceedings of a Judgment obtained agst him by James Cowden & the same is Granted. Elisha Blankinship is allow'd 2 Days Attendance as a Witness for William Austin vs Samuel Webb. Hook vs Vincent & Wright. A Jury sworn, to Witt, Robert Cowin, Samuel Calland, William Thompson, Thomas Hale, Thomas Crump. David Barton, John Woods, William Fowler, Stephen Goggin, Edw'd Wilson, John Kemp & John Boswell. Verdict returned for the Defs & O. R. Mary Dillion is Allow'd 5 Days Attendance as a Witness for William Austin vs Sam Webb. Mary Dillion is allow'd 2 Days Attendance as a Witness for Wm. Dillion ads of Farley. Danl. Perdue is allowd 2 Days for the same. Same is allow'd 2 days for Austin vs Webb. Thos. Cragg is allow'd 9 Days attce as a Wits. for James agst Gordon. John Bird is allow'd 16 days for the same.

PAGE TWO HUNDRED TWENTY-SEVEN

May Court 1788—A Deed of Trust from William Cowden to Samuel Caland Ack'd & O. R. A Power of Attorney from Danl. Richardson to Sam'l Calland Prov'd & O. R. Brown vs Radford, Thomas Arthur Spl. Bail & Spy Imp. Ferguson vs McGrady cont'd. George Wright vs David Stewart, Jacob Boon Garnishee being sworn sayith he hath in his hands as much Corn of the Def. as will amount to 21/6 at 12/6 P. Barrell & 6 Shillings in Cash & Order Condemnation. Danl. Brown & Co. vs William Kelly Judgt. on Repy Bond Accg to Spl & Costs. John Edwards vs Francis Kerbey Sec'y for Edmondson. Judgt. on Repy Bond accg to Spl. & Costs. Johnson vs Doggett and Doggett vs Johnson, Agreed & dismissed. William Christopher is allow'd 2 Days Attce as a Wits. for Trent vs Jones. James Dillion is allow'd 4 Days Attce & 2 Coming & returning as a Witness for Dillion ads Farley. Welch vs Kelleys Admrs, Cont'd. Meshack Perew is allow'd 2 days Attce as a Wits. for Dillion ads Farler.

PAGE TWO HUNDRED TWENTY-EIGHT

May Court 1788—James McVey vs William Miller, John Rentfro & Thomas Prunty Spl. Bl. & Spl. Impl. It is ord. by the Court, that Jeremiah Early, Jubal Early & John Sullin be fined £10 each for offering a Comtempt to the Order of the Court & for their Rid'ous behavior & that they be Comm'd to Custody till Paid & Costs & to give Security for their Good behavior. Callaway & Co. vs Blain & Rentfro, William Akers a Guarnishee sworn sayth he owes the Def. the arnch of the Pltfs Claim. Judgt. for £2.13.9 w'th Int. till Paid & Costs. & O. C. I. Webster vs I. Rentfro. a Jury sworn, to wit, Plumnee Hairston, John Bird, Thomas Cragg, Israel Standifer, Rich'd Radford, Elijah Hatcher, Law McGeorge, John Ferguson, Mordecai Mosley, Isaac Bates, David Barton & William Akers. Verdict returned for the Pltf. for £7.10.10/ & Costs & O. R. Jamison vs Gordon, A Jury sworn, to Wit, Samuel Calland, Moses Rentfro, Plummer Thurston, Israel Standifer, Rich'd Radford, Elijah Hatcher, Law McGeorge, Mordacai Mosley, Isaac Bates, Ste. Wood, James McVey, Elisha Keen. Verdict return'd for Plf for £9.6.8. & the same was ordered to be Recorded. The Court is Adjourn'd till Tomorrow at 8 o'Clock.—T. ARTHUR.

PAGE TWO HUNDRED TWENTY-NINE

May Court 1788—At a Court Cont'd & held for Franklin County the 7th. May 1788. Present: Swinfield Hill, John Smith, Moses Greer, John Rentfro & John Dickerson, Gent. Hook vs Whitworth atta. on hearing Judgt. for £16.15.7. and Costs of Condemnation. William Swanson a Garnishee in the Suit Hook vs Whitworth being Sworn says he has nothing. The order of Yesterday imposing a fine on Jere Early for Reasons appearing to the Court is Remitted by his Paying the Costs & Cont'd as to the Others. Hook vs Wm. Mead Atta. on hearing. Judgt for £174.10.6. w'th Int. from the first of April 1787, till Payment the Same Subject to Mead Costs on Hook Atta in Bedford Court. Danl. Farley a Garnihee being sworn saith he owes the Def. £207.14. to be Sealed at 2½ ford with Int. from 23 day of June 1786 O. C. & Costs & Cont'd for Garshces. It is Considered that the Debt due from Farley to Mead is not finally settled but subject to future Settlement if the Law Shall institute a Just on James

123

Farley Penn and their Garnishee being sworn saith he owes the
Def. nothing & John Ferguson another Garshee saith he owes
the Def. Nothing. A Division of the Estate of John Pinkard
Dec'd Returned & O. R. Will Cowdin is allow'd one Days
Atta. as a Wits. for E. Keen vs Grimmit.

PAGE TWO HUNDRED THIRTY

May Court 1788—Thomas Doggitt vs William Rentfro Atta.
on hearing Judg. for £5.4. & William Akers, a Garnishee being
sworn, saith he Owes the Def. a Sufficiency to satisfy the Ptf.
Demand. & O. C. & Costs. Common Wealth vs Benja. Hale a
Jury sworn, to Wit, Samuel Calland, Ste. Wood, Isaac Bates, John
England, Thomas Miller, Law McGeorge, Rich'd Radford, Elijah
Hatcher, John Kemp. Joel Estes, James McVey & Mordicai
Mosley, who returned a True Bill & it is the opinion of the Court
that the Def. be fined Damages & to be Imprisoned Twenty four
hours & to pay Costs. It is ordered by the Court that the Shf.
take in to his Possession a Negro Man named Daniel now at
Spencer James & to Imprison & advertise him accordg to Law.
Ordered that a Negro named Danl now in Gaol of this County
after Staying in Gaol 2 months from the time of his Commitment shall be hired to the highest bidder to pay the Prison
Charges &c. Elianer Hill is allow'd 12 Days attce as a Wits. for
the Commonwealth agst Hale. Swinfield Hill, Gent. is allow'd
8 Days Attce as a Wit for the Same. Commonwealth vs Toney,
A Jury sworn, to Wit, John Hook, William Maveaty, Amos Richardson, Israel Standifer, Robert Jones, Law McGeorge, Sam Calland, Jacob Oldakers, Thomas Lewis, Mordecai Mosley, Rich'd
Radford & David Barton & not Agreeing in their Verdict, they
are Discharged.

PAGE TWO HUNDRED THIRTY-ONE

May Court 1788—William Akers is allow'd 8 Days Attce as
a Witness for Com Wealth vs Toney. Doley French is allow'd 3
Days Attce as A Wits. for Toney ads Commonwealth. James
McVey is allow'd 9 Days Attce ads Same. Mary McVey is allow'd 9 Days Attce ads Same. Martin Delancy 9 days ads Same.
Joshua Wilson is allow'd 4 days Attce. as a Wits. for the Commonwealth vs Toney. Mary Henderson is allow'd 9 days Attce

as a Wits for the Same. Isabella McClure is allow'd 9 days for the same. Phebey McClure is allow'd 9 Days for the same. Joseph Ritter is allow'd 3 days for the same. Eliza Kelly is allow'd 7 Days for the same. Rosannah Wilson is allow'd 4 days for the same. Thos. Prunty is allowed 10 Days for the same. Mary Ritter is allow'd 1 Day for the same. Mary Miller is allow'd 9 Days Attce as a Wits for Toney ads Commonwealth. Rebecca Scruggs is Allow'd 7 days as a Wits for the same.

PAGE TWO HUNDRED THIRTY-TWO

May Court 1788—Aberiller Thompson is allow'd 9 Days attce as a Wit's for Toney ads Com. Wealth. John Rodgers is allow'd 4 Days Attce as a Wits. for Edw's Wilson vs John England. Andrew Thompson is allow'd 4 days for the same. Smith Webb vs John England, Wm. Thompson Spl. Bl. Present: Jonathan Richardson, Thomas Arthur, Swinfield Hill & Moses Greer, Gent. Absent: John Smith & John Rentfro. Choice vs Finney Peter Finney Spl. Bl. & Spl. Impl. Farley vs Dillion, Dism'd. The Court is adjourned till Tomorrow 8 o'clock—T. ARTHUR. At a Court of quarterly Sessions Cont'd & held for Franklin County on Thursday the 8th. Day of May 1788. Present: Thos. Arthur, Jonathan Richardson, Swinfield Hill & John Rentfro, Gent.

PAGE TWO HUNDRED THIRTY-THREE

May Court 1788—Robert Jones is allow'd 3 Days Attce & 1 Coming & Returning 25 Miles as a Wits. for Prunty ads Jones. Amos Richardson is allow'd 11 Days Attce. as a Wits for Eusebus Hubbard ads Patterson. Stokes vs Goggins a Jury sworn, to Wit, John Hook, Stephen Woods, Thomas Jones, Isaac Bates, Israel Standifer, Amos Richardson, James McVey, William Akers, Willaim Walton, John Craighead, John England & Thomas Miller. Verdict Returned for Def. & O. R. William Bartee is allow'd 4 Days. Attce 1 Coming & Returning 24 Miles as a Witness for Stokes vs Goggins. Black vs Swanson. a Jury sworn, to wit, John Hook, Stephen Woods, John Craghead, Thos. Jones, Isaac Bates, Israel Standifer, Amos Richardson, James McVey, William Akers, William Walton, John England & Thomas Miller. Verdict returned for the Plf. £3.6.18 Damages & O. R. that Black the Ptf. at Law Pay the Costs at the Injo. & half the Costs at the suit of

Common Law & O. R. It is ordered that the fine imposed on
John Sullin for Offering an Insult & his Riotous Behavior to the
Court be remitted by paying Costs. Hunt vs Bartee, Dism'd for
want of Procution. Delany vs Bates, Cont'd at the Ptf. Costs.
Leave is Granted Martin Delany to take the Depo. of Frale
Nicholes, John Kelly & Thos. Bell in a Suit agt Bates.

PAGE TWO HUNDRED THIRTY-FOUR

May Court 1788—Delancy Ham vs Bates D. the Ptf being
nul'd to—Tryal the Witnesses not attendg. by Ptf order the same
Dism'd. Stinson vs Livesay Dism'd for the same. Livesay vs
Anderson Cont'd. Callaway vs Guthery Admx, Cont'd. Callaway
vs Brooks &c Cont'd. Chitwood vs Coleman, Same. Quigley vs
Miles a Jury Sworn, to Wit, Isaac Rentfro, Law McGeorge, Edw'd
Wilson, Lewis Davis, Wm. Thompson, William Maviaty, Jere.
Holliday, John Kemp, Mordecai Mosley, Jas. Webb, John Jamison
& Rich'd Bailey. Verdict Returned for the Ptf. 14/ O. R. Stokes
vs Dueas Judgt for Costs. Thomas Jones is allow'd 1 day Attce
as a Wits. for Miles ads Quigley. John Chambers is allow'd 5
Days Attce. as a Wits for Quigley vs Miles. Abraham Jones is
allow'd 7 Days Attce. as a Wits. for Quigley vs Sam Miles.
Edw'd Beck is allow'd 6 Days for the same. Martha Beck is allow'd 6 Days for the same. James Greer is allow'd three Days
for Miles ads Quigley. Enos Miles is allow'd 7 Days for the
same. Rentfro vs Doggitt, Cont'd. Sam Calland is allow'd 4 days
attce & 1 Coming & going 21 Miles as the Wits. for Livesay
ads Barton.

PAGE TWO HUNDRED THIRTY-FIVE

Hill vs Early Robert Williams a Garnishee Came in Court &
Ack'd to pay the Ptf £8, Ten Shillings when it comes into his
hands & O. C. & Cost. John Hale vs John Craghead. A Jury
Sworn, to wit, John Hook, Thos. Jones, Isaac Bates, Israel Standifer, Amos Richardson, James McVey, William Akers, William
Walker, Thomas Miller, David Barton & John England————
be attend the suit is Cont'd. Lettoy Oldakers is allow'd 7 Days
attce. as a Wits for Quigley agst Miles. John Camp is allow'd
5 Days attce. as Wits. for Craghead ads Hale. Elijah Hatcher is
allow'd. 3 Days Attce for the same. Asberry vs Clutcher Leave is
granted to take the Depo. of Rich'd Watts, John Pane, Charles

Anderson, Jas. Young, James Chafin & Jas. & Charles Bratcher. James Hale is allow'd 3 Days attce as a Witness for Craghead ads Hale. It is ordered that John Dickerson, Hugh Innis, John Martin & Hugh Martin, or any three of them, Divide the Lands comprised in the Last Will & Testament of John Ramsey Dec'd, among his Children agreeable to their father's Will & make report thereof to next Court. Thos. Watts is Allow'd 4 Days Attce as a Wits. for Bott vs Chitwood. Also 3 days for Trent vs Jones. Absent: T. Arthur, Gent.

PAGE TWO HUNDRED THIRTY-SIX

Bott vs Chitwood a Jury Sworn, to Wit, Lewis D———————, William Thompson, Jere. Holliday, Wm. Maveity, Samuel Calland, John Craghead, Robert Jones, Mordecai Mosley, John Camp, Rich'd Baily, Thomas Jones & Samuel Miles. Verdict returned for Pts. £8 Damages & O. R. Errors filed, & being Argued, are over ruled wth Cost. William Swanson is Allow'd 5 Day Attce as a Wits. for Craghead ads Hall. Law McGeorge 5 Days Attce & 2 Comig & returning 25 Miles as a Witness for Trent vs Jones. The Court is Adjourn'd till Tomorrow 8 oClock.—JONATHAN RICHESON. At a Court of Quarterly Sessions Cont'd & held for Franklin County on Friday the 9th Day of May 1788. Present: Jonathan Richardson, Moses Greer, Swinfield Hill & John Rentfro, Gent. William Call vs John Short. a Jury Sworn, to Wit, John Hook, Thomas Watts, Mordecai Mosley, Will. Menefee, Jun., Thomas Wilson, William Walton, George Simmons, Thomas Doggett, Joseph Webb, George Asbury, John Levisey & James McVey. Verdict Returned for the Plf. £9.11.3 O. R.

PAGE TWO HUNDRED THIRTY-NINE

May Court 1788—Hook vs. Geo. Simmons a Jury sworn, to Witt, Thomas Miller, Thomas Watts, Mordecai Mosley, William Menefee, Jun., Thomas Wilson, William Walton, Thomas Terry, Thomas Doggett, Joseph Webb, George Asberry, John Livesey & James McVey. Verdict returned for the Ptf. & O. R. Hook Assee of Callaway vs Theodorick Webb. A Jury sworn, to Wit, Thomas Miller, Thomas Watts, Mordecai Moseley, William Menefee, Jun., John Leftwich, William Walton, Thos. Terry, Thomas

*Pages 237 and 238 are blank.

Doggett, John England, George Asberry, John Livesey & James McVey. Verdict returned for the Ptf. & O. R. Errors filed & being Argued an over ruled with Costs. William Akers is allow'd 9 Days Attce as A Wits. for Ste. Wood ads Hook. Hook Assee of Thomas Watts vs Theodorick Webb. A Jury sworn, to wit, Robert Hollerday, Isaac Bates, Stephen Rich'd Radford, Samuel Calland, Israel Standefer, Daniel Brown, Jeremiah Hollerday, Lewis Davis, Edw'd Willson, Samuel Dillion & Joseph England. A Verdict returned for the Ptf. & O. R. Present: Thomas Arthur. Webb vs Hook a Jury sworn, to Wit, Thomas Miller, Thos. Watts Mordecai Mosley, William Menefee, Jun., Wm. Walker, Thomas Terry, Thomas Doggett, John England, George Asberry, John Livesey, James McVey, & Thomas Kay. Verd. Ret. & O. R'd. Errors filed & being Argued are overruled w'th Costs. Isaac Bates is allow'd three Days Attce as a Wits. for Theodorick Webb vs Hook.

PAGE TWO HUNDRED FORTY

May Court 1788—Rich'd Radford is allow'd 8 Days Attce. as a Witness for Hook ads Webb. Hollerday vs Wilson, a Jury sworn, to Wit, George Simmons, John Vanmaple, Lewis Davis, Israel Standefer, Isaac Rentfro, Edward Choat, Jacob Kingery, John Craghead, Stephen Wood, Lawrence McGeorge, Rich'd Radford & Rich'd Copeland. Verdict returned for the Deft & O. R. Thomas Wilson is allow'd 14 days Attce as a Wits. for Wilson ads Hollerday. Mordecai Moseley is Allowed 10 days for the Same. Thomas Hill is allow'd 1 Days Attce. for the Same. Hook vs Wood A Jury sworn, to Witt, Jeremiah Hollerday, George Simmons, John Vanmaple, John Craghead, Rich'd Copland, Mordecai Mosley, Thomas Miller & Edw'd Choat. Verdict returned for the Def. & O. R. Hook vs Wood on the trial of this Cause the Pet. mov'd by G. Hancock his attorney, that the within article of agreem't on whch the Suit was brought and which was heretofore lost or mislaid, and this day found among the pages of a former Suit brought by Jno. Hook agt the said Wood on an obligation for the Delivery of three horses, on which Judg't was heretofore obtained, should be admitted as Evidence to the Jury. The Court were of opinion the said Instrument of writing should not be admitted as Evidence, It being proven by three of the Jurors in the former Suits that they then took under their con-

128

sideration the Damages Sustained by the pltf by reason of the Deft. failing to perform on his contract aforesaid, a Duplicate of the said Agreemt being Given in to them for information, Evidence to which opinion the Pltf by his Attorney Excepts, & prays the Presiding member may Seal & sign the same, which is accordingly done, & prays an appeal to the ——— day of the succeeding Genl. Court from the Judge aforesaid, which is granted him, whereupon he entered into Bond with Security as the Law directs.

PAGE TWO HUNDRED FORTY-ONE

May Court 1788—Law McGeorge is allow'd 6 days Attce & 2 Coming & Returning 25 miles as a Wits. for Hook ads Webb. William Walton is allow'd 10 days Attce as a Wits. for Wood ads Hook. Lewis Davis is allow's 3 Days Attce as a Wits. for Graham vs Graves. Lewis Davis is allow's 3 Days Attce. as a Wits for Edward Wilson vs England. Israel Standefer is allow'd 9 Days Attce as a Wits for Ste. Wood ads Hook. James McVey is allow'd 7 Days Attce. as a Wits for the Same. Wilson vs England, Referred to Thomas Arthur & Swinfield Hill & in case they do not agree, they are to Chuse an Umpire whose award shall be the Judgt. of the Court. Moses Greer is allow'd 3 Days Attce. as a Wits. for Hudgins ads Simmons. The Court is adjourned till Court in Course.—T. ARTHUR.

PAGE TWO HUNDRED FORTY-TWO

June Court 1788—At a Court held for Franklin County on Monday the 2nd Day of June 1788. Present: Peter Saunders, Jonathan Richardson, Moses Greer, George Turnbull & John Dickinson, Gent. A Deed Charles Roason from Thomas Huston Prv'd & Agnes the wife, being Privily Examined, Relinguish'd &c & O. R. Also Henry Sands from Charles Roason Ack'd & Hannah the wife, be'g Priviley examd'd, Relinguish'd &c & O. R. Paid 12/6. The Last Will & Testament of Benjamin Greer Dec'd was Exhibited in the Court by Mary Greer Ex'x &c. Martin Greer Executor, W'ch was Prov'd by Wits & w'th Shelton Taylor & Moses Greer & Amos Ellison their Security entered into Bond according to Law & Ack'd the same & O. R. Alexander Ferguson, Oaty Procer, Anthony Pate & John Hook, or any three thereof, are appointed to appraise the said Estate & return

129

an Inventory thereof to the Court. On the Mot. of Anthony Pate, his Negro Wench Judith is Ex'd from the Payment of the County & Parrish Levy. A Deed of Gift from Jane Pinkard to Elizabeth Ryan is Prov'd & O. R. A Bill of Sale from Moses Hudgins to Danl. Hudgins Ack'd & O. R. A Deed William Spencer to Isaac Miller Pro'd. & O. R. Also Wm. Thompson to Benja. White Ack'd & Sarah the wife, being Privily Examined as the Law Directs, reling'd her right of Dower & O. R.

PAGE TWO HUNDRED FORTY-THREE

June Court 1788—Owen Ruble & Leonard Gearheart are Exempted from the fine Imposed on them for not Attending as Grand Jury men on Paying Costs & that the Execution be with-drawn. A Deed from James Young to Samuel Dent Ack'd & O. R. Also Rich'd Watts to Thomas Watts Pr'd by Wits. & O. R. Also Solomon Davis from John Grimmit, Same. Also Danl. Rich-ardson to James Prunty, Prov'd & O. R. Also James Rodgers to Robert Prunty Pro'd by 2 Wits & O. C. Also Isaac David to Phillip Bailey Pro'd by 2 Wits & O. C. Also Joel Chitwood from Rich'd Bailey same. Also John Arthur from Rich'd Bailey further Pr'd by 1 Wits & O. C. Also William Boyd from Joel Chitwood Ack'd & O. R. Absent: Peter Saunders, Gent. A Bill of Sale Joel Innis to William Thompson Pr'd & O. R. Thomas Arthur, Gent. is Recomded to his Excellency the Governor to Serve as Colo. in place of Hugh Innis, Gent. who hath Resigned. Also John Rentfro is appointed Lieut. Colo in the Place of Colo. Ar-thur who is Promoted. Jonathan Richardson is appointed a Maj. in the Place of John Rentfro Who is Promoted. George Thomas is appointed Lieut. & James Myer Ensign in the Cumpny of Capt. Greer.

PAGE TWO HUNDRED FORTY-FOUR

June Court 1788—Elisha Keen is app'd Insign to Capt. Dick-inson Cumpy of Militia. Israel Standifer is appointed Lieut & Martin Young Insign. to Capt. Reives Cumpy of Militia. Joseph Hodges Sur'y of the Pigg River Road is Directed to Turn the s'd Road as he shall be Directed by John Dickinson Gent. Peter Geerheart is appointed Surveyor of the Road from Blackwater to Pigg River in the Place of Joshua Rentfro & the list to be fil'd be his Gang. George Peery is App'd Surveyor of the Road from

Tittle Creek to Magotty, in the place of Tobias Miller, & the list fil'd to be his Gang. Eusebus Hubbard is Allow'd 7 Days Attce as a Wits. for Swanson ads Black. John Law, Israel Standefer, James Marcum, & John Smith, or any three of them, are App'd to view way for a Road from the Chestnut Creek Road to Cross Pigg River, Black Water & Stanton, in as Straight Direction to Medow Road as can be with Convenience. Ordered that Rachel Huff, Daughter of Ste. Huff, be bound to Danl. Spangler. Also Ruth Huff be Bound to Nathan Sellers. Ordered that an Additional list of hands filed be Added to the hands of Robt. Prunty.

PAGE TWO HUNDRED FORTY-FIVE

June Court 1788—Spencer James is appointed Surveyor of the Road from the County line to Peter Saunders in the Place of John Sneed & the former hands to be his Gang. It is ordered that Sarah Huckerby be Bound to Danl. French. Abraham Abshire is app'd Surveyor of the Road in the Place of David Morgan & the fil'd list be his Gang. Hugh Innes Gent is Permitted to Keep a Retail Store. Danl. Barnhart is app'd Surveyor of the Road in the Place of William Walton & the list filed be his Gang. Joel Meddow, Jr. is app'd Sur'y of the Road in the Place of Peter Wood & the s'd Wood hands to be his Gang. William Walton is app'd Sur'y of the Road from Abrham Abshire to the 3rd ford of Black Water. John Taylor is App'd Lieut. in the Cumpy of Skelton Taylor & Sam'l Cockrum Insign. David Stewart Came in to Court & made oath that he is Charged by the Sheriff with more land than belongs to him, he being owner of but 100 Acres. Lewis Davis is App'd Sur'y of the Road from Story Creek in the place of Luke Standifer & his hands he his Gang. Thomas Prunty Came into Court & Quallified to his Collection Since his last Return & Ord. to be Certif'd. It is ordered that the Clk Certify to the Solicitor that Asa Holland made oath Accordg to Law that he stands Charged w'th 96 Acres of Land more than belong to him.

PAGE TWO HUNDRED FORTY-SIX

June Court 1788—William Ryan, Deputy Shf, Came into Court & Quallified accordg. to Law to his Collection sence his last Return & the same was ordered to be Certifyed. John Dickerson Gent. is allow'd 2 Days Attce. as a Wits. for John Hook vs

Vencent & Wright. The Court is Adj'd till Court in Course.—
JONATHAN RICHESON. At a Court held for Franklin County
on Monday the 1st day of June 1788 for the Examination of
Reuben Pursel and James Lyon, alias Thompson, for Feloniously
Stealing a Sorrel Horse & a Bald Eagle Horse, the Property of
Thomas Arthur. Present: Robert Hairston, Jonathan Richeson,
Swinfield Hill, Moses Greer, And George Turnbull, Gent. The
said Reubin Persel bing led to the Bar in the Custody of Hugh
Innis Gent. Sheriff of the said County, and to whose Custody he
had been Comitd for the Crime aforsaid, & it being Demanded
of the said Prisoner whether he is Guilty of the fact wherewith
he stands Charged or not guilty, answered that he is in no wise
Guilty. Whereupon the Court Proceeded to Examine Divers Witnesses as Well on behalf of the Com. Wealth as the Prisoner at
the Bar, on Consideration Whereof the Court are of Opinion that
the said Ruben Parsel is Guilty of the facts wherewith he stands
Charged & that he Ought to Receive a further Tryal before the
Honble the Genl. Court in the City of Richmond On the first
day thereof in October next, whereupon he is Remanded into
the Custody of the Shff Aforesaid.

PAGE TWO HUNDRED FORTY-SEVEN

Chas. Thomas, who Prosecutes on Behalf of the Com. Wealth,
Saml. Mannin And James McCutcher Came into Court and Acknowledged themselves Severally Indebted to the Com Wealth
of Virginia in the Sum of £100 each to be Levied their Respective
Goods & Chattles, Lands & Tenements on Condition they do not
Appear before the Hble the Genl. Court in the City of Richmond on the first day thereof in October Next, as Witness on
behalf of the Com Wealth Against Rubin Pursel & James Lynn,
alias Thompson. The Depo. of Charles Thomas of Lawful Age
being Sworn Saith that the 29th. day of May Last he in Company with Others Apprehended and took a Certain James Lynn,
Alias Thompson, on Suspicion of his being a Horse-thief. This
Depo further Saith that he found Two Horses with him & one
which he Claimed as his Own Property both of w'ch horses was
Claimed by Thomas Arthur. The Depo of Saml. Mannin, being
first Sworn, Saith that in the 29th. day of May last he in Company with Others Apprehended & took a Certain James Lynn,
alias Thompson, on Suspicion of his bing a Horse Thief. This

Deponent further Saith that he found Two Horses with him &
One of w'ch he Claimed as his Own Property both of w'ch
Horses was Claimed by Thomas Arthur. This Depo. further Saith
be Verily believes that Rubin Pursill, the other Prisoner, to be
An Accomplice of Lynn & that he is the Other Person who made
his Escape when Lynn was Apprehended. The Depo. of Jas.
McCutchin, being first Sworn, Saith that on the 29th Day of
May last he in Compy. w'th Others apprehended & took a Cer-
tain Jas. Lynn, Als Thompson, on Suspicion of his being a Horse
Thief, that he found 2 horses w'th him, One of w'ch he Claimed
as his Own Property, both of w'ch horses was Claimed by Thomas
Arthur, That he Verily believes that Rubin Parsell the other
Prisoner to be an Accomplice of his & that he is the Person who
made his Escapte when Lynn was Appehended.

PAGE TWO HUNDRED FORTY-EIGHT

June 1788—The Said James Lynn, Alias Thompson, being
led to the Bar in the Custody of Hugh Innes Gent. Sheriff of
Said County, to whose Custody he had been Commited for the
Crime Aforsaid, & it being Demanded of the Said Prisoner
whether his is Guilty of the facts wherwith he Stands Charged
or not Guilty, Answered that he is in no wise Guilty whereupon
the Court Proceeded to Examine Divers Witness as well as Behalf of the Com. Wealth as the Prisoner at the Bar, on Consideration whereupon the Court are of Opinion the said Lynn, Alias
Thompson, is Guilty of the fact wherewith he stands Charged
& that he Ought to receive a further Tryal before the Honble
the Genl. Court in the City of Richmond on the first day thereof
in October Next whereupon he is Remanded into the Custody
of the Shff afores'd.—ROBT. HAIRSTON.

PAGE TWO HUNDRED FORTY-NINE

At a Court held for Franklin County on Monday the 7th.
Day of July 1788. Present: Thomas Arthur, Jonathan Richard-
son, John Smith, George Turnbull & Moses Greer, Gent. Thomas
Arthur Gent. Produc'd a Com. from his Excellency the Gover-
nor Appointing him Colo. of the Militia of this County who
Qualified according to Law. John Rentfro, Gent Produced a
Com. from his Excellency the Governor, appointing him a Lieut.
Colo. for the Milita of this County who Quallif'd Accorg. to Law.

133

Also Jonathan Richardson Quallif'd as a Maj. of the Militia. Also Moses Greer, Gent. Qual'd as a Capt. of the Militia. A Deed Edgcomb Guilliam from Henry Bohannan Ack'd & O.R. Mary the Wife Being Privily Examined as the Law Directs Rel'd &c. Brown & Co. vs Menefee as Sur'y for Livesey Judgt. accg. to Repy Bond & Costs. Joseph Price Came into Court and Made Oath that he was Chag'd with 7 head of Horses & 1 Cow More than Was his Own in the Tax of 1786 & Ord. to be Certify'd to the Solicitor.

PAGE TWO HUNDRED FIFTY

July Court 1788—Israel Standifer Gent Produc'd a Com. from his Excellency the Governor appointing him a Lieut. for the Militia of this County, who Qual'd accordg to Law. Swinfield Hill, coroner for this County, return'd to the Court an Inquest taken on the Body of Ste. Evans & the Jurors for that Purpose inpanneled. Brougt in their Verd. w'ch was ordered to be Recorded. Saunders vs Miller. Judgt Conf'd by Rentfro on a Repy Bond. w'th Costs. A Deed Peter Holland from Ashford Napier Atto. for Peter Gillams & Israel Standifer Ack'd & Susannah the wife of Standifer, Being Priviley Examined, Reling'd her Right of Dower. Samuel Cockram Pro'd a Com. from his Excellency the Governor appointing him an Ensign for the Militia of this County who Qual'd accordg to Law. A Deed from Benja. Griffith to John Ferguson Ack'd & Catherine the wife, being Privily Examined as the law Directs, Reling'd as her Right of Dower & O. R. A Deed from Thomas Arthur to Rob. Ellison & Thos P. Jourdin Ack'd & O. R. Thomas Arthur vs Thomas Doggett. Dism'd.

PAGE TWO HUNDRED FIFTY-ONE

July Court 1788—John Cooper, Anthony Pate, Jubal Early & George Kelly, or any three of them, are appointed to View the nearest & best way from the Mouth of Praters Run on Staunton River to the Blackwater Road where Early Road Crosses the same & make a Report thereof to the Court. Mathew Kidd Came into Court & Claimed the Advance to go of the Insolvent Act & giving a schedule of his Estate & O. R. A Bill of Sale from Danl. Farley to John Hook Prov'd by 2 Wits & O. R. Hancock vs Williah Rentfro, Wm. Akers a Garnishee being Sworn sayith he hath

Sufficient in his hands to Satisfy the Plfs Demands for 35/6 Pay-able the 25th Day of Dec. 1787 & O Conda & Judgt for the same & Costs. Woods vs Jamison Cond. Thorp vs Gipson, Con'd at the Defs Costs. Warring vs Harris leave is Granted the Ptf a Deds to take the Depo. of Rhody Cooly Giv'g. 10 Days Notice to the Def. Hollerday vs Christian Cont'd at the Defs Costs. Bitting vs Jamison Judg for £3.7.6 Jn. agreeable to Spl. & Costs. Hurt vs Young Dism'd. Edmonson vs Burns, Judgt accorg. to Spl & Costs. Parker vs Coleman Judgt for 40. & Costs.

PAGE TWO HUNDRED FIFTY-TWO

July Court 1788—Hook vs Sowing Judgt for £2.13.47 & Costs. Isaiah Turner came to Court & made oath that he is Charged with fourteen Shillings in his Tax for the Year 1786, w'ch is Wrong, & the same is ordered to be Certif'd to the So-licitor. Ross & Hook vs Mead. Judgt for £43.18.9 w'th In. from the 12th of April 1787 & Costs. Robert Head a Garnishee being sworn sayith that he has Bonds in his Possession Deeded to the Def. to the amount of near £300, Due from Sundry Persons, w'ch are to be valid whenever the said Robert Mead is inabled to con-vey the Title for Certain Lands which he had sold in Trust for the Def. & for wch these bonds were Given. The Garnishee fur-ther sayith that he has a full Power from the Def. to make a good Right to these Lands & Cont'd for Proof. Garishees Danl. Foster & A. Fralin. Braidon vs Marcum Ashford Napier Spl. Bail. Samuel Bird came into Court & Made Oath that he is charg'd with the Tax on 173 Acres of Land for the Years 1786 & 1788 w'ch is not his own & the same is ordered to be Certified to the Solicitor. Danil Graham is fined 10/ for Swearg. 2 Oaths before the Court & that the Sh'f Keep him in Custody till he pays the same with Costs. Stanup Richardson Came into Court and made Oath that he is Charged w'th the Tax of 100 Acres of Land for the Year w'ch is not his own & the same is ordered to be Certi-fied to the Solicitor.

PAGE TWO HUNDRED FIFTY-THREE

July Court 1788—Samuel Hairston came into Court & En-tered into Bond with Hugh Innis his Security for one hundred Pounds for the faithfull Administration of the Goods & Chattles of Gideon Smith Dec'd who Qualif'd accordg. to Law. Swinfield Hill Gent. entered into Bond wth. Security accord'g to Law, for the Faithfull Performance of the Duties of a Coroner for this County, who Qualif'd accordg. to Law. Absent: John Smith, Gent. Present: Robt. Hairston, John Dickerson, Swinfield Hill, Gent. Thomas Hale Joel Estes, John Early, are Recommended to his Excellency the Governor as Proper persons to Serve as Magis- trates from the County of Franklin. The Court is Adj'd till Court in Course.—ROBT. HAIRSTON.

PAGE TWO HUNDRED FIFTY-FOUR

August Court 1788—At a Court of Quarterly Sessions held for Franklin County on Monday the 4th. Day of August 1788. Present: Jonathan Richardson, John Smith, Moses Greer & George Turnbull, Gent. Trent vs Jones, Dism'd. Same vs Same, Same. Callaway & Co. vs Jones & Taylor, same. Boulton Adm'x vs Hubbards, Same. Peter Saunders from John Rentfro. Ack'd & Abigail the wife, being Privily Examined, Reling'd her Right of Dower & O. R. Same from Same, Same. Peter Saunders Gent, Present. A Deed David Stewart from James Stewart Prov'd 2 Wits. & O. C. Also Thomas Boulton from Robert Boulton for- merly Prov'd &c Mary the wife this Day Reling'd her Right & O. R. Hook vs Key George Asberry Spl. Bl. Deliv'd hereupon Whereupon he is Pray'd Commit'd & Ashford Napier further Spl. Bl. & Spl Impl. Non Asse & Issue therefore he is Discharged out of Custody. Bramblett vs Cowdin, Ashford Napier & James Burns Spl. Bail & Impl.

PAGE TWO HUNDRED FIFTY-FIVE

August 1788—James Callaway & Co. vs Stephen Wood, Judgt Conf'd According to Spl & Costs & Stay Exon. till Xmas next. Mathew Boulton vs Boultons Admx. Judgt Conf'd for Twenty Seven Pounds Eighteen Shilling & Ord. Callaway & Co. vs Robt. Boulton Judgt. Conf'd accdg to Spl. & Stay Exon till November. Thomas Arthur, Gent, Present. Federick Rives Fore- man. A Grand Jury, to Wit, James Pinkard, Elisha Estes, Jas. Bottom Estes, David Willis, John Wilks, John Martin, Samuel Bird, William Menefee, Sen, Mordecai Mosely, John Hunter, Josiah Turner, Burwell Rives, Phillip Sutherland, Thomas Hale, George Simmons, Israel Standifer, Richard Booth & Thos. Miller, who were Sworn as Grand Jury of Inquest for the Body of this County, Whereupon they Withdrew to Consult upon their presentments. Christopher Henderson Clark Produced a License from under the hands of Edmond Prathon, John Blair & Henry Tazwell to Practice as an Attorney in the Superior & Inferior Courts, Who quallified according to Law Robert Williams, Jr., the Same.

PAGE TWO HUNDRED FIFTY-SIX

August Court 1788—Mary Craighead Came into Court & made oath that Peter Craghead's Orphans is Charged w'th 70 Acres of Land & but 10/0 of the same belong to the said Orphans & Ordered to be Certified to the Solicitor. Stover vs V. Davis. Notice Ack'd by the Def. Attc & C. O. set aside. Braiden vs the same, Dism'd at Defs. Costs. John Hook vs J. Booth, Peter Booth Spl. Bl. & Spl. Impl. Perryman vs Cook, Cont'd at the Plf Costs. Cook vs Roger & Tuggle. Allen Ridley Young Spl. Bl. Set a Side & Gl Issue. Callaway & Co. vs William Martin Jr. Dism'd. James McVey Produced a Commissioner from his Excellency the Governor Appointing him Ensign of the Militia for this County Who Quallif'd &c. Redd vs McWilliams & Jamison Judgt. Conf'd as to Jamison According to Spl & Costs. Stay Exon. till Xmas & Dism'd as to McWilliams. Same vs Sams, same. Talbott vs Hugh * * * Same. Dillin Spl. Bl & Judgt Conf'd accorg to Spl. & Cost Stay Exon. 3 Months. Greer vs Cook & Prunty, John Rentfro Spl. Bl for Prunty, Notice given & the Plf. Rule to Give Security for Costs accordg to Law. McVey vs Braiden, Isaiah Willis Spl. B & Spl. Imp.
* * * Missing.

PAGE TWO HUNDRED FIFTY-SEVEN

August Court 1788—William Bennett came into Court & made oath that he is Charged w'th a Tract 40 Acres of Land w'ch is not his Property & it is ordered to be Certif'd to the Solicitor. Christopher Agt. Dillin Judgt for £4.7.6 & Costs Subject to the Credit of £3.8.9. Chitwood vs Deuvalt Judgt Conf'd Accordg to Spl. & Costs & Stay Exon. till the 20 of Decemb. next. Flowers vs Jones Award Returned for the Def. for £29.10 & O. R. The Grand Jury Returned into Court, & made Several Presentments, Whereupon Process is ordered to Issue. Samuel McCoy came into Court & with William McCoy & Rich'd Copeland, his Surities

& Ack'd themselves Severally indebted to the Overseers of the Poor in the Sum of Forty Pounds to be levied on their Respective Goods & Chattles, Lands & Tenements, on Condition the said Samuel fail to Pay to the said Overseer of the Poor the Sum of Three Pounds P. Year for 6 Years, in Quarterly Payments, for the Support of a Bastard Child begotten on the Body of Tabitha Jones. The fine imposed on Bolton Estis for not Attending as a Grand Juryman in May Last is Remited w'th Costs. Leftwich vs Houzer. Jas. Ballard Spl. & Spl. Impl.

PAGE TWO HUNDRED FIFTY-EIGHT

August Court 1788—Commonwealth vs William Nowlin Judgt According Same vs Stewart, same Obadiah H. Trent is al- low'd Two Days Attce as a Wits for Pucket ads Asberry & One Comg & Ret. 26 Miles. Samuel Patterson vs E. Hubbard is Referd to Benja Cook & Robert Prunty & in case they do not Agree they are to Chuse an Umpire & their award to be the judg- ment of the Court. Commonwealth vs Asberry & Obidiah H. Trent Spl. Bl. & Spl. Impl. The Court is Adjourned till tomor- row 8 oClock.—PETER SAUNDERS. At a Court of Quarterly Sessions Cont'd & held for Franklin County on Tuesday the 5th. Day of August 1788. Present: Peter Saunders, Thomas Arthur, John Smith & Moses Greer, Gent. Absent: Thomas Arthur. Anderson vs Clutcher, Answer filed, Replication & Ded's for Wits. Ferguson vs Mead & Callaway, on hearing the Bill & Answer read It is ordered & Decree'd that 200 Acres of Land in the Bill mentioned, lying on Little Creek, be visited in the Com- plaint & that he Recover his Costs, In that behalf Expended.

PAGE TWO HUNDRED FIFTY-NINE

August Court 1788—Hook vs Jones &c Deft, having stood out all Proposes of Contempt, it is ordered that the Prayer of the Bill be Taken as Confised, that 250 Acres of Land more or less lying on Stanton River in the County of Franklin be hereforth Visted in the Complaiment & that the Def's be Produced after 3 Months form any Benefit Reduction & that the Complatient recover the Costs. Callaway & Co. vs Foster Hatcher Judgt. Conf'd accorg to Spy & Costs. Stay Exon. til Xmas. Hook vs Ray Continued for Depo. Farley vs Martin, Judgment on Repy Bond accorg to Sp. & Costs. On the Motion of John Keyley by his Attorney for an Inj'n to stay the Proceedings of a Judgt. at Com. Law by John Hook the same is Rejected With Costs. Thorp vs Jo. Rentfro & Thos. Prunty Judgment on Repy Accordg. to Spl & Costs. John Hook vs Poteet (On Atta) Judgt. for £4.16. & Order Condennation in the hands of John Divers & Costs Armstrong vs Spangler Ex'x Rule to give Security for Costs at next Turm or to be Dism'd. Callaway & Early vs. Hensley Security for Jas. Wm. Condy Judgt. on Repy Bond accordg to Spy & Costs. Geo. Ferguson vs Alex. Watson, Atta. Judgt. for £3.18.9. w'th Costs & on Condinination. Present: Robert Hairston Gent. Absent: P. Saunders.

PAGE TWO HUNDRED SIXTY

August Court 1788—Saunders vs Radford, David Barton Spl. Bl. & Delivered him up whereupon he is Prayed Committed. David Barton & Moses Rentfro further Sp. Bl. & Released. Commonwealth vs Toney, a Jury Sworn, to Wit, John Keay, John Kemp, Thomas Demoss, William Poteet, James Burns Eusebus Hubbard, Richard Booth, Robert Napier, Thomas Jones, Peter Finny, Jonathan Davis & Thomas Lewis. Verdt. Return'd for the Ptf. Whereupon the Def. Pray'd a new Tryal & the same is Granted him by his Paying the Costs of the Day. William Akers is allowed 2 Days Attce as a Witness for the Com. Wealth agt. Toney. Joshua Wilson is Allow'd. 2 Days for same. Rosannah Wilson is Allow'd 2 Days for the Same. Eliza. Kelley is allow'd 1 Day for the same. Jas Ritter is Allow'd 1 Day for the same. John Van Maple is Allow'd 1 Day for the Same. Thomas Miller is allow'd 2 Days for the same. Isabella McClure is allow'd 1 Day for the same. Phebey McClure is Allow'd 1 Days for the same. Thomas Prunty is allow'd 2 Days for the same. Mary Henderson is allow'd 2 Days for the same. Jacob Webster is allow'd 2 Days for the same. Martin Delancy is allow'd 1 Day for Toney ads ComW. Mary McVey is allow'd 2 Days for the same. Amos Ellison is allow'd 2 Attce, as a Wits. for Hook vs Key.

PAGE TWO HUNDRED SIXTY-ONE

August Court 1788—Saunders vs Radford Judgt Conf'd Accorg to Spl & Costs Stay Exon. till Xmas. ConWealth vs Smith Webb, Ordered to be reinStated & set for Tryal. Hale vs Craghead a Jury Sworn, to Wit, Bird Smith, William Mavity, John

Ferguson, Robert Prunty, Wm. Kelly, Ashford Napier, Joel Chitwood, Samuel Henderson, John Choice, Smith Webb, John Kerby & Wm. Walton. Verd. Returned Jury not agreed in Verdt. Callaway & Co. vs Hubbard & Jas. Prunty. Spl. Bl. Judgt Conf'd accordg. to Spl. & Costs Stay Exon. Till the 24th of Decemb. Next. Mary Miller is Allow'd 2 Days Attce as a Wits for Toney ads Commonwealth. Early vs Gillaspy Dism'd at the Defs Costs. Mathew Miller is allow'd 11 Days Attce as a Wits for Johnson vs Doggett, to the exclusion of all their Attendance. Mary Hartwell, the same. Isaac Bates is allow'd 1 Days Attce as a Wits for ComWealth vs Toney. Cook vs Green, Jas. Edmondson & Nathan Sellers Spl. Bl. & Delivered him therefore he is Prayed Committed.

PAGE TWO HUNDRED SIXTY-TWO

August Court 1788—Elijah Hatcher is allow'd 1 Day Attce. as a Wits for John Craighead ads Hale. Richard Robertson is allow'd 1 Days Attce as a Wits for John Hale vs Craghead. Simmons vs Hudggins, Refered to Jonathan Richardson & Moses Greer & their award to be the Judgment of the Court, & in case can not agree, they are to Chuse an Umpire. John Kemp is Allow'd 1 Days attce as a Wits for Craghead ads Hale. James Hall the same. David Preston, William Mavity, Wm. Rentfro & Owen Ruble, or any three of them, are appointed to Appraise the Estate of Gideon Smith Dec'd & make Return thereof to the Next Court. The Court is Adj'd till toMorrow 8 oClock.—PETER SAUNDERS. At a Court of Quarterly Sessions Continued & held for Franklin County on Wednesday the 6th. Day of August 1788. Present: Peter Saunders, Thomas Arthur, Jonathan Richardson & John Rentfro. William Smith is allowed 2 Days Attce as a Witness for John Hook vs Poteet. Same 1 Day for Hook vs Key.

PAGE TWO HUNDRED SIXTY-THREE

August Court 1788—William Smith is allow'd 2 Days Attce as a Witness for Obediah Henry Trent vs Thos. Jones. P. Guthrey vs. J. Hook Jubal Early Spl. Bl. & Sp. Jn. Same vs Same, Same, Same. It is the Opinion of the Court. that the Tonys ads ConWealth do Pay the Costs of Yesterday before they shall have the Benefit of a New Tryal & In Case that the said Costs is not Paid during the Turm that then the new Tryal shall be rejected. Hale vs Craghead, the Jury of Yesterday being Call'd & not ap pearing they are Discharged. Present: Robert Hairston. Absent: John Rentfro. McGuffey vs Underwood, Atta. Dis'd. McVey vs William Miller Atta. a Judgt for £26.7 Int. for 21 Apl 88 & Wm. Menefee a Garnishee being sworn Sayeth that he owes the Def. a Ton of Iron Payable in October 1788, & he acknowlegds that there will be a Sufficiency in his hands to Satisfy the Plfs. Demand Payable October cum 12 months & O. C. James McVey vs Miller. Ordered that an Atta Issue vs Peter Holland named as Exrs in the last Will & Testament of Elisha Lyon Dec'd for Contempt, for not appear'g here being Summon'd to quallify as Ext. of S'd Will.

PAGE TWO HUNDRED SIXTY-FOUR

August Court 1788—Cook vs Greer (Attce) Dism'd at the Plf Costs. Holliday vs Duvall Cont'd. Livesey vs Davis Same. John Rentfro vs Jesse Rentfro Dism'd. Holliday vs Calland Jud on the Motion of the Def to Dissolve the Injo. of a Judgment wch obtained a Garnishment of the Attce Effects, Calland vs Kimmins. Callaway & Early vs D. Richardson, Dismiss'd. Jubal Early vs Same, the Same. Dickenson vs Perryman Cont'd. Stegall vs Jinkins the Ptf. failg. to appear, Dismissed. Mullinden vs Bebee Dism'd Agreed. Doggett vs Gipson Continued. Chavers Finney the Plt Ruled given Security for Costs in 60 Days or be Dism'd. Ferguson vs McGrady Atta. Judgment for £30.9.7 w'th Int. from the 28th. Day of Apl. 1788 & O. C. in the hands of the Garnshee formerly Sworn. Jubal Early is allow'd 2 Days Attce as a Wits for Ferguson vs McGrady. Johnson vs Stewart Cont'd.

PAGE TWO HUNDRED SIXTY-FIVE

August Court 1788—Stover vs Davis a Jury Sworn, to Wit, James McVey, George Asberry, Ed'd Choat, Robert Mason, John Kyle, David Barton, Jubal Early, Thomas Jones, Robert Johns, Samuel Kerby, John Bates & Lewis Davis. Verd. Returned for Plf. & O. R. On the Motion of Jonathan Davis it is ordered that Meshack Hodges & William Dillingham be fined According to Law for not Attndg as Witness for S'd Davis Ads Stoner. Choice vs Finney Robert Napier Surity for Costs Stover vs Davis Judgt. on Repy Bond accorg. to Spl. & Costs. Holden McGee is allow'd 2 Days Attce & 1. Cuming & returng 20 Miles as a Witness for Stover vs Davis. Jeremiah Stover is allow'd 2 Days as a Wits for the same. Samuel Calland is allow'd 3 Days attce & 1 coming & Reurning 21 Miles as a Witness for Livesey ads Barton. Pate Assee vs Wright, a Jury sworn, to Wit, Thomas Hale, David Barton, James McVey, Robert Mason, Sam'l Kerby, Wm. Maviety, Wm. Mullins, Edw'd Choat, John Bates, Lewis Davis, John Kyle & George Asberry. Verdt Return'd for Plf. & O. R. Joshua Starkey is allow'd 2 Days Attce as a Witness for May Lyon ads Eda Lyon. Ste. Pate is allow'd 7. Days attce as a Witness for Wright ads Pate.

PAGE TWO HUNDRED SIXTY-SIX

August Court 1788—Hollerday vs Calland, Injo. On Motion to Desolve the Inj. of a Judgt. & on hearing the Bill & answer read, the Court are of the opinion the same should be Disolved. Mary Troup Widow of Jacob Troup Dec'd who was recom- mended to the Governor as a Pensioner, it is ordered that it be Further Certif'd to the Executive that the said Jacob Troup be- longed to General Lason's Brigade of Militia in Colo. Skipwith Regiment. Com. Wealth vs Jubal Early the fine w'ch was Leveyed for £10. for Contempt to the Court is Remitted. Cox Greer vs Webb (on Appeal Bond) a Jury sworn, to wit, Samuel Kerby, David Barton, John Ferguson, Joel Chitwood, William Mullins, Willm Maviety, John Kyle, John Bates, John Robertson, Lewis Davis, William Walton, & Robert Mason. Verdt. Returned for the Plf. & O. R. Errors offered in arrest of Judgt. & it is the Opinion of the Court they should be Rejected with Costs. Where- upon he Prayeth in Appeal to 8th Day of Next General Court, by his Giving bond & Security in the Clks Office. Rich'd Rich- ards Assee vs Wm. Kelly & Thos. Miller, Thos. Miller Jr. Spl. Bl. & Spl Jent. The Court is Adj'd till toMorrow 'oClock.— T. ARTHUR.

PAGE TWO HUNDRED SIXTY-SEVEN

August Court 1788—At a Court of Quarterly Sessions Cont'd & held for Franklin County on Thursday the 7th. Day of Au- gust 1788. Present: Thos. Arthur, Jonathan Richardson, John Smith, Swinfield Hill & Jno. Rentfro, Gent. Early vs Martin, Cont'd. Rentfro Assee vs Callaway, Cont. Bell vs Rentfro, Cont. Early vs Martin Cont'd. Rentfro Assee vs Callaway, Cont. Bell vs Rentfro, Cont. Hollerday vs Bartee, Atta. a Jury Sworn, to

Wit, Bird Smith, John Ferguson, John Fewson, William Menifee, William Maviety, Philemon Greer, Guy Smith, John Bates, Samuel Kerby, John Hall, David Barton & George Asberry. Verd. Retur'd for the Def. & O. R. Greer vs Cook & John Cox, Security for Costs. Present Peter Saunders. Underwood vs Slone, George Hancock, Gent. Su'y for Costs, & a Jury Sworn, to Wit, John Hale, John Fuson, Bird Smith, John Ferguson, William Menefee, William Mavity, Philmon Greer, Guy Smith, John Bates, Sam'l Cockran, David Barton & Geo. Asbury. Vert. Return'd for the Plf. & O. R. & the Def. by his Atto. Offered the Papers Slone vs Underwood in a former Suit of Chancery had offered for Evidence & the same is Rejected, with Costs. Trent vs Bandy, Cont. Callaway & Early, vs Clower, Pleas waved & Judgt. accordg. to Spl. & Costs, Allow'd all Just Credits.

PAGE TWO HUNDRED SIXTY-EIGHT

August Court 1788—Callaway & Co vs Cockram, Cont'd. Evans vs Harmon Cook a Jury Sworn, to Wit, John Hall, John Fuson, Bird Smith, John Bates, Samuel Cockran, David Barton, & George Asbury. Verd. Retur'd for Plf. & O. R. Brown & Co. vs Choat Plea Wavd & Judgt award to Spl & Costs & to be Credit for £20.5 Accg 1788. Bates vs Callaway Rule to Give Security for Costs in 60 Days or to be Dismiss'd Richardson vs Cook Dismiss'd. Murray Assee vs Brown Pleas Waved as to Brown & Judt agt him by non Sum, information, & Dismiss as to Callaway. Cowan vs J. Rentfro. Cont. Webb vs Austin Cont. forward. Webb vs Dillon a Jury Sworn, to wit, John Fuguson, John Fuson, Samuel Cockrum, Samuel Hairston, Joel Chitwood, David Jones, Isaac Rentfro, Samuel Patterson, Phillman Greer, Wm. Maviety, Lewis Davis & David Barton. Verdict return'd for the Ptf for £100. w'ch is to be Discharg'd by a Compliance with the Contract. Cook vs Whitworth Judgt. for Costs. Grymes vs Asberry Dismiss Agreed. Grayham Jt. vs Graves. a Jury Sworn, to wit, Samuel Hairston, John Hale, John Bates, Ashford Napier, Joel Chitwood, Robt. Napier, David Jones, Lewis Davis, John Fuson, Robert Perryman, David Barton & William Mullins. Verdt return'd for the Ptf, & O. R.

PAGE TWO HUNDRED SIXTY-NINE

August Court 1788—Foster vs Dillion leave is Granted the Deft to Take the Depo. of Ste. Heard, Thomas Foster & Farris Foster & Wm. Perdue, giving Legal notice. Asberry vs Stokes. Award returned & O. R. Callaway & Early vs Stokes Cont. Callaway & Trents vs William Wright Cont. for Ptf. Barton vs Livesey Cont. Asberry vs Devine. Cont. at the Def's Costs. Lewis Davis is allow'd 4 Days Attce as a Wits for Grayham vs Graves. Edmond Wilson is allow'd 7 Days for the same. William Mullins is allow'd 5 Days for the same. Samson & George Mathew vs Livesey, Cou'd. Craig, Assee vs Bandy's A Jury sworn, to Wit, Samuel Hairston, George Radford, Isaac Rentfro, John Apperson, James Brummitt, Edward Wilson, Joseph Hale, Samuel Kerby, Samuel Patterson, Elisha Keen & Stephen Stone. Verdt. return'd for the Ptf & O. R. McKensey Ex'rs &c vs Patterson. Judgt Conf'd for £50 With Int. from the 25th. Day of Dec. 1774 & Costs, all just Credits to be Allow'd. Edmondson vs Napier, Abates by the Ptfs death. Richardson vs Boyd & Dillin a Jury sworn, to Wit, George Radford, Isaac Rentfro, John Epperson, James Brammitt, Edward Wilson, Joseph Hale, Robert Prunty, Samuel Hairston, Samuel Kerby, Samuel Patterson, Elisha Keen & Stephen Slone. Verdt returned for the Plt. The Debt Declaration within men—

PAGE TWO HUNDRED SEVENTY

August Court 1788—Warren & ux. vs Harris a Jury Sworn, to Wit, George Radford, Isaac Rentfro, John Epperson, James Brimmett, William Maviety, Joseph Hall, Robert Prunty, Samuel Hairston, Joel Chitwood, Elisha Keen, David Jones & Stephen Slone we the Jury find for the Plf. 40/6 Damages. & O. R. George Thomas came into Court & Qualif'd as a Lieut in the Militia of this County. Keen vs Grimmett. W. E. set aside & General Issue. Austin vs Webb. Cont'd for Award. Heard &c vs Webb. A Jury sworn, to Wit, Amos Richardson, Lewis Davis, Robert Perryman, Samuel Kerby, George Asberry, Robert Mason, John Choice, John Bates, Robert Foster, John Fuson, John Hook, & William Toney. Jury return'd & the Plf called & not Appearing is non Suited. Rhody Colley is allow'd 4 Days Attce & One Coming & returning 40 Miles as a Wits. for Warran & ux vs Harris. Michel vs Hollerday Postponed. Callaway & Early vs M.

Rentfro. Jury sworn, to wit, Joseph Hale, William Maviety, George Radford, Joel Chitwood, Amos Richardson, Davis Jones, Robert Prunty, Isaac Rentfro, Ste. Stone, Samuel Hairston, John Epperson, & James Brummitt, Verdt. Returned that they find no Part of the within Bond Paid & O. R. A Bill of Sale from Thomas Livesey Sr. to William Menifee Sr. Prov'd & O. R.

PAGE TWO HUNDRED SEVENTY-ONE

August Court 1788—Joseph Webb is allow'd 8 Days Attce as a Wits for Webb vs Dillon. Richards Assee vs English &c Jas. Ritter Spl. Bl. & Sp. J. William Kelley ads Millers. Choice vs Finney, A Jury sworn, to Wit, Robert Perryman, Edward Choat, Samuel Kerby, George Asberry, Robert Mason, Joel Chitwood, Bird Smith, William Mavity, John Fuson, Elisha Keen, Lewis Davis & Joseph Hall, the Jury not Agreed on Verd. It is ordered that Amos Richardson & Robert Prunty be Appointed as Commissioner of the Exon'x Law & Valuers of Property for this County in Place of John Martin & John Woods, Who Quallified according to Law. John Ferguson Came into Court & made oath to his Collection sence his last Return & the Same is ordered to be Certified &c. Joel Estes is allow'd 5 Days Attce as a Wit. for Choice vs Finny. Amos Richardson is Allow'd 5 Days for the same. On the Motion Lewis Davis by his Atto to Injoin the Judgt obtained agt. him by Harmon Cook, the same is Rejected with Costs. Ashford Napier is allow'd 12 Days Attce as a Wits. for Williams vs Chitwood. Zachariah Bryant is allow'd 7 Days Attce One coming & returning 75 Miles for Wits. Finny ads Choice.

PAGE TWO HUNDRED SEVENTY-TWO

August Court 1788—Choice vs Finney Referd to John Dickerson & George Turnbull & in Case they Disagree to chuse An Umpire & their award to be the Judgment of the Court. John Choice is allow'd 6 Days Attce. as a Wits for Choice vs Finney. Cyrus Choice is allow'd 1 Days Attce for the same. Ann Choice 5 Days for the same. James Brummitt is Allow'd 5 Days for Finney ads Choice. Joseph Webb is allow'd 8 Days Attce as a Wits for Webb ads Heard &c. Samuel Patterson is allow'd 6 Days Attce as a Wits for Choice vs Finney. The Court is adjourned till Tomorrow 8 o'clock.—PETER SAUNDERS. At a Court of

Quarterly Sessions Cont'd & held for Franklin County on Friday the 8th Day of Augt. 1788. Present: Peter Saunders, Thomas Arthur, John Dickerson & John Rentfro, Gent. Choice vs Finney, award returned for Plf. £4. &c. Party to Pay his own Costs & O. R.

PAGE TWO HUNDRED SEVENTY-THREE

August Court 1788—Jackson vs Frith, a Jury sworn, to Wit, Guy Smith, Bird Smith, Samuel Kerby, Amoss Richardson, George Asberry, John Hook, Daniel Brown, Thomas Watts, Isaac Rent-fro, John Kelly, Joseph Webb, & William Maviety. We the Jury find no Part of the within bond Paid. Willis & Campbell vs Thomas Dugliss, a Jury Sworn, to Wit, Guy Smith, Samuel Derby, Amos Richardson, George Asberry, John Hook, Dan'l Brown, Thomas Watts, Isaac Rentfro, John Kelly, Joseph Webb, & William Maviety. We the Jury find no Part of the within bonds Paid. William Woods vs Jamison Judgt. for £4. & Costs. Robert Perryman is allow'd 4 Days Attce, as a Wits for Barton vs Livesey. Brown & Co. vs Dillon, a Jury sworn, to Wit, Guy Smith, Bird Smith, Samuel Kerby, Amoss Richardson, George Asberry, John Hook, Samuel Hairston, Thomas Watts, Isaac Rentfro, John Kelly, Joseph Webb, & William Maviety. Verd Ret'd that We the Jury find no Part of the Within Bond Paid. Stewart vs Dillon &c a Jury sworn, to Wit, Guy Smith, Bird Smith, Samuel Kerby, Amos Richardson, George Asberry, John Asberry, John Hook, Samuel Hairston, Thomas Watts, Isaac Rentfro, John Kelly, Joseph Webb & William Maviety. We of the Jury find for the Plf. £20. Damages to be Discharged by the Payment of an Execution Stewart vs Dillon, likewise the Cost of an Injo. Dillon vs Stewart & the Cost of this Suit & O. R.

PAGE TWO HUNDRED SEVENTY-FOUR

August Court 1788—Will Brown vs Radford &c a Jury sworn, to Wit, Guy Smith, Bird Smith, Samuel Kerby, Amos Richardson, Arthur Grayham, John Hook, Thomas Watts, Isaac Rentfro, John Kelly, Joseph Webb, William Maviety & Sam'l Hairston. The Ptf being called & not Answering is non Suited & Verd. Return'd for the Def. George Asberry is allow'd 3 Days Attce as a Wits for Radford ads Brown. John Epperson 3 Days for the same. Samuel Hatcher 3 Days for the same. Taylor vs

Woodcock, A Jury sworn, to Wit, Guy Smith, Bird Smith, Samuel Kerby, Amos Richardson, Arthur Grayham, John Law, Thomas Watts, Isaac Rentfro, John Kelly, Joseph Webb, William Maviety, Samuel Hairston & Daniel Brown. We the Jury find no Part of the Within Bond paid & O. R. James Callaway vs John Kelly leave is Granted the Ptf. to Take the Depo. of Flail Nicholes Gives the Def. 10 Days Notice. Webb vs England Cont. Greer vs Cook & Prunty, Dismis'd as to Prunty. Miller vs Kelly, Dismissed for want of Surity for Costs. Delany vs Bates Cont'd. Welch vs Kelly's Admirs Cont'd.

PAGE TWO HUNDRED SEVENTY-FIVE

August Court 1788—Gordin vs Heard Cont'd. Livesey vs Anderson a Jury Sworn, to Wit, Guy Smith, Bird Smith, Samuel Kerby, Amos Richardson, Arthur Grayham, Thomas Lewis, Robert Napier, Thomas Watts, Joseph Hale, William Mavity, John Law. & John Hale. We the Jury find for the Def. Chitwood vs Coleman, Cont'd. Callaway vs Guthery Exors, Cont'd. Commonwealth vs Mary Lyon, C. O. Lewis vs Willis leave is Granted the Plf to Mend the Bill on Paying the Costs thereof. Joseph Webb is allow'd 4 Days Attce as a Witness for Anderson ads Livesy. Joel Chitwood is allow'd 2 Days for the same. John Hale, 12 Days for the same. Clay vs Willson, Cont. Rentfro D. vs Dogget, same. Samuel Cockrum is allow'd 9 Days Attce as a Wits for Anderson ads Livesey. Martin vs Spearpoint, Cont'd. Thomas Arthur is allow's 23 Days Attce. as a Wits. for Anderson ads Livesey. Jinkins vs Winn & Ramsey Cont'd. Prunty vs. Jones'd Admrs. a Jury Sworn, to wit, Joel Chitwood, Robert Napier, William Walton, Thomas Lewis, Samuel Cockrum, John Law, Guy Smith, William Brown, William Mosely, Edw's Choat, Bird Smith, & Richard Brown. Verd. Returned for the Def. * * * and is Granted the * * * the Costs * * *

PAGE TWO HUNDRED SEVENTY-SIX

August Court 1788—Moses Greer Gent is allowed 7 Days Attce as a Wits for Hudgins ads Simmon. On the Motion of George Asberry by his Atto. to Stay the Proceeding of Judgment, obtained agt. him by William Woods the same is Granted,

---

* * * Missing.

Whereupon Thomas Prunty & Thomas Arthur his Security's entered into Bond & Ack'd the same. Sterling vs Kinzey Judgt, for Note & Jn. & Costs. On the Motion of Thomas Livesey by his Atto. to Stay the Proceedings of a Judgment Obtained agt. him by James Callaway & Early, the same is Rejected with Costs. Joseph Ritter is allow's 1 Days Attce as a Wits for Kelly ads Miller. Zachariah Davis is allow'd 9 Days attce & 3 Coming & Returng. 35 Miles as a Wits for Prunty vs Jones's Admr's. Arthur Grayham is allow'd 2 Days Attce. as a Wits for Prunty vs Jones's Admrs. On the Motion John Kelly his Atto. to Stay the Proceeding of a Judgment Obtained against him by Nathan Demsey, the same is Granted, Whereupon Lewis Davis, John Fuson, & Joseph Ritter entered into Bond & Acknowledged the same. Thomas Watts is allow'd 3 Days Attce as a Wits for Trent vs Jones. Hugh Innis vs Isaac Rentfro, J. Rentfro & Edw'd Choat, Isaac Rentfro Accordg. to Delivery Bond & Costs.

PAGE TWO HUNDRED SEVENTY-SEVEN

August Court 1788—Susannah Griffith is allow'd 5 Days Attce as a Wits for Jones's Admrs ads Prunty. William Griffith 5 Days for the same. Joseph Hale is allow'd 4 Days Attce. as a Wits for Prunty vs Jones's Admr's. The Court is Adjourned till Court in Course.—PETER SAUNDERS. At a Court held for Franklin County on Monday the 1st Day of Sept. 1788. Present: Jonathan Richardson, Swinfield Hill, Moses Greer & John Smith, Gent. Patterson vs Hubbard, James Prunty Sp. B. Came in Court & Deliv'd the Def Where upon he is Prayed Committed. An Inventory of the Estate of Gidion Smith Dec'd Ret'd & O. R. Same of Benja Greer. Ret. & O. R. A Deed from David Barton to George Stanton Ack'd & O. R. Also a Deed from John Keele to William Standley Ack'd the wife being Priv'y Examined Rel'd & O. R. by 1 Wits. Also James Dillion to William Boyd Pro'd & O. C. * * * vs Hubbard Aw'd Rent. & O. R.

PAGE TWO HUNDRED SEVENTY-EIGHT

September Court—On the Motion of Penelope Guthery by James Penn her Attorney to stay the Proceeding of a Judgment obtained agt. her By John Hook, the same is Granted, Where-

* * * Missing.

upon she Came into Court with John Hook & Rich'd Booth her Sec'y & Ent'd into Bond accordg to Law & Ack'd the same. The last Will & Testament of Richard Edmundson was Exhibited into Court & Prove by 2 Wits. Daniel Dillmon came into Court & made oath that he is Charged with 280 Acres of Land, that he Pay Tax on land wch is not his own Property & the same is Ordered to be Certif'd to the Solicitor. Peter Holland one of the Exectors named in the last Will & Testament of Elisha Lyon Dec'd came into Court & Refusd to take upon himself the Burden of the Ex'ship. A Deed Michael Gilbert from Jesse Law Ack'd & Mary the wife being Privily Examined as the Law Directs Relin'd her Right of Dower & the same is Or'd to be Re'd. Also William Mullins from John Keele, Ack'd & Ann the Wife being Privily Examined Rel'd & O. R. William Standley is allow'd 7. Days Attce as a Wits for Jones Agt. Spangler. On the Motion of James Slone by Robert Williams Jr. to stay the Proceeding of a Judgment Obtained against him by Joseph Underwood & It is the Opinion of the Court, that the Costs of a Suit in Char'g Presented in this Court, the said Slone agt. Underwood on wch he ob'd a Decree for 225 Acres of Land & the Jn. Decree on the Bond from Slone to Underwood be Enjoind & that the Judg. in Com. Law, be Confirmed whereupon he ent'd in to Bond wth Su'y & Ack'd the same Acc'd to Law.

PAGE TWO HUNDRED SEVENTY-NINE

September Court 1788—On the Motion of Richard Randy by James Penn his Attorney to Stay the Proceed'gs of a Judgt Obtained against him by Toliver Craig Assee w'ch is Granted him, on his Ent'g Into Bond w'th Security at Next Court. Thomas Prunty came into Court & Quallified to his Collection for the Tax of 1787, Since his last Return, the same is ordered to be Certified. On the Motion of William Graves Sr. by James Penn his Attorney, for a New Tryal ads Arthur Grayham for Slander w'ch is Rejected Orderd by the Court that the Exon should be stayed till Novemb. On the Motion of Rich'd Booth, by Robert Williams Jr. his Atta. to Stay the Proceedg of a Judgment obtained against him by John Hook, the same is Rejected w'th Costs. Robert Prunty is allow'd 3 Days Attce as a Wits for Patterson agt. Hubbard. John Cooper is app'd Overseer of the Road from Praters Run to the Lower end of Jno. Earlys Lane, & the list fil'd to be his Gang. William Charter is app'd overseer of the Road from the Lower end of Earlys Lane to Slones Mill & the list fil'd to be his Gang.

PAGE TWO HUNDRED EIGHTY

September Court 1788—George Kelly is app'd overseer of the Road from Slone's Mill to Blackwater Road & the list filed to be his Gang. A View of a Road from the Road above Wm. Marcum Shop to the Road below Rich'd Booths & the list filed to be his Gang. On the Mot. of John Hook, it is ordered that Danl Foster be Summond to appear at next Court to answer as a Garnishee Ross & Hook vs Mead. The Court is adj'd till Court in Course.—THOS. ARTHUR. At a Court held for Franklin County on Monday the 6th. Day of October 1788. Present: Peter Saunders, Thomas Arthur, Jonathan Richardson, Moses Greer, Gent. Leave is Granted Thomas Livesey a Dedim's to Take the Depo. of James Baker ads Mathews, Giving Legal notice. Same & ads Barton the same. Simmons vs Hudgins award Ret. & Ordered to be Recorded. A Deed from Thomas Watts to John Hook Ack'd & O. R. Also a Deed from John Furrow to Sarah Furrow Prov'd & O. R. A Ded's for the Relingt of Dower of Dan'l Richardsons wife to Champion Napier Ret. & O. R.

PAGE TWO HUNDRED EIGHTY-ONE

Ordered that the Overseers of the Poor do Bind William Fram a Bastard Child of Happy Frame to Lewis Bryant. Ordered that the Clerk Certify to the Governor & Council that James Powell Edmundson an Inhabitant of the County of Franklin is the Person who is intitled to the position allow'd him on the Pention list of Continental Sold'rs. Alex'r Ferguson is app'd Survyor of the Road from the Ford of Gills Creek to Thomas Watts in the Room of Thomas Charter & the list filed to be his Gang. Bandy vs Craig On injo. the Ptf. failg. to Give bond & Security Agreeable to a former order of this Court, the same is Desolved & the Ptf. at Law to have the Benefit of his Judgt. A Deed Joel Chitwood from John Robertson Prov'd by 1 Wits. & O. R. Copland vs Boulton Judgt. accordg. to Spl & Costs. A Deed James McKinsey from Joseph Hambrick Prov'd by 1 Wits. & O. R. Grayham v. Graves ordered that the Plf. have the Benefit of his Judgt. & the former order of the Court to be Resinded. The Last Will

& Testament of John Lumsden Dec'd was Exhibited in Court by Willmouth Lumsden ex'd & Jeremiah Lumsden & Jonathan Price Ex'rs & Proved the same & O. R.

PAGE TWO HUNDRED EIGHTY-TWO

From the best Informa. he has, Percen Hale came into Court & Made oath that he was under the Years of Twenty one when listed by James Cannon for the Year 1780; Therefore the Specee & Certificate &c is Remitted to the s'd James Cannon wch is Ordered to be Certifyed. Mary Ballard came into Court & made oath, that she is Taxed for the year 1787 with 30 Acres of Land wch is not her Property & the same is ordered to be Certified to the Solicitor. Leave is granted Joel Chitwood a Dedim's to take the Depo. of William Turnbull Jr. William Nolin, William Martin, William McKennon & Ste. Parkey, he giv'g legal notice. vs Brown & Callaway. A Deed from Daniel Richardson to Amos Richardson Prov'd by 1 Wits & O. R. On the Motion of Samuel Patterson by his Atto, Rich'd Nath'l Veneble for to stay the Proceedg. of a Judgt Obtaind against him by William &c the same is rejected with Costs. The Clerk Produced a list of his fees for the Year 1787 as also the list of his Taxes & ordered to be Certifyed. A Deed from James Stewart to Samuel Patterson Prov'd & O. R. Danl. Dillmon came into Court & made oath that he is charged with Tax's for 280 Acres of land for five Years wch is not his Property & the same is ordered to be Certified to the Solicitor. Rich'd Ballard came into Court & made oath that he is Charged with the Tax of one hundred & forty Seven Acres of Land w'ch is not his Property & the same is ordered to be Certifyed to the Solicitor. A Power of Atto. from Edw'd Lyon to John Chitwood Prov'd & O. R.

PAGE TWO HUNDRED EIGHTY-THREE

A Deed from Robert Mason to Nath. Mason Ack'd & O. R. On the Motion of John Chitwood to stay the Prcedg. of a Judgt. Obtained agt. him by Conrad Betts the same is Granted, Whereupon James Slone his Security entered into Bond & Ack'd the same. A Deed from William Martin & Wife to John Hook further Proved by 1 Wits & O. R. Also from Robert Grimmit to Nath'l Mason Prov'd by 1 Wits. & O. C. A Deed from Thomas Jones to Alex' Sutherland Ack & O. R. Also Dillion to Boyd further Prov'd by 1. Wits & O. C. William Swanson came into Court & Qualified to his Collection for the Year 1787 & same is ordered to Certifyd. John Ferguson, the same. Thomas Prunty, the same. Williams vs Mead ordered that John & Robert Anderson be Sum as Garshee to the next Court. Ross & Hook vs Mead, it is ordered that Danl. Foster be Atta. for Contempt, for not Attendg. as a Garnishee said Ross & Hook vs Mead. Yuell vs I. Rentfro (Atta) John Rentfro a Garnishee being sworn sayith, he owes the Def. nothing & Cont. for G'shee & Subject to Jno. Rentfroes Jud. for £43.19.5.

PAGE TWO HUNDRED EIGHTY-FOUR

John Rentfro vs I. Rentfro Judgt. for £43.19.5. Atta James Rentfro a Garnishee being sworn sayith he owes the Def. 80 Bushels of Salt to be Delivered at French Beard after Deductg. his Acct. not Excudg. £5 & O. C. & Costs. William Ryan D. S. came into Court Quallified to his list of Collection Sence his last Ret. for the Year 1787 & the same is ordered to be Certifyed. Hugh Woods the same & also his list of Insolvents. It is ordered that the Clk furnish the Court with a State of all Exeon of the C.Wealth & the Shf. Ret. thereon. Thomas Arthur, Swinfield Hill & Moses Greer are app'd to let the Repairg of the Gaol of this County the lowest Bidder. It is ordered that Shf. Give notice that a Court of Claims is to be held for this County the 21st of next month. The Court is Adj'd till Court in Course.— PETER SAUNDERS.

PAGE TWO HUNDRED EIGHTY-FIVE

November Court 1788—At a Court of Quarterly Session held for Franklin County on Monday the 3rd Day of Nov. '88. Present: Thomas Arthur, Jonathan Richardson, John Rentfro & John Dickerson, Gent. Hook vs Baily James Callaway Spl. Bl Pay & Issue. A Bill of Sale William Menifee Jr. to William Menifee Sr. Ack. & O. R. A Deed William Menefee to William Crump Ack'd & O. R. A Deed of Gift from Mary Spangler to John Nofsinger Ack'd & O. R. A Deed William Menefee Jr. to Callaway & Early Ack'd & O. R. Eliza. Greer being Craved the Peace Agt. Noel Battles, the said Noel Battles came into Court w'th Charles Sebrett his Securitys and Ack'd themselves Severally Indebted to the Com. Wealth that is to say the s'd

Battles in the sum of £10 & his Securitys in the sum of £5 to be Levied on their Respective Goods & Chattles, Land & Tenenants on the Condition the said Battles does not act with good Behavior for one year & a Day Especially to the said Eliza. Greer. John Litteral came into Court & w'th Sam. Letteral his Securities & Ack'd themselves Severally Indebted to the Overseers of the Poor in the sum of Fifty Pounds to be levied on their Respective Goods & Chattles, Land & Tenements on Condition the s'd Litteral shall fail to Pay to the S'd Overseers of the Poor the sum of Six Pounds Per Year for six years for the Support of a Bastard Child begotton on the Body of Sarah Elliott.

PAGE TWO HUNDRED EIGHTY-SIX

Owen Ruble Foreman, John Wilks, Robert Sherwood, Benja. Chandler, Elisha Easter Jr. Samuel Patterson, Anthony Pates, George Simmons, Jacob Prilliman, Nathan Sellers, Peter Holland, John Kemp, David Clackson, John Ferguson, Rich'd Sharp Barnaba Arthur, William Maviety & William Thompson who were Sworn as a Grand Jury of Inquest for the Body of this County, Whereupon they withdrew to Consult upon their presentments. John Johnson came into Court & made oath that he is Charged with the Tax on Six hundred & fifty eight Acres of Land w'ch is not his Property & the same is ordered to be Certif'd to the Solicitor. Robert Hairston Gent Present. Black vs Smith Security for Swanson Judgt. on Repl. Bond Notice Confest w'th Costs. Hugh Innes Gent is appointed Gardian for Thomas & Jane Pinckard Orphans of John Pinkard Deceased, whereupon he Came into Court & entered into Bond with his Security & Ack'd the same accordg. to Law. Meade Assee vs Clybourn . . . Amos Ellison Spl. Bl. & Spl. Imp. Jeremiah Lumsden one of the Executors of John Lumsden Deceased came into Court & with Swinfield Hill & James Burns his Securities entered into Bond & Ack'd the same accordg. to Law. James Burns, William Poteet, John Arthur & Martin Binnion, or any three of them, are App'd to Appraise the Estate of John Lumsden Dec'd & Make Return thereof to the Court. Hook vs Baily, Pleas wav'd & Judgt Conf'd by note for £33.3.6 & Two & Twenty Pounds of w'ch is to have Int. from the 10th. May 1788 & Costs.

At a Court held at Franklin Courthouse on Monday the 3rd Day of Novem. 1788, for the Examination of Josiah Turner who was Committed on Suspicion of Stealing from John Finney, Sundrey hogs. Present: Robert Hairston, Thomas Arthur, John Rentfro, John Dickerson & Hugh Martin, Gent. The said Isaiah Turner was led to the Bar in the Custody of Hugh Innes Gent, Sheriff of the County of Franklin to whose Custody for the Cause aforesaid he was Committed, and it being Demanded of the said Prisoner whether he is Guilty of the Fact wherewith he stands Charged or not guilty answered that he is in no wise guilty. Whereupon the Court Proceeded to Examine Divers Witnesses as well on Behalf of the CommonWealth as the Prisoner at the Bar, on Consideration whereof the Court are of the Opinion the said Prisoner is Guilty of the fact wherewith he stands Charged, It is ord. that he be find Accorg. to Law & that the Sheriff take the S'd Turner into his Custody & Keep till he find Sec'y on the Payt. of the s'd fine at March next, who fail'g to give Sec'y it is Ordered that he receive 25 lashes on his bare back at the Public Whip'g Post & that the Shff amediately execute the same.— ROBT. HAIRSTON. Court dissolved—

PAGE TWO HUNDRED EIGHTY-EIGHT

Miller vs Brown Judgt. for 33/4 & Costs on hearg. Mary Miller is Allow'd 4 Days attce as a Wits for Thomas Miller vs Danl. Brown. The Grand Jury Return'd into Court & not having whereof further to present are discharged. Ord. that Process Issue against the several Persons this day presented by the G. Jury. Thomas Terry is allow'd 15 Days Attce as a Wits for Miller vs Brown. James Edmondson & Priscilla Edmondson one of the Exor's & Ex'x named in the last Will & Testament of Rich'd Edmondson deceased came into Court, and on their motion Cer-tificate is Granted them for Obtaining Probate thereof in due form, Who made oath & Gave Bond & Sec'y Accordg. to law, Liberty being Reserved the other Exors named in the said Will to join in the Probate when they shall think fit. The Court is Adj'd till tomorrow 8 oClock.—ROBT. HAIRSTON. At a Court of Quarterly Sessions Cont'd & held for Franklin County on Tues-day the 4th. Day of Novemb. 1788. Present: Robert Hairston,

Thomas Arthur, Moses Greer & John Dickerson, Gent. A Deed Jas. Callaway Heir at Law of Wm. Callaway Dec'd to John Finney Ack'd & O. R.

PAGE TWO HUNDRED EIGHTY-NINE

John Cox vs Jones's Admrs, Cont, for the Ptf, Costs Wm. Mavity vs same the same. Elisha Keen Produced a Com'n from the Governor Appoin'g him Ensign of the Militia of this County Whereupon he Qualif'd Accordg. to Law. Prunty vs Jones Admrs Cont. at the Plf Costs. Welch vs Kelly's Admrs. Cont. Williams vs Mead (on Atta) Robert & Jno. Anderson Garshee's are Dis' charged & Cont'd for Garshees. Callaway vs Guthery's Admrs, Cont. at the Deft Costs William Griffith is allow'd 2 Days Attce as a Wits for Jones's Admr's ads Prunty. Susanah Griffith, the same. Bramblet vs Cowdin Plea wav'd Judgt. Conf't Accordg to Spl. & Costs stay Exon till March 1789. Rentfro Assee vs Calla' way a Jury sworn, to Wit, Benja. Griffith, Jas. Slone, Sansford Hall, Wm. Cowden, Elisha Keen, Robert Mason, Thomas Parker, Anthony Pate, Stephen Slone, John Camp, Edw'd Williams & John Booth. We of the Jury find for the Ptf. the within Bond Due & on the Mot. of the deft. a new Tryal is Granted on Payment of the Costs. A Deed from Thomas Terry, Sr., to Moses Greer Jr. Ack'd & O. R. Delancy vs Bates, Cont, at the Ptf's Costs & the suit is set for hear'g the Second Day of Next Term.

PAGE TWO HUNDRED NINETY

John Chitwood vs Williams Case Dism'd at the Ptf's Costs. A Deed from Thomas Jones to Alexander Sutherland formerlly Acknowledged by Thos. Jones & now Mary the Wife being Privily Examined Reling'd her right of Dower & O. R. Hale vs Craghead, A Jury sworn, to Wit, Moses Rentfro, Daniel Hickson, Wm. Griffith, Joseph Miller, William Right, Absalom Branson, John Roberts, Peter Gearheart, Lewis Davis, George Ferguson, Jacob Prillamon & Wm. Bell. Verd. Ret. for the Def. & O. R. Callaway & Early vs Samuel Cockrum Dism'd at the Ptf. Costs. Prunty vs Bates Dism'd at the Defs. Costs by Consent of Parties. Isaac Bates is allow'd 2 Day's as a Wits, for the Com. Wealth vs Toney. John Camp is allow'd 2 Days Attce. as a Wits for Craigh'd ads Hale. Elijah Hatcher is allow'd 2 Days for the same. James Hale is allow'd 2 Days for the same. James Hale is allow'd

2 Days for the same. Zachariah Davis is allow'd 1 Days Attce
& one Com'g & Ret'g. 35 Miles as a Wits. for Prunty vs Jones
Admr's.

PAGE TWO HUNDRED NINETY-ONE

On the Mot. of Tolliver Craig by George Hancock his Atto.
for a Judgt. Agt. Absolom Jordan who was Security for the de-
livery of Property taken in Execution to satisfy a Judgment &
Costs the Said Craig vs Rich'd Bandy. & fails to deliver the same
at the day of Sale Jud. for the Amt of said Jd. & Co. including
Sheriffs Comn. & the Costs of this Motion. Notice proved.
Rich'd Robertson is allow'd 1 Day Attce as a Wits for Hale
vs Craig. Rice Mead (Atta) Judgt, for Ten Pounds Sixteen
Shillings & Two Pence & Costs & Cond'd in the hands of Danl.
Foster who was sworn as a Garnishee, but Subject to the Atta.
Hook & Ross, Agt. Mead. The Court is Adj'd till tomorrow 8
oClock.—ROBT. HAIRSTON. At a Court of quarterly Sessions
Cont'd & held for Franklin County on Wednesday the 5th. Day
of Novemb. 1788. Present: Robert Hairston, Thomas Arthur,
Jonathan Richardson, Moses Greer, John Rentfro, Jno. Dickerson
& Hugh Martin, Esqrs. Wits: Bell vs Isaac Rentfro Cont.

PAGE TWO HUNDRED NINETY-TWO

Ross & Hook vs Mead—Atta. Daniel Farley & Garshee & it
being Proved to the Court Saith that he oweth the Deft a Suf-
ficiency to Satisfy the Plaintiff, Demand—Judg. for £43.18.9 & Int.
from the 12th. Day of Apl. 1787. & Order of Conda. & Costs.
Absent: Thos. Arthur, Moses Greer, Jonathan Richardson, Jno.
Rentfro. Jno. Dickerson, Gent. Present: George Turnbull & Swin-
field Hill. On the Motion of Robert Woods late Sheriff by his
Atto. for the Judgt. agt. Thomas Prunty D. S. John Rentfro,
Thos. Arthur, Mark Rentfro his Su'ys for Seven hundred &
Seventy Pounds Three Shillings Eleven Pence for the Balance of
Taxes is Collected by him in this County for the Year 1786 pur-
suant to the Act. of Assembly for establishing a permanent Reve-
nue being part a Balance due on an Execution the Common
Wealth against Said Woods Jud. is Granted for the Same with
Damages & the Costs of this Motion Notice Proved & the Ptf
to be allow'd all Just Credits Exempted. On Argument and over

Rul'd whereupon they Pray'd an Appeal to the 8th. Day of Apl. next usual Court w'ch is Granted ret'd into Bond & Ack'd the same. A Deed Thomas Doggitt to James Callaway Prov'd by 2 Wits & Sarah Arthur, Wife of Thomas Arthur, came into Court & Voluntarily Reling. her Right of Dower in & to four hundred & Seventeen Acres of Land, sold by her S'd Husband to Thos. Jurdin & Rob. Ellison. Robt. Woods late Sheriff vs Will Ryan D. S. Judgt. Confes'd for Eight hundred & Six Pounds, Six Shillings & a Penny with Security P. O. Damages, & All Just Credits to be allow'd. A Deed Robert Ellyson to George Thomas Ack'd & O. R. A Deed of Conveyance from George Thomas & Sarah Thomas to Robt. Ellison Ack'd & O. R. Robert Wood state Sheriff vs John Ferguson, Judgt. for £569.19.6½ w'th 20 per ct. Damages & all Just Credits to be allow'd agt. the said Judgt.

PAGE TWO HUNDRED NINETY-THREE

Fuson vs Thompson—Judgt. Conf'd accord'd to Spl. Stay Exon till 1st day of Feby & the Costs to be Equally divided between the Parties. It is ordered that Samuel Jones a bastard Child of Samuel Jones be bound to Danl. Jones. Skinner Devalt is allow'd. 6 Days Attce. & one cuming & Retur'g 45 Miles as a Wits for Walton ads Thorp. William Miller is allow'd a Days Attce. as a Wits for the ComWealth vs Toney. Callaway & Trents vs Wm. Wright Cont'd. Williams vs Mead (Atta.) It is ordered that the Shf. Sum'n Danl. Foster a Garshee. Mary Miller is allow'd 2 Days Attce as a Wits. for Toney ads ComWealth. Joshua Willson is allow'd 2 Days Attce as a Wits for the Com. Wealth vs Toney. Rosannah Willson is allow'd 2 Days Attce as a Wits. for the Com. Wealth vs Toney. William Akers is allow'd 3 Days Attce for the same. John Vanmaple is allow'd 2 Days Attce. for the same. Eliza. Kelley is allow's 2 Days Attce. as a Wits for the ComWealth vs same.

PAGE TWO HUNDRED NINETY-FOUR

Phebey McLain is allow'd 2 Days Attce. as a Wits. for the ComWealth vs Toney. Isabella McLane is allow'd 2 Days for the same. Jacob Webster is allow'd 2 Days for the same. Thomas Miller Jr. 2 Days for the same. Mary Henderson is allow'd 2 Days for the same. Mary Henderson 2 Days for the same. Mary McVey is allow'd 2 Days Attce as a Wits for Toney ads ComWealth.

157

Obediah. Henry Trent vs Rich'd Bandy. A Jury sworn, to Wit, William Thompson, Jas. Webb, John Booth, Sanford Hall. Thomas Parker, Thomas Miller, Jr., William Bell, Smith Webb, William Crump, John England, Jacob Prilliman, & James Wray. Verd. Ret. for the Ptf £1816.18.11 Damages & Judgment Accordgly. Sarah Terry the wife of Thomas Terry came into Court & Voluntarily reling'd her right of Dower in & to 190 Acres of Land sold by her said Husband to Moses Greer. Cowan Assee vs Rentfro Cont'd. Callaway vs Kelly William Kelly Jr. Spl. Bl. Jud. Issue. Davidson vs Jones James Prunty Spl. Bl.

PAGE TWO HUNDRED NINETY-FIVE

On the Mot. of Hugh Innes Shf. John Choice is admitted a Depy Shf. who Qualif'd Accord'g to Law. Jonathan Richardson came into Court & administer'd upon the Estate of Elisha Lyon Dec'd who quallif'd accord'g to Law & w'th Skelton Taylor his Sec'y entered into Bond & ack. the same. John Divers, Danl. Ward. John Smith, Gwin Dudley or any three of them are Appointed to appraise the said Estate & make Return thereof. Court is Adj'd till Tomorrow 8 oClock.—PETER SAUNDERS. At a Court of Quarterly Sessions Cont'd & held for Franklin County on Thursday the 6th. Day of Novemb. 1788. Present: Peter Saunders, Swinfield Hill, Jonathan Richardson, Moses Greer & George Turnbull, Esqrs. William Swanson is allow'd 6 Day's Attce as a Wits for Cragh'd ads Hale. Hook Agt. Keay, Pleas Wav'd & Judgt. cont'd for £19.6.3 & Costs with Int from this Date. with Stay of Exon til after the 10th Day of Decembr. 1788. Thomas Terry came into Court & made oath, that he is Charged with the Tax on 180 Acres of Land W'ch is not his Property & the same is orderd to be Certif'd to the Solicitor.

PAGE TWO HUNDRED NINETY-SIX

Thomas Hill came into Court & made Oath that he is Charged w'th the Tax of 209 Acres of Land w'ch is not his Property & the same is ord. to be Certif'd to the Solicitor. Keen vs Grimmett a Jury sworn, to Wit, Isaiah Willis, Smith Webb, Jas. Webb, Jas. Griffith, Littleberry Leftwich, James Martin, John Booth, Jno. Ferguson, Thos. Parker, David Morgan, Thomas Lewis & Thos. Miller Jr. We the Jury find for the Ptf £3.7.6. Damages Judgt for the Same & Costs. A View of a Road from Terrys

Glade up Black Water to Joshua Rentfros Returne'd & O. R. Brown & Co. vs Joel Chitwood, Injo Disolved By Consent of Parties Except £15 & Cont. for the Balance for the Determination of the Court. Guthery vs Hook Notice to Dis at next Court. Richards vs English & Ritter, a Jury sworn, to Wit, Ashford Napier, Wm. Cowden, Absalom Branson, Joel Chitwood, Samuel Davis, Elisha Keen, Sanford Hall, Jno. Keen, John Hale, William Crump, Jno. Toney, Wm. Thompson & John England. Ret'd a Verd for Plt. We of the Jury find no part of the within Bond Paid. Cook vs Reazer & Tuggle. A Jury Sworn, Viz, the same as in the case Richards vs English & Return'd a Verd. We of the Jury find no part of the Within Bond Paid Except £2.16.7. Judgt. Accordgly. A Division of the Estate of John Ramsey Dec'd Ret'd & O. R.

PAGE TWO HUNDRED NINETY-SEVEN

McRea vs Braiden Pleas Wav'd & Judgt. Conf'd Accord'g to Spl. & Costs. Stay Exeon til Xmas. John Ferguson is App'd D. S. under Hugh Innes high Sheriff, who Quallif'd Accordingly to Collect the arrearages of Trent D. S. from William Cowdin is allow'd 4 Days Attce as a Wits. Keen vs Grimmett. Leftwich vs Houzer a Jury sworn, to Wit, Ashford Napier, William Cowden, Absolom Branson, Joel Chitwood, Samuel Davis, Elisha Keen, Sanford Hall, John Keen, William Crump, Wm. Thompson, John England & John Booth. We the Jury find for the Def. Thomas Parker is allow'd 3 Days Attce as a Wits for Hook ads Guthery. John Keen is allow's 3 Days Attce as Wits for Keen vs Grimmett. Sansford Hall, 1 Day for the Same. John Ferguson came into Court & Quallifd to his list of Collection sence his last Return & the same is orderd to be Certif'd to the Solicitor. James Martin is allow'd 4 Days Attce as a Wits for Howser ads Leftwich. Harris Ballard is allow's 4 Days Attce as a Wits for Howser ads Leftwich. William Swanson came into Court & qualf'd to his list of Collection for the Tax of 1787 & the same is ord. to be Certif'd.

PAGE TWO HUNDRED NINETY-EIGHT

Hugh Woods D. S. came into Court & Quallif'd to his Collection for the Tax of 1787 Sence his last Return & the same is orderd to be Certif'd. Ste. Slone is allow'd 4 Days Attce. as a Wits for Leftwich vs Howzer. John Smith, Peter Holland, John

Divers, & Danl Ward of any three of them, being first Sworn, are Appointed to lay out the third of the Estate of Elisha Lyon Dec'd the Dower of May Lyon the Widow of the S'd El. Lyon Dec'd. William Ryan D. S. came into Court & quallif'd to his Collection for the Tax 1787, Sence his last Return & the same is ordered to be Certif'd. William Thompson is allow'd 1 Days Attce as a Wit's for England &c ads Willson. William Ryan came into Court & Quallif'd to his list of Insolvents for the Year of 1786 & ordered to be Certif'd. Will. Swanson Prov'd his list also of Insolvents also from the Year 1787 & O. C. Thomas Prunty the same & Also for the Year 1786. Davidson vs Jones, James Prunty his Spl. Bl. came into Court & Deliv'd him up Whereupon he is Prayd Committed. Richd. Radford Came into Court & Ack'd given to his Son George one negro Girl named Luce. Asberry vs Divers leave is Granted for the Ptf. to take the Dep's of Joseph Webb Debene Esse. The Court

PAGE TWO HUNDRED NINETY-NINE

The Court is Adjourn'd till Court in Course.—JONATHAN RICHESON. At a Court held for Franklin County on Monday the 1st. Day of Decemb. 1788. Present: Thomas Arthur, Jona- than Richardson, John Smith & Moses Greer, Esqrs. Thomas Hale Produced a Commission from his Excellency the Governor Appointing him a Justice Peace for this County, Whereupon he took the Oath to the ComWealth as also the oath of A Justice of the Peace. Thomas Hale Gent. Present. Abraham Abshire Quallified as a Lieutenant of the Militia of this County. An In- ventory of the Estate of John Lumsden Dec'd was Return'd & O. R. Charles Walden, Peter Gearhart, Moses Rentfro & Charles Minnex, or any three of them, being first sworn, to view & Mark the nearest & Best way for a Road from this X Road to Joshua Rentfros & Make Report thereof. Isaac Miller is app'd Surveyor of the Road in the Place of Benj. Griffith & the list Filed to be his Gang.

PAGE THREE HUNDRED

A Deed Benja. White to Faithful Luke Ack'd & Susannah the wife being Privily Examined as the Law Directs Reling'd &c & O. R. Also Robert Napier to William Godsey Ack'd & O. R. Also Thomas Flower to Thomas Hoff Prov'd by 2 Witses. Joseph

Greer came into Court & made oath that he was from the best Information under 21 Years of Age when he Tax'd with Poll Tax & 2 Years, to Wit, 1786 & 87, w'ch was ordered to be Certifyed to the Solicitor. Hugh Walton is Exempted from the Payment of the County & Parrish Leveys for the Future. Benja. Chandler came into Court & made oath that he is Taxed with 145 Acres of Land wch he has no Patent & the same was ordered to Certify'd to the Solicitor as Also the Poll Tax for his Son who was under Age for the Year 1786. Thompson vs Rodgers Dis'd at Def. Costs. John Epperson came into Court & made Oath that he is taxed with 150 Acres Land w'ch is not his Property, Also a Poll Tax for a Negro under 12 Years of Age w'ch is Ordered to be Certify'd to the Solicitor. John Mattox, made Oath that his is Taxed for Three Years w'th 140 Acres of Land w'ch is not his Property & the same was ordered to be Certifyed to the Solicitor. Edward Willson made oath that he is Taxed for 154 Acres of Land for the Year 1787 W'ch is not his Property & the same was ordered to be Certifyed to the Solicitor.

PAGE THREE HUNDRED ONE

Leave is Granted to John Craghead to build a Water Grist Mill on the Gills Creek he being Proprietor on both Sides of the said Creek. John Faris Administratrix vs Robert Anderson on Replevy Bond Judgt. Accog. Spl. & Costs. Absent: Thomas Arthur. George Hancock vs William Ferguson Judgt. Conf'd for £2.8.0 & Costs. Stay Exeon One Month. John Ferguson came into Court & Quallified to his Lists of Insolvents, As Also his List of Collection for the Year 1786 Sence his last Return & O. C. Jeremiah Lumsden came into Court & took the Oath of Fidelity to the Commonwealth & ent'd into Bond with Swinfield Hill Surety as the Law Directs for Solemnizing Marriages. Robert Prunty Came into Court & made Oath that he is Tax'd with 623 Acres of Land for Three years Past w'ch is not his Property & the same was ordered to be Certifyed to the Solicitor. On the Mot. of John Hook by his Atto. to Dissolve the Injo. of a Judgt. obtained agt. him by Penelope Guthery, on Hear'g & the Bill & Answer Read the same is Disolved with Cost & that the Def. have the Benefit of his Judgt. at Common Law. The Ptf. not Appearing.

PAGE THREE HUNDRED TWO

A Deed of Gift from Rich'd Radford to George Radford Ack'd & O. R. A Deed Joel Chitwood from John Robertson further Proved by 1. Wits & O. C. John Rodgers is allow'd 1. Day's Attce as a Wits for Wilkson vs England. Charles Sebert is recommended to his Excellency the Governor as an Ensign for the Militia of this County & the same ord. to be Certifyed. A List of Insolvents in the County of Franklin for the Year 1786, Prov'd in Court & O. C. An Inventory of the Esta. of Elisha Lyon Dec'd is Ret. & O. R. Jonathan Richeson, John Smith, Federick Rives, & Israel Standifer or any three of them, being first Sworn, do Appraise the Estate of Rich'd Edmunson Dec'd & make Ret. Thereof to the Court. Rich'd Booth is app'd Surveyor of the Road in the Place of William Martin & his list to be his Gang, w'ch he is to Keep in Good Repair according to Law. It is ord. that James Stewart & Sam Bird do work on the Road on w'ch William Shearwood is overseer. Hancock vs Marcum Jud. for £1.10 & Costs. Present: John Dickerson, Gent.

PAGE THREE HUNDRED THREE

On the Mot. of Thomas Watts by his Atto. for a Jud. Against Hugh Innes, Sheriff of for this County, on a Return of an Execon the said Watts vs Hambrick the same is Rejected with Costs. On the Mot of Tolliver Craig Assee by his Atto. for a Judgt. agt. Hugh Innes Gent. Sheriff for this County Notice Proved & Cont till next Court.* On the Mot. of Robert Woods late Sheriff of for this County by his Atto. for a Judgt. agt, Isaac Rentfro on the Securities of Thomas Prunty D. S. for the s'd Woods for Seven hundred & Seventy six Pounds three Shillings & Eleven Pence for the Ballance of Taxes Collected by him in this County for the Year 1786. Pursuant to an Act of Assembly for Establishing a Permanent Revenue being a Part of a Balance Due on an Execution the CommonWealth against the said Woods, Judgt is Granted him for the same with 20 P. cent Damages & the Cost of this Mot. Notice Proved & the Ptf. to allowance Just Credits. The Court is Adj'd till to Morrow 8 oClock.—T ARTHUR.

---

* This paragraph is marked X X X X X.

PAGE THREE HUNDRED FOUR

At a Court held & Cont'd for Franklin County on Tuesday the 2nd Day of Decemb. 1788. Present: Thomas Arthur, Mose Greer, Swinfield Hill & Thos. Hale, Esqrs. Thomas Prunty came into Court and Made Oath that he is Taxed with 236 Acres of Land which is not his Property & the same was orderd to be Certifyed to the Solicitor. On the Mot. of Joseph Under-wood by Geo. Hancock Gent his Atto. to Disolve an Injo. ob-tained agt. him by James Slone to Stay the further proceeding of a Judgt. Underwood vs P. Sloan. On hearing the Bill & Argu-ments on both sides It is considered & Decreed that the Int. from the Sender of the Money be Perpetuly Enjoyned is also £2.17. part of the Cost of the former Suit in Chy. from which Decree the Def pray'd an appeal to the first day of the ensuing High Court of Chancery whereupon he by his Attorney entered into Bond with Stephen Smith his Security conditioned as the Law Directs. Thomas Arthur is Allowed Twenty five Days Attce as a Witness for George Asberry vs Stokes &c. Thomas Prunty came into Court & made oath to his List of Insolvents for the Year 1787, & the same is ord. to be Certifyed. William Ryan D. S. came into & Quallified to his Collection for the year 86 & 87, Sence his last Ret. & the same was ordered to be Certi-fyed. Leave is Granted Thomas Prunty to amend this Ret. Craig of Exeon also agt. Bandy. It is Ord. that the Exon on the Grand Jury's Prest. agt Wm. Griffith for Gam'g. be Quasht, the Pro-ceedings thereon being Contrary to Law.

PAGE THREE HUNDRED FIVE

Peter Lanfield came into Court & made oath from the best Information he has that he was under the Age of 21 Years when he was Charged w'th a Poll Tax for the year 1786 & the same was ord. to be Certifyed. Hugh Woods Came into Court & Qualify'd to his List of Insolvents for 1786 & O. C. Thomas Prunty D. S. came into Court & quallifyed to his Collection of for Tax's for the Year 1787. Hugh Woods D. S. the same for the year 1786. The Court is Adj'd till Court in Course.—T. ARTHUR. The County of Franklin for the Year 1788 is made Debtor To the Clerk for his annual Sallery, 1248. To the Dpy. States Atto. same, 1248. To John Dickerson Surveyor for open'g

& Clos'g the Prison Bounds, 100. To Peter Gearheart for Damages done a horse in convey'g Pursel to the P. Gaol, 264. Total 2860. At a Court held for Franklin County on Monday the 5th. Day of January 1789. Present: Thos. Arthur, Moses Greer, John Dickinson, Tho. Hale, Peter Saunders, Swinfield Hill, Gent.

PAGE THREE HUNDRED SIX

The County Levey Brought forw'd, 2860. To the Jailor for Commitment & Relesmt of Edward Lyon, 20. To Ditto for the same, 10. To Do for 14 Days Board for Reubin Pursell & Thompson, 40. To Ditto for the same, 40. To Jonathan Graham for 8 Days Guardg Reubin Pursell & Jas. Thompson for Brown & Callaway, 200. Joseph Webb for 8 Days, Do, 200. To Jesse Terry for 14 Days, Do, 350. To Thomas Doggett, 7 Days, Do, 175. To the Jailor for Commitmt. & Releasmt, of Nathan Dempoy, 20. To the Jailor for Comt. of Howell Jones, 10. To Williston Talbott for 14 Days Guard'g Prisoners for Brown & Callaway, 350. To Ditto for Robert Graham 8 Days, Do, 200. To Thomas Crutcher for Guarding the Prisoners for Brown & Callaway, 350. To Doct'r Daniel Brown for Repairing the Jail, 840. To Indian Tom for Making 2 Pr. Hancuffs for Brown & Callaway, 80. To Carparter James to the Damages his horse Sustaind In Conveying Hensley to the Publick Jail for Brown & Callaway, 160. To John Law for Killing an Old Wolf, 100. To Samuel Webster 1 Old Wolfs head, 100. To the Clerk for his Services & for Attend'g the Com. &c, 1920. To Ste. Smith for the Carrag. of a Pris, 120. To Ditto, for Attend'g 6 Call Courts, 1200. To the Sheriff for his Ex oficia Servises, 1248.

PAGE THREE HUNDRED SEVEN

A Deed from Joshua Rentfro to Theo. Webb Ack'd & O. R. Also from Geo. Sanford to Joshua Noales prov'd by 2 Witnesses & O. C. Also Daniel Farley to Geo. Turnbull Prov'd & O. R. Also, the Same to John Short Prov'd by 2 Witnesses & O. C. Joseph S. Price Came into Court & made Oath that he is Charged w'th a Black Iythe Mare that belongs to him w'ch is Ordered to be Certifyed to the Solicitor. Also John Woods the Same. Also John Bates the Same. Ordered that the Overseers of the Poor do bind Out Peter Miller to George Medley. A Deed from Danl. Farley to Thos. Crump Prov'd by 2 Wits & O. C.

Also from Philip Sheridan to Ann Neal Prov'd & O. R. Also from Evan Price to Jonathan Price Prov'd & O. R. Ordered that John Craghead, William Swanson, Philip Raley, William Clay or any 3 of them do View & mark out a Way for a Road, the Nearest & best Way from the Chesnut Road X Pig River & Black Water to Stanton to Intersect the Meadow Road Leading to Lynches Ferry & make Report thereof to the Court. Jonathan Richeson, who formerly Administered on the Estate of Elisha Lyon Dec'd Came into Court & Prayed to be Discharged from the s'd Trust, which is Granted him & Mary Lyon Widow of the s'd Dec'd Prayed Adm'x of the said Estate, w'ch is Grant'd her, whereupon she entered into Bond w'th Security for the Faith-ful Performance of s'd Trust & Ack'd the same & made Oath Accord'g to Law.

PAGE THREE HUNDRED EIGHT

An inventory of the Estate of Rich'd Edmundson Dec'd Re-turn & O. R. Franklin County for the Year 1788 is made DR. Tobacco. Brought Forward, 10.18.17. To the Sheriff for Attend-ing Called Court, to Wit, 1 Over Jno. H. Jones, 200. George Lamb, 200. Benja. Hensley, 200. James Martin, 200. Edw'd Lyon, 400. Drusilla Hoff, 200. Reubin Purcell, 200. Isaiah Turner, 200. To Owen Ruble for Damages Done a Mare in Conveying Lynn Alias Thompson to the Publick Gaol, 264. Total, 12881.

PAGE THREE HUNDRED NINE

On the Motion of Robert Woods Gent. late Sheriff of this County for a Judgment Against Moses Greer & William Menifee Securitys for Thomas Prunty D. Sheriff for the Said Woods for Seven hundred and Seventy Six Pounds Three Shillings and Eleven Pence for the Balance of Taxes Collected by him for the Year 1786. Pursuant to Act of Assembly for Establishing a Per-manent Revenue being Part of a Balance Due on an Exeon the ComWealth against the Said Woods. Judgment is Granted him Against them for the Same, with 20P-Cent. Damages & the Costs of this Motion nothing Proved & the Pll. to give All Just Credits, whereupon they Prayed an Appeal to the ———— Day of the Next Genl. Court & that the Def's have leave to Give Security at the next Court. The Court is Adjourn'd till Court in Course.—ROBT. HAIRSTON. At a Court held for Franklin

County on Monday the 2 Day of February 1789. Present: Robert Hairston, Thomas Arthur, John Rentfro & Moses Greer, Gent. Leave is Granted Thomas Ruble to build a Water Grist Mill on Nicholas's Creek, the Proprietor on the one Side Consenting to the same.

PAGE THREE HUNDRED TEN

Samuel Hairston Foreman, John Webbs, Daniel ————,* James Parberry, Sam'l Bird, Luke Standifer, Thomas James, Edw'd Choat, Daniel Spangler, Joseph S. Price, Jacob Prilliman, Peter Holland, Israel Standifer, David Clarkson, Benja. Griffith & John Richardson were Sworn as a Grand Jury of Inquest for the Body of this County wherewith they withdrew to Consider their Presentments. Callaway & Co vs Compton Dismiss'd by Order———— Jean Akers Came into Court and Prayed Administration of the Goods & Chattles of James Akers Dec'd wch is Granted her ————She entered into Bond with John Jamison & Wm. Cow—— Securitys & Ack'd the Same According to Law. John Law, John Dickerson, Swinfield Hill & Fred Rives, or any of them, being first Sworn, Do Appraise the s'd Estate & Return &————thereof to Court. On the Motion of John Chitwood for a Judgment Lewis Duval Marcum Duvall on a Delivery Bond is Granted him for 1200.18 Inspected Tobo. w'th the C————, a former Suit & the Costs of this motion. notice Proved. A Deed John James to Randolph Hall Prov'd & M———— the Wife being Privily Exam'd Relinguished & O. R. Bird vs Jemeson Thos. Jameson & John Bird Spl. Bl. & Spl. Impl. Samuel Hatcher Came into Court & Craved the Peace of Jesse Martin, the said Martin Came into Court & with Joel Meadows & Jesse Meadows his Securitys Acknowledged them selves Indebted to the ComWealth in the Sum of £200 that is to say the Martin in the Sum of £100 & each of his Securitys in £50 on Condition the Jesse Martin be not of Good behavior to all Persons for 12 Months & 1 Day, but more especially to the s'd Saml. Hatcher.

PAGE THREE HUNDRED ELEVEN

ComWealth vs Jno Simmons Obediah H. Trent Spl. Bl. & Oyer of the Present. Callaway & Co. vs Ferguson. Jud. Confess'd Accg. to Sply & Costs. Hudgins Trustee &c vs King (Atta for Rent) Jud. for Plf. for £4.2.6 & Costs whereof the Plf. is to

*Missing.

have the Benifit of an Exeon Immediately & the Bal'c the agrees
to wit One Month for & it to be Optional in the Def. to Perform the Repairs Stipulated in the Agreement in that term, to wit,
1 month, or to Pay the s'd Balance at his Dismiss & O. Condema.
The Grand Jury returned into Court & made Several presentments
whereupon Procss is Ordered to Issue. A Deed from John Jones to
Royal Wade Prov'd & Mary the Wife being Privily Ex'd Relinguished &c O. R'd. Thorp vs Walton—Dismiss'd on hearing.
Kelly vs Kellys Adms. All matters in Dispute between the Parties are Refered to Geo. Hancock & Robt Williams & in Case
they Disagree to Chuse an Umpire & their or his Award to be
the Jud. of the Court. Thos. Miller Jr. is allowed 5 Days Attce
as a Witness for Thos. vs Levi Willis. Thos. Miller Sr. is
Allow'd 3 Days for the Same. John Hale by the Approbation of
Hugh Innes is Admited a D. Sheriff, who Qualifyed Accordgly.

PAGE THREE HUNDRED TWELVE

Austin agt. Webb & Webb agt. Austin, Award Returned
& O. R. John Early Produced a Comn. from his Excellency the
Governor Appointing him a Justice Peace for this County, Where-
upon he Took the oath to the Commonwelth as Also the oath
of a Justice of the Peace. Present: John Early Gent. A Deed
from Martin Key to John Bowman Prov'd & O. R. Present
Thomas Hale & John Smith Gent. A Deed from Hills Legatees
to Thomas Hill Ack'd & O. R. Also the same to the same Ack'd
& O. R. Also the same to David Barton the same. Absent: John
Rentfro, Gent. Present: Swinfield Hill. A Bill of Sale from
James Ray to Moses Ray Ack'd & O. R. Present: Hugh Martin,
Gent. On the Motion of Robert Woods Gent. late Sheriff of
This County for a Judgment against Joshua Rentfro & Mary
Spangler Executrix of Daniel Spangler Deceased Securities for
Thomas Prunty Depy Sheriff for the said Woods for seven Hun-
dred & Seventy six Pounds Three Shillings & Eleven Pence for
the Balance of Taxes Collected by him for the Year 1786 Pur-
suant to an Act of Assembly for Establishing a Permanent Reve-
nue being part of or Balance Due on an Execution the

PAGE THREE HUNDRED THIRTEEN

ComWealth against the said Woods, Judgt. is Granted him
against them for the same w'th 20 P. Cent Damages & the Costs

of this Motion Never Prov'd & the Plf. to give all Just Credits. Robert Hairston Gent. is allow'd £30.18 for his Services as a Com. for this County. Moses Greer Gent is allow'd £27. for the same. The Court is Adj'd till to Morrow 8 oClock.—T. AR' THUR. At a Court Continued & held for Franklin County on Tuesday the 3rd Day of February 1789. Present: Thomas Ar' thur, Swinfield Hill, Moses Greer & Thomas Hale, Gent. The County of Franklin for the Year 1788 is made Dr. Tob. Brought Forward, 12881. To Peter Gearheart 14 Diets & horse for Lynn & Purcell & horsefeeding 148. To George Livsey 5 Young Wolf heads, 250. To Thomas Hill for 10 Days Attendc. as a Guard over Pursell & Thompson, 250. To Stephen Smith assee of Dog' gett for Old Wolfs head 100. To Thomas Prunty DS. for Sum a Jury of Inquest on the Body of John Geerheart & One Days Attce 200. To Swinfield Hill, Coroner, Takg an Inquest on the same 153. To William Campbell for a P. large hand Cuff, 144. To Hugh Woods for 28 Insolvents for 1786 at 22 Tobo, 616. To Ditto for 21 Insolvants for 1787 at 14, 294. (Total) 15015.

PAGE THREE HUNDRED FOURTEEN

Franklin County Dr. Bro. forward, 15010. To William Ryan 21 Insolvents for 1788 1418 Tobo, 294. To Thomas Prunty 82 Insolvents for 1788 1518 Tobo. 1092. 16.40.2. To the Sheriff for Collecting the Above at 6 P. ct., 984. 17380. To A Depo' sition in the hands of the Sheriff, 892. 18,276. 1400 Tythes at 13 18 Tobo is, 18278. Thomas Prunty Quallify'd to his list of Insolvants for the year 1787 & O. C. Ord. That Thomas Prunty be allow'd 40 Tobo. out of the Depositum for puting William Ingram twice in the Stocks. David Hughes & Wm. Austin each of them once. Ord. that William Ryan be allowed 20 Tobo. out of the Depositum for Puting Baldwin Nowlin & Thos. Quigley in the stock. Hugh Woods DS. Quallify'd to his list of Insolvents for the Year 1787. Abraham Abshire is appointed Surveyor of the Road in the Place of David Morgan & his list to be his Gang. The Court is Adj'd till Court in Course.—THOS. ARTHUR.

PAGE THREE HUNDRED FIFTEEN

At a Court of Quarterly Sessions held for Franklin at the Courthouse On Monday the Second Day of March 1789. Present: Thomas Arthur, John Smith, Moses Greer, Thomas Hale, Gent.

A Dedamus for the Relinguishment of the Dower of Susannah Wilks wife of Miner Wilks in & to 334 Acres of Land Sold by her Husband to John Wilks Ret'd. & O. R'd. A Deed William Bradley from Mathew Farley Prov'd by 2 Witnesses & O. C. Also Peter Kingery from George Earnest Prov'd by 2 Witnesses & O. C. Also Valentine Iles from Skelton Taylor Ack'd & Sarah the Wife being Privily Exam'd Relinguished her Right of Dower & O. R. Also John Richardson from Jas. Prunty Ack'd O. R'd. Callaway & Co. vs Jas. Prunty Thos. Townsend Spl. Bl. A Deed Thos. Hoff from Thos. Flower further Prov'd & O. R. A View of a Road from the X-Roads to Joshua Rentfros Returned & O. R. Callaway & Co. vs Asberry Jud. Confess'd Stay Exeon till Order'd by the Plf. A Deed, Jas. McKinzey from Joseph Hambrick further Prov'd by 2 Witnesses & O. R.

PAGE THREE HUNDRED SIXTEEN

Skinner Duvall is Allowed 1 Days Attce. as a Witness for Wm. Walton ads Thorp & Once Coming 21 Miles & Returning. The Court is Adj'd till Tom. 11 oClock. At a Court held & Continued for Franklin County on Tuesday the 3rd of March 1789. Present: Peter Saunders, Swinfield Hill, Moses Greer, Thomas Hale, Gent. Ross & Hook vs Hale, Dismiss'd. Ordered the Clerk Certify to the Executor, that James Powel Edmondson is an Inhabitant of the County of Franklin And is the Person Entitled to the Pention Allowed him the Pention List, he having lost a Legg in the Engagement At Somerset Courthouse and did belong to the 9th Virginia Redgmt. but Detached in the Case of Rifleman under Colo. Morgan Aged 34 Years. Chitwood vs Brown & Co (On Injo.) on hearing the Bill And Answer Read & Argued the Court are of Opinion that the Injo. aforesaid Shall be Disolved and that the Plf. at Law have the Benefit of his former Jud. Wth Costs. Danl Brown & Co. vs Wm. Chitwood & Joel Chitwood Jud. on Replevy Bond w'th Costs. On the Mot. of Danl. Brown & Co. Jud. is Granted him for £4.11.1 Agst. Rob. Woods late Sheriff & Costs Due in form the Cty Levey. Guthery vs Hook. S.B. & also Impl. A Jury Sworn, to Wit, Samuel Hairston, David Barton, James McVey, Absolom Branson, Robert Holliday, Wm. Maviety, Isaac Rentfro, Nathl. Tate, Stephen Lee, Thomas Parker, Joel Chitwood & Mark Rentfro. Verd. Ret. for £9.19.11.

169

PAGE THREE HUNDRED SEVENTEEN

Webb. vs England Dismiss'd at Deft Costs. Theodorick Webb is Allow'd 5 Days Attendce as a Witness for Webb vs England. Sutherland vs Ruble, Wm. Maviety Spl. Bl. & Impl. Willson vs England, It is Ordered that the Referees Proceed Exparte in Giving Lawful Motive. Bramlet vs Cowden Jas. Burns Spl. Bl. & Delivered him up & Pray'd Commited. Dillon vs Fralin Jno. Chitwood Spl. Bl. Field'g Jones is Allowed 3 Days Attendance as a Witness for Webb vs England. Sam'l Davis is Allow'd 5 Days for the Same. A Deed from Wm. Mead & Isham Talbot, to Jno. Hook Ack'd Robert Meed Atto. for Wm. Mead & Proved by 3 Witnesses as to Talbot who Saw Talbot Sign & Acknowledge the Same the 23rd Feb. 1789 & O. R'd. John Ferguson is Allowed 4 Days Attce as a Witness for Hook ads Guthery. The ComWealth vs Toney on an Indictment & it Appearing to the Court that the Indictmt. & Papers Relative thereto in Sd. Suit are Lost, therefore the D. States Atto. is Directed to enter a Nole Prosigne & It is the Opinion of the Court that the Def. Pay the Costs of the Indt. & it is the Opinion of the Court that there be Only Six Witnesses Attendance Taxed in the Bill of Costs, the Jury having formerly bought in a Verdict in favor of the ComWealth.

PAGE THREE HUNDRED EIGHTEEN

Isaac Bates is Allowed 2 Days Attce. as a Witness for the Com. Wealth vs Toney. Joshua Willson is Allow'd 2 Days for the Same. Rosannah Willson is allow'd 2 Days for the Same. Eliza Kelly is Allow'd 2 Days for the same. Isabella Crawford is Allow'd 2 Days Attce One Comg. & Ret. 21 Miles as a Witness for the Same. Pheby McClure is Allow'd 2 Days for the Same. William Akers is Allow'd 2 Days for the same. Mary Henderson is Allow'd 2 Days for the Same. Jacob Kingery is allow'd 2 Days for the same. Rachel Kelly is Allow'd 4 Days for the Same. Thomas Miller Jr. is Allow'd 2 Days for the Same. John Vanmaple is Allow'd 2 Days for the same. Jacob Webster is Allow'd 2 Days for the Same. Mary McVey is Allow'd 2 Days for Toney ads ComWealth. The Court is Adj'd till Tomorrow 10 oClock. —PETER SAUNDERS. At a Court held & Continued for Franklin County On Wednesday the 4th Day of March 1789. Present:

Thomas Arthur, John Smith, Swinfield Hill & John Rentfro, Gent. Frances Graves is by the Aprobation & Consent of Hugh Innis Gent. Admited D. Sheriff, who Qualified Accordg. to Law. Thomas Prunty & William Swanson are Permited to finish their former Collections. Present: Peter Saunders Gent.

PAGE THREE HUNDRED NINETEEN

Delancy vs Bates, a Jury Sworn, to Wit, John Booth, David Barton, William Mavity, Thomas Hunt, Michael Coats, James Slone, William Griffith, John Bates, Rob. Perryman, Stephen Lee, Isaac Rentfro & Absolom Branson. Verd. Ret'd We the Jury find for the Def. & O. R'd. Hugh Rentfro vs Jas. Callaway, A Jury Sworn to Wit John Booth, David Barton, William Mavity, Thomas Hunt, Michael Coats, William Griffith, John Bates, Rob. Perryman, Absalom Branson, John Kelly, John Orr, & John Fuson. A Juror Withdrawn & the Parties Agree to Refer the matters in Dispute to George Hancock & Rich'd N. Venable & In Case they Disagree to Chuse an umpire & his or their Award to be the Jud. of the Court. Hubbard vs Perryman Jud. Confess'd Accordg. to Sply & Costs with Stay of Exeon till May Court. Caleb Tate is Allow'd 9 Days Attce & Three times Coming & Return'g 50 Miles as a Witness for Callaway ads Rentfro. Isaac Rentfro is Allow'd 3 Days Attce & One Coming & Returning 28 Miles as a Witness for Rentfro vs Callaway. Stephen Lee is Allow'd 3 Days Attce. & One Comg. & retg. 18 Miles as a Witness for the Same vs the Same. Guttery vs Hook on the Mot. of the Def. by Geo. Hancock his Atto. for a New Tryal the Same is Reject w'th Costs and Atto for Excepted. Hugh Innis Gent Sheriff Came into Court & with Jas. Calland & Saml. Patteson his Security enterd into Bond for the Collection of the Revenue Tax & Ack'd the Same Accorg to Law & O. R'd. Same for the Collection of the County Levy, the Same. Same for the Collection of Officers the Same.

PAGE THREE HUNDRED TWENTY

Prunty vs Jones Admrs a Jury Sworn to Wit, Robert Holleday, James Slone, John Smith, William Campbell, George Ferguson, Robert Perryman, George Kelly, James Blair, George Simmons, John Booth, David Guttery & James Wray. Verdict Ret'd for the Def. & O. R'd. John Hale is Allowed 4 Days Attce. as a

Witness for Prunty vs Joneses Admrs. Zachariah Davis is Allow'd 3 Days Attce & One Comg. & Retg. 35 Miles as a Witness for the Same. John Key is Allow'd 5 Days Attence & Twice Comg. & Retg. 20 Miles as a Witness for Guttery vs Hook. Youell vs Rentfro. Jud. Confessed, Accordg. to Spy & Costs. Stay Exeon till August & then the Ptf. to Take Property At ¾ of its Value in the Opinion of the Comrs. of this County. William Ryan is Allow'd 5 Days Attce. as a Witness for Hook ads Guttery. William Ryan Qualifyed to his Collection sence his last Return. William Swanson, the Same. William Griffith is Allow'd 3 Days Attce. as a Witness for Jonese Admrs ads Jas. Prunty. Ordered that Wm. Swanson DS have leave to Amend the Ret. of an Exeon. Anderson vs Livsey. The Court is Adjourn'd till Tomorrow 10 oClock.—PETER SAUNDERS.

PAGE THREE HUNDRED TWENTY-ONE

At a Court held & Continued for Franklin County on Thursday the 5th. Day of March 1789. Present: Jonathan Richeson, Swinfield Hill, Moses Greer & Thomas Hale, Gent. Inquisition on the Body of John Gearheart Dec'd Returned by the Coroner & O. R'd. On the Complaint of Robert Williams, Gent, Deputy States Attorney for this County, It is Ordered that George Radford & Richard Radford be taken into the Custody of the Sheriff untill they give Security for their appearance at the next Court to answer the Complaint of the Said Williams for rescuing Sundry Property taken by Wm. Swanson Dpy Shf on an Execution Trent vs Asberry & also that the Sheriff be Authorized to Summon a Sufficient Posse to carry his Order into Effect to retake the Property where found. Mavity vs Jones Admr. Depo Plt not further prosecuting Callaway & Trent vs Wright, Cont'd. A Deed from Thomas Watts to Samuel Arrington Proved by 2 Wits & O. C. J. Hook to Pay Tax. Jones vs Prunty, Ans. filed & notice to Desolve. Barton vs Livesey, a Jury Sworn, to Wit, John Fuson, John Smith, Philemon Greer, Merun Duvall, John Orr, Lewis Duvall, John Hook, John Booth, John Bates, Richard N. Venable, Robert

PAGE THREE HUNDRED TWENTY-TWO

Williams & John Clybourn. Verd. Ret'd that we of the Jury find the Def. Guilty of the Trespass in the Decl. Mentioned &

172

Assess the Ptfs Damages to 12 d & O. R'd. Armstrong vs Spang-
ler Adm'x Dismissd for want of Security for Costs. Robert Perry-
man is Allow'd 7 Days Attce as a Witness for Livsey ads Barton.
Mathews vs Livseay Cont'd at Defts Costs. Greer vs Cook Pleas
& Issue & Dismiss's at the Plfs Cost. Hook vs Booth Plea Waved
& Jud. Confess'd Accordg, to Sply & Costs. John Fuson is Al-
low'd One Days Attce as a Witness for Greer vs Cook & Prunty.
Ordered that a Summons Issue Against Arch'd Gordon, Obediah
Stewart & Frances Farley to Appear here at the May Court as
Garnishee of Wm. ads Williams. Richards Assee vs Kelly &
Miller. A Jury Sworn, to Wit, Jacob Prillamon, David Spangler,
John Orr, John Clyborn, Skelton Taylor, Luke Standifer, John
Fuson, Thom's Prunty, William Griffith, Joseph Griffith, John
Booth & Philmon Greer. Verd. Ret. that We of the Jury find
no part of the Bond Paid & O. R'd. Mead vs Clyborn, Rule to
give Su'y for Costs Accorg. to Law or to be Dismiss'd. Farler vs
Dillion, Cont'd at the Pltf Cost. Webb vs Arthur, Aw'd Ret. &
P. R'd.

PAGE THREE HUNDRED TWENTY-THREE

Callaway & Earlys vs Stokes. A Jury Sworn, to Wit, Jacob
Prillaman, Daniel Spangler, John Orr, John Clyborn, Skelton Tay-
lor, Luke Standifer, John Fuson, Thomas Prunty, William Grif-
fith, Joseph Griffith, John Smith & Philmon Greer. Verd Ret.
for £5.7.4. Damages & O. R'd. Guttery vs Hook Cont'd. Rentfro
Qtm. vs Doggett. Cont'd. Clay vs Willson, Cont'd. Jenkins vs
Lynn &c Cont'd. Ord. that David Barton, Thos. Jones, Henry
Jones & Joseph Davis are App'd to View a Way for a Road from
David Bartons to Peter Saunderses & make Report thereof. Michie
vs Holliday. Jud. for Costs. Smith vs Griffin, Jud. for Costs.
Callaway vs Kelly, Dism'd. Martin vs Spierpoint, Jud. for Costs.
Asberry vs Clutcher, Jud. for Costs. Keepler vs Hodges, Jud. for
Costs. J. Smith, Exors. vs Guy Smiths Exors, Continued. Hueston
vs Livsey, a Jury Sworn, to Wit, George Ferguson, Daniel Brown,
Saml. Cockrom, Joseph Greer, James McVey, John Fuson, Wm.
Griffith, Thomas Prunty, David Barton, George Asberry, Phil-
mon Greer, & Joseph Griffith. Verdt. Ret. for the Ptf. for
£104.18.0. Damages & O. R'd. Moses Rentfro vs Callaway. Cont'd.
Hancock vs Rentfro. Dismiss'd, Agred.

Hancock vs Stewart, Jud for £2.15.6 & Costs. Woods vs Prunty & His Securitys, the Appeal, Relinguish by Consent of Partys Staying Exon. till the first Day of July Against Such as Shall give Sufficient Security in the Opinion of Rich'd N. Venable & Stephen Smith for the Delivery of Sufficient Property to Robert Woods, high Sheriff, to Indemnify him Against the failure of Thomas Prunty, his late Deputy, but it is the Intention of this Order, Not to Sever the Demand Agt the Several Securitys but that the Same remain Joint as formerly & that Exeon Issue Accordingly. Thomas Prunty Came into Court & Qualify'd to the Collection Sence his last Ret. The Court is Adj'd till Tomorrow 9. oClock.—T. ARTHUR. At a Court of Quarterly Sessions held & Continued for Franklin County on Friday the 6th, Day of March 1789. Present: Jonathan Richaeson, Swinfield Hill, George Turnbull, Thos. Hale, Gent. Present: Thomas Arthur. On the Motion of Conrad Bott to Desolve the Injo. of a Jud. Obtained Against him by John Chitwood & on hearing the Bill & Answer Read the Court are of Opinan that the Injo. afores'd Shall be Desolved & that the Pf. at Law have the Benefit of this Jud. at Law w'th Costs.

Ryan vs Ramsey (in Chancery- on Reading the Bill and after Papers filed in the said Cause it is the Opinion of the Court and therefore ordered and Decreed that the said William Ryan is entitled to one half of the Land which Sr. levid on at his death, known in his Will by the name of the Manner Plantation and that s'd Ryans Part of the land be the part laid off for him by the Commissioner appointed for that purpose, And as to the other half of the s'd Land, it is Decreed that John Dickerson, Hugh Innes, Hugh Martin and John Martin or any three of them sell the same & for the Purchase money take bonds with good Security (Viz) for one third of the Purchase money a bond to Thomas Ramsey payable when he shall arrive at the age of 21, for another third a bond to James Ramsey payable when he shall come of age, and a bond for the remaining third to Mr. Ramsey payable when he shall come of age, and make report to the Court how they have executed this trust, and that the s'd John, George

& William Ramsey do make a Deed from their Part of the s'd Land to the Purchaser. Holliday vs Christian Con'd for Plf. Johns vs Keen, Dismiss'd. Lewis vs Hale, Dismiss'd by the Oaths of Tho. Prunty. Blankenship vs Perdue, Cont'd.

PAGE THREE HUNDRED TWENTY-SIX

Stewart vs Haynes Dis'd for want of Acct. Holliday vs Willson, Cont'd. Blankenship vs Godsey Dismiss'd. Thorp vs Gipson. Cont'd. Howel vs Hicksen, Cont'd. Callaway & Co. vs Hunt. Jud. Proceed'g to Note & Costs. Asberry vs Woods Abates by the Defdts Death. Orr. vs Fryth, Jud. for £3.0.9 & Costs. Kellys Jr. vs Kelleys Aw'd Jud. for £3.14.2 & Costs. Hancock vs Chitwood—Dismiss'd, Agred. Same vs Sherwood Woodson, Jud. for £1.10. & Costs. Stogden vs Clower, Cont'd. Willson vs Kellys Adm'rs Cont'd. Asberry vs Divers a Jury Sworn, to Wit, John Hook, Saml. Henderson, John Fuson, Jas. McVey, Thos. Hill, Bird Smith, Thos. Prunty, Wm. Griffith, Danl. Brown, Jas. Wray, Hugh Woods, & Frances Graves. Verd. Ret. for the Plf. for £1.4.9 Damages & Rd. for the Same w'th as much as Damages. Joseph Webb is Allow'd 7 Days Attce as a Witness for Asberry vs Devien. Hook vs Wray Cont'd.

PAGE THREE HUNDRED TWENTY-SEVEN

Greer vs Cook & Prunty, Abates as to Cook. W. E. agst Prunty Set Aside, Robert Williams Spl. Bl. & Genl Issue, Rule to Give Sec'ty for Costs Jno. Cox Security for Costs & Cont'd. William Griffith is Allow'd 2 Days Attce. as a Witness for Joneses Adm'rs ads Cox. A Deed from James Callaway to R. Mead Ack'd & O. R. Thomas Prunty is Allow'd 11 Days Attendance as Witness for Cox vs Jamses Adm'rs. The Court is Adjourn'd till Court in Course.—THOS. ARTHUR. At a Court held for Franklin County on Thursday the XII Day of March 1789 for the Examination of Isham Hall & Anthony Owens, Charged with Feloniously breaking Open the House of Amos Ellison & Stealing therefrom A Quantity of Meat & a Sack Bagg. Present: Thomas Arthur, Jonathan Richeson, Moses Greer, George Turnbull & Thomas Hale & Swinfield Hill, Gent. The Said Isham Hall & Anthony Owens being led to the Bar in the Custody of Hugh Innes Gent. Sheriff of Said County, to whose Custody for the Crimes aforesaid they were Commited & It being Demanded of

175

the Said Prisoners afores'd whether they are Guily of the facts, wherewith they Stand Charged or not Guily, Answered, that they are not Guilty, whereupon the Court Proceeded to Examine Divers, Witnesses as Well on Behalf of the ComWealth as the Prisoners at Bar, On Consideration whereof the Court are of Opinion that the Said Hall Shall give Security for his Appearance at the next Grand Jury Court to be held for this County, & stands Comtd until he gives Su'ty of

PAGE THREE HUNDRED TWENTY-EIGHT

himself in the Sum of £100. & his Security in the Sum of £50 each to be Levied on their Respective Goods & Chattles, Lands & Tenemts On Condition the s'd Hall Does not Appear before the Next Grand Jury Court & the s'd Owen is Discharged. Amos Ellison, John Chitwood, William Nolen & John Arthur Came into Court & Severally Ack'd them Selves Indebted to the Com. Wealth of Virginia in the Sum of Ten Pounds each to be Levied on their Respective Goods & Chattles Lands & Tene- ments on Condition they do not Appear before the Next G. Jury Court as Witness for the Com. Wealth Against Isham Hall.— T. ARTHUR. At a Court held for Franklin County on Monday the 6th. Day of April 1789. Present: Thomas Arthur, John Smith, Swinfield Hill, Thos. Hale, Moses Greer & Jon'th Rich- ardson. A Deed Tunbull Johnson to Jacob Boon Ack'd & Cath- arine the Wife being Privily Ex'd Reling'd & O. R. Ferguson vs Delaney on Atta. Dismiss'd. A Deed from Benja. Potter to Lewis Potter Ack'd & O. R'd. Also from G. Daniel Richardson to Thos. Long, the Same. Also from G. Danl. Richardson to Geo. Brock, Same. Leave is Granted Joel Chitwood to Take the Depo. of Jesse Starke in his Suit vs Jno. Hook. John Cook, his ear Mark, to Wit, a Crop & under Ked in the Right ear & a Slit in the left & O. R'd (Paid).

PAGE THREE HUNDRED TWENTY-NINE

A Deed from William Young to Benja. Potter Ack'd O. R'd. Also from Daniel Richardson to Amos Richardson further Prov'd & O. R'd. Also from Arthur Edwards to Jas. Brummit Ack'd & O. R'd. Benja. Cook is Recommended to his Excellency the Gov- ernor as a Proper Person to Serve as A Justice in the Com. of the Peace for this County. A Deed from Thos. Dimoss to Philemon

Saunders Ack'd & O. R'd. Also the Same to Granberry Greer, the Same. Also Isham Hall to Jas. Bell Prov'd 1 Witness & O. C. Ordered That Brown & Callaway be Paid the Sum of £9. by the Sheriff out of the Depositum of Last Year for Repairing the Gaol of this County & it is Ordered that the Tobo. Allow'd them for the Same Servce in the County Proportion of this Year be Ex- pended & that the same be Considered at a further Deposit. On the Motion of John Cox Clk of Henry a Jud. is Granted him vs John Martin as Security for Rob Woods Late Sheriff of this County for £20.8. w'th the Balance of his fees put into his hands to Collect & Costs. Notice Prov'd & this Jud. to have Credit for £3. On the Motion of Danl. Brown & Co. Jud. is Granted him Against John Martin Security for Rob. Woods, Late Sherff of this County, for £4.11.1. Also 15, & 100, Tobo. Due the S'd Brown in the County Levy, & Costs & this Jud. to be Credited for 8/. Isaiah Willis is Appointed a Com'r in the Place of Thos. Watts who Qualify'd According to Law. Jas. vs Rentfro, Cont'd. A Deed Geo. Sanford to Joshua Noles further Prov'd & O. R. Hugh Woods Qualy'd to his Collection Sence his last Ret. & O. C.

PAGE THREE HUNDRED THIRTY

A Deed from John Smith to Danl Hixon Ack'd & O. R'd. Parker vs McGuire. Atta. Jud. £5.10. & O. Con'd & Costs. Wil- liam Swanson Qualify'd to his Insolvents & O. R'd. Also to his Collection Same his Cost Return. On the Motion of Thomas Prunty Issued Jud. vs No Finney Security for Jas. Brummit on Delivery Bond the Same is Granted Accordg. to Sply & Costs. A Deed from Sanford to Saneed further Prov'd by 2 Witness & O. R'd. A Deed of Trust from Arch'd Gordon to Campbell Prov'd by 1 Witness & O. R. A Deed Wm. Austin to Sam'l Hairston Prov'd by 1 Witness & O. C. Also Nath'l Simmons to Jno. Kannady Prov'd by 2 Witness & O. C. The Court is Adj'd till Court in Course.—JONATHAN RICHESON.

PAGE THREE HUNDRED THIRTY-ONE

At a Court held for Franklin County At the Courthouse On the XX Day of April 1789 for the Examination of John Burgess on Suspicion of Feloniously Breaking open the house of John Prewitt & Stealing therefrom ¾ Yards of Linen And Cash to the Amount of 29/ & on pr of Shoe Buckles. Present: Robert

Hairston, Jonathan Richison, Moses Greer, Swinfield Hill &
Thomas Hale, Gent. The Said John Burgess being Led to the
Bar in the Custody of Hugh Innes, Gent. Sheriff of Said County
to whose Custody he had been Commited for the Crime Afore-
said & it being Demanded of the Said Prisoner whether he was
Guilty of the fact wherewith he Stands Charged or not Guilty
Answered that he was in No Wise Guilty, whereupon the Court
Proceed to examine Divers Witnesses, as well on behalf of the
Comm. Wealth as the Prisoner at the Bar and on Consideration
whereof the Court were of Opinion the Prisoner Afors'd is Not
Guilty of the Crime Aforss'd and that he be Discharged Out of
Custody.—ROBT. HAIRSTON. At a Court of Quarterly Sessions
held for Franklin County On Monday the 4th. Day of May 1789.
Present: Peter Saunders, Jonathan Richeson, John Smith and
Moses Greer. Callaway & Co. vs Kemp Dis'd by Plfs Ord. Same
vs Jno. Guttery, Dis'd.

PAGE THREE HUNDRED THIRTY-TWO

A Deed from Thomas Jones to Mary the Wife of Robt.
Hairston Ack'd & O. R. Also from Thomas Prunty to Same
Ack'd & O. R'd. Also from Robert Mead to Thos. Edwards,
Same. Also from John Ellis to Caleb Hundley Prov'd by 1 Wit-
ness & O. C. Also Caleb Hundley to John Peter Hudson Prov
by 2 Witness & O. C. Also from Wm. Spencer to Wm. Walton
Prov'd by 2 Witness & O. C. Also from Isaac Bates to Shores
Price Ack'd & Eliza. the Wife being Privily. Ex'd Relingt &
O. R. Also from Caleb Hundley & Isham Hall to Jas. Roberts
Prov'd by 2 Witness & O. C. Also from Allen R. Young to Jas.
Roberts Prov'd by 2 Witness & O. C. Also from Rob. Mead to
Wm. Dodd Ack'd & O. R. Callaway & Co vs Bandy, Jud. Con-
fess'd Accordg. to Spy & Costs. George Thomas, Foreman, John
Wilks, Arthur Edwards, Bottom Estes, John Kemp, Page White,
Philemon Sutherland, James Strange, Barnabas Arthur, Robert
Napier, Jonathan Price, William Griffith, William Wright, Peter
Finney, Jacob Prillaman, John Taylor, Thomas Jones Jr. William
Maviety, Thomas Craig, & Rich'd Copland, Were Sworn as a
Grand Jury for the Body of this County whereupon they with-
drew to Consider their Presentments. The Last Will & Testa-
ment of Jacob Hickman Dec'd was Exhibited in Court by Jacob
Kinzey & Jacob Sowder. Executors therein Named was Proved

by the Oaths of Two Witness Whereupon they Entered into Bond w'th Security Accordgly w'ch were Ordered to be recorded & John Naufsinger, Danl. Barnhart & Peter Gearheart & Jacob Prillaman are Appointed to Appraise the S'd estate & Make Return thereof to the Court.

PAGE THREE HUNDRED THIRTY-THREE

Thorp vs Gipson Cont'd for Def. Howell vs Hickson. Cont'd. Callaway & Co. vs Jno. Martin Jud. Accorg. to Sply & Costs. On the Mot. of Eliza Menifee it is Order'd that a Negro Named Harry on Acc't of Age & Infirmity be Exempt from the Payt. of the County & Parish Levies. Callaway & Co. vs Simmons Jud. Accg. to Sply & Costs. Same vs Coleman. the Same. Same vs John Chitwood, Same. Same vs Jno. Brodie, Same. Smith vs Pettyjohn, Dism'd. Leftwich & Co. vs Jno. Payne. Jud. Accg. to Sply & Costs. Stogdon vs Clower Jud. Accorgl to Sply & Costs. Slone vs Kelly Jud. for £5 & Costs. A Deed from Jas. Callaway to Danl. Barnhart Ack'd & O. R. A View of a Road from Chestnut Road to Stanton River Ret'd & O. R. Talbott vs Early Jud. for £1.5.11 & Costs Ordered that George Asberry, Hercules Ogle & James Hunt be Summond to Appear before the Next G. Jury Court to Answer the Compt. of ComWealth for abuse given to Allen R. Young. Jones vs Spanglers Exex. Jud. for £1.6.4 & Costs. James vs Rentfro, Joshua Rentfro Spl. Bl. Never Absconded Issue (replecation). A Deed from Wm. Austin to Saml. Hairston further Prov'd by 2 Witnesses & O. R. Brown & Callaway vs John Rentfro on Atta Jud. for 31/11 & Costs. John Arthur is Allow'd 1 Days Attce as a Witess for the Com. Wealth vs Isham Hall.

PAGE THREE HUNDRED THIRTY-FOUR

The Grand Jury Came into Court & made Several Presentments on W'ch Process is Orderd to Issue. Calland Assee vs Napier &c Robt. Napier Spl. Bl. & Spl. Impl & Gl. Issue. A Deed from Martin Binnian to Saml. Webb Further Prov'd & O. R. Ordered that an Atta for Contempt Issue vs Farleys as G. Issue An Atta, Wm. vs Mead. Bott vs Chitwood & Slone, John Hale Spl. Bl & Delivered the Def. Slone up whereupon he is Pray'd Commited, Thos. Slone & Wm. Wright further Spl. Bl. & Spl. Impl. Sutherland vs Ruble. Dismiss'd at Plfs. Costs. Bird vs

Jamison Dismiss'd Agreed. On the Motion of Harmon Cook to Disolve the Injo. of a Jud. obtained Against him by Absalom Branson, on having the Bill And Answer Read & Arguments on both Sides, It is Ordered & Decreed that the Injo. Afores'd be perpetually injoined for 15/ w'th the Costs of s'd Injo. be Ord. that Exon go for the Plt. at Law for the ballance of the Judmt. Inventory of the 2/3 of the Estate of Elisha Lyon Ret'd & O. R. A Deed from Jno. Thornton to Walter Dent Prov'd & O. R'd. Parberry vs Edwards. Thomas Townsend & Jno. Bird Spl. Bl. & Spl. Impl. Same vs Same, the Same. Court is Adj'd till Tomorrow 8 oClock.—ROBT. HAIRSTON.

PAGE THREE HUNDRED THIRTY-FIVE

At a Court Continued & held for Franklin County on Tuesday the 5th. Day of May 1789. Present: Robert Hairston, Jonathan Richeson, John Dickinson & Thomas Hale, Gent. Anderson vs Clutcher (In Chy) on hearing the Bill & Answer Read and Arguments on both Sides, it is Ordered and Decreed that the Land in the Pltfs Bill mentioned Containg 93 Acres to hence forth Visted in the Complaint Reserving the Equity of Redemption in the Def. for 12 Months & in Case the Def. Pay to the Plt. the sum of £26.0.0. W'th Int. thereon from the 21st. Day of Dec. 1785 until paid, in that Case the Compl. reconvey the Said Land to the Def. Otherwise that Compl Sell the Said 93 Acres of Land for the best Price in Ready Money W'ch Can be gotten After having Advertized the Sail for One Month & After Satisfying himself the Debt & Int. Afores'd the Costs of this Suit & the Costs of Advert'g to refund the Surplus of the Money Arising from S'd Sail to the Def. If anye. Adam Young, vs Perryman. Dis'd at Def. Costs. Present: Jno. Early, Gent. Smith Executrs vs Smith Excrs a Jury Sworn, to wit, Isaac Rentfro, James Hines, David Willis, John Martin, Rob. Holliday, William Wright, Robert Perryman, Isaiah Willis, John Johnson, Robert Mead, William Griffith & Stephen Wood. Exception to Evidence offerd & filed. Verd. Ret'd for the Plf for £138.4.8. Damages & O. R'd from W'ch the Def. Appealed to the first Day of the District Court in September next to be held at New London whereupon he entered into Bond w'th Security & Ack'd the Same Accordg. to Law. Wm. Austin is Exempt from the Pay't of County & Parish levies. William Kelly Sr. the Same.

PAGE THREE HUNDRED THIRTY-SIX

Joseph Ritter is All'd 8 Days Attce. as a Witness McLain vs Toney. Hoge vs Davis (An Atta) Jud. for £40 w'th Int from the 5th. December 1785 Attach'd Effects Released. Hook vs Loving. Wm. Swanson Spl. Bl & Detn'd the Def up Joel Chitwood further Spl. Bl. & Co. McVey vs Delaney—Jud. for £6.9.10 & Wm Kelly Is. a Gshee being Sworn Saith he Owes the Def. £4.3.0 & O Con'd & Costs. Guttery vs Hook, a Jury Sworn, to Wit, Charles Sebret, Thomas Boulton, John England, Joseph Cook, Anthony Pate, John Willis, John Burgess, Joshua Brock, James Coleman, William Johnson, Mordecai Mosely, & James Prunty. Verdt. Ret. for the Plf. for £7.10 whereupon the Def. Pray'd a new Tryal w'ch is Granted on Paying the Costs of the Day w'ch was Accordgly pd. Holliday vs Christian Dismiss'd on hearing. Henry Lyne is Allow'd 2 Days Attce & one coming & Returning 28 Miles as a Witness for Jno. Cox against James Adm'rs. David Guttery is Allow'd 7 Days Attce as a Witness for Hook ads Guttery. John Guttery is Allow'd 4 Days Atta. as a Witness for the Same. Ann Guttery is Allow'd 4 Days for the Same. Thomas Parker is Allow's 4 Days for the Same. John Key is Allow'd 2 Days for Guttery vs Hook & One Comg. & Retg. 20 Miles. Edw'd Willson is Allow'd 3 Days Attce as a Witness for Christian ads Holliday. Clayborn ads Mead Assee. Rob. Mead is Allwd 2 Days Attce & Comg. & retg. 30 Miles.

PAGE THREE HUNDRED THIRTY-SEVEN

Moses Rentfro vs Callaway, Isaac Rentfro is Allow'd 1 Days Att'ce & Once Comg. & Retg. 28 Miles. The Court is Adjourn'd till Tomorrow 8 oClock.—ROBERT HAIRSTON. At a Court Contin'd & held for Franklin County on Wednesday the 6th May 1789. Present: Robert Hairston, Moses Greer, John Smith, John Dickerson & Swinfield Hill, Gent. Thomas Booth a Pensioner in this County having Prov'd to the Satisfaction of the Court, that he is the Person Entitled to the S'd Pension for £6. the same is O. Ca. Ryan vs Woods Ref'd to R. N. Venable & Hugh Innes & in Case they Disagree to Chuse an umpire & their Award to be the Jud. of the Court. Richards Asse of Kellys Adm'rs vs Wm. Kelly & Thomas Miller On Detr on wch there is a Jud. Same vs English & Ritter in Debt on wch Jud. is Obtained It is their Opinion that the Judgmts, be Confirm'd where Judgmts

181

are Obtained & where not Obtain'd we Award the Defts Respectively pay the Debts & Int. in their Several Bonds mentioned to the said Richards as Assee of the Adm's Except in the Suit Richards vs Wm. Kelly, it is Our Opinion that the Def. have Credit for 20/ for Funeral Expences &c Accordg. to his Acct. £1.17.0 w'ch he paid John Hoff as P. Receipt. Wm. Kelly Sr. vs Kellys Adm'x we find for the Deft. John Elsweek vs Same we find for the Deft. John Watts. vs Same we find for the Defts. Abram Ritter vs Same we Award the Pts. £4.8.0. & Costs except An Atto fee (when Assetts).

PAGE THREE HUNDRED THIRTY-EIGHT

Robert English vs Kellys Adm'x we find for the Def. Wm. Kelly Jr. vs Same we find for the Ptf. 279 but failing to Claim a Credit on her Bond Executed to the Ptf. on W'ch there is a Jud. Also failg to Produce his Acct. at the Sale when the Creditors were requested by Advertisment to do so, we Aw'd that the Ptf. pay the Costs. Jesse Willson vs Same Award for the Ptf. for £1.14.0 when Assetts except as Atto fee. Ordered that the Sheriff Summon a Guard over Isham Hall a Prisoner in the Gaol of this County, to serve in the night & one in the day. (A line is drawn through this order). Isaac Rentfro vs Mead (Atta) Robert Mead a Garshee being Sworn Saith that he hath a Sufficiency in his hand of the Defts to Satisfy the Plfs Demand. Jud. for £30 & Costs & O. C. but exeon to be Staid till the further Order of this Court. Johnson vs Lewis. Jud. for £4 & Costs. John Johnson is Allow'd 3 Days Attce as a Witness for Johnson vs Lewis. Jacob Johnson, the Same. Patrick Johnson, the Same. Haynes Morgan vs Smith Exetr: Jud. for £2.6.3. when Assets & Cost. Hancock vs Radford Jud. for £3.0.0 & Costs. James Prunty vs Jones, Dismiss'd by Ptfs Order. John Ferguson Qualif'd to his Collection Sence his last Return & O. C. Wm. Ryan Qualifyed to his Collection Sence his Last Ret. & O. C. John Law is Allow'd 2 Days attce as a Witness for Heard vs Webb. Daniel Perdue is Allow'd 4 Days for the Same.

PAGE THREE HUNDRED THIRTY-NINE

Hook vs Ray (in Chy) on hearing the Bill Answer & Dep's read and Arguments on both Sides. It is Ordered & Decreed by the Court that the Agrements between the Parties be Specifically

Perform'd and that George Turnbull, John Early, John Knaufsinger & Skelton Taylor, Or any three of them, Attended by the Sur'v of the County Do go the Land in the Bill mentioned, and After Laying it off accordg. to the Agrement in the Bill Mention'd, Do make report of the Same to this Court in Order for a final Decree, & that the Expence Attendg the Laying off s'd land is to be satisfyed by the Complainant & that they make report at or before August Court Next. On the Motion of Thomas Prunty to Desolve the Injo. of a Jud Obtained Against him by Thomas Jones & on hearing the Bill, Answers & Affidavits read & Arguments on both sides, it is Ordered & Decreed by the Court that the Injo. Afors'd be not Desolved but that the Same be Perpetually enjoyn'd. Elijah Lyon, orphan of Elisha Lyon Dec'd, Came into Court & Chose Joseph Greer his Guardian whereupon the S'd Greer entered into Bond w'th Security & Ack'd the Same Accordg to Law for a Breach of the Peace. Order'd that John Pruit be Taken into Custody by the Sheriff till he find Sufficient Security for his Good behavior for 12 Mo. & a Day. Wills vs Herd Atta. Dismiss'd. On the Motion of Peter Saunder Gent License is Granted him to Keep a Retail Store. Thos. Prunty Qualify'd to his Collion Since his last Ret.

PAGE THREE HUNDRED FORTY

On the Motion of William Cockram to Stay the Proceeding of Jud. Obtained Against him by Wm. Holley, the Same is Rejected w'th Costs. Jenkins vs Wynne & Al. Cont'd. Clay vs Willson. Cont'd. Rentfro Qtm vs Doggett, Nole Proseque. Richards Assee vs Kelly Dismiss'd. Heard vs Webb W. E. Set Aside & G .Issue A. Jury Sworn, to Wit, John Fuson, Robert Johns, Thomas Simmons, William Ferguson, William Martin, Joseph Greer, William Dillion, Amos Richardson, Samuel Cockram, Walter Bernard, Robert Mead & Casper Houzer. Vert. Ret. We of the Jury find for the Ptf. £5. Damages & O. R'd. On the Mot. of Sam'l Hairston, Leave is Granted him to Keep a Retail Store. Samual Hairston is Allow'd 4 Days Attce as a Witness for Jones vs Spangler Exrs. On the Mot. of Thomas Simmons, Leave is Granted him to take the Depo. of Uriah Ferguson ads Hook & Graham vs Simmons & Martin. The Affidavit of Wm. Smith & Wm. Martin Respecting the Tender & Delivery of a Mare & Cash from Jno. Hook to James Wray filed at the request & Costs of the S'd Hook & O. R'd. Hugh Woods Qualify'd to his Collection Sence his last Ret. & O. C. Also to his List of Insolvents, the Same.

PAGE THREE HUNDRED FORTY-ONE

Orderd that John Dickinson & Swinfield Hill Gent. do let the Puting up Posts round the Prison Bounds to the Lowest Bidder & Report. William Griffith is Allowed 3 Days Attce as a Witness for Jones ads Cox. Susannah Griffith 3 Days for the Same. Nicholas Brown is Allow'd 3 Days Attce as a Witness for Ryan vs Woods. Ord. William Harris & Absalom Dillingham be Added to Smith Webbs List of Hands. Ord. that William Griffith be Sum. to Answer the Informa. of the D. States Atto. for Twice Voating at the last Election. The Court is Adjourn'd till Court in Course.—ROBT HAIRSTON. At a Court held for Franklin County at the Courthouse on Tuesday the 12th Day of May 1789 for the Examination of Isham Hall on Suspicion of Feloniously Stealing from Clayborn Blankenship One Feather Bed & Sundry Other Articles. Present: Peter Saunders, Swinfield Hill, Moses Greer & Thomas Hale, Gent. The said Isham Hall being led to the Bar in Custody of Hugh Innis Gent, Sheriff of the Said County to whose Custody for the Crime Afors'd he had been Commited, & it being Demanded of the S'd Prisoner whither he is Guilty of the Fact wherewith he Stands Charged or Not Guilty, Answered that he was in no wise Guilty, whereupon the Court Proceeded to examine Divers Witnesses as well on behalf of the Common Wealth as of the Prisoners at the Bar.

PAGE THREE HUNDRED FORTY-TWO

On Consideration whereof the Court are of Opinion that the S'd Prisoner Should be Bound over to the Next Grand Jury & that he find Sufficient Security for his Appearance & that he Stand Commited until he find Security, Whereupon the Said Hall Put himself on the Mercey of the Court & Agreed to Receive Punishment as the Court should think Proper or Abide by any Other Jud. of the Court, whereupon the S'd Hall do Pay the Costs of the Com. Wealths Protection & Also Pay unto Clayborn Blankenship Five pounds 6/10 for his Bed, whereupon he entered into Bond w'th Security for the Paymt. of the Jud. Afors'd. Clayborn Blankenship, Mary Blankenship, Thos. Parker, & Joseph Webb Came into Court & Severally Acknowledged themselves Indebted to the Com. Wealth of Virginia in The Sum of Twenty five Pounds each to be Levied on their Respective Good & Chattles on Condition they do not Appear before the Court on the First Monday in August Next as Witness for the Com. Wealth vs Isham Hall.—PETER SAUNDERS.

The last 7 lines of page 342 are marked X X X X.

THE HARE CASE

Most Franklin County boys of the past century have heard their fathers or grandfathers tell tall tales of Hare the highwayman. No two men ever told their stories alike, for Hare, soon after his appearance in Franklin County, seemed to become a mythical figure. One story had it that he was the son of a prominent Lynchburg family and that he robbed and murdered a lone traveler in Franklin County for which he was hanged. Another story was that Hare wrote his confessions of many crimes while awaiting execution at Rocky Mount, and that the confessions were published in a book which was suppressed by his wealthy family. Nobody seemed to know when his crime in Franklin was committed, or when he was hanged. Some even said there never was such a man, that Hare was an imaginary character used to frighten several generations of small boys.

When the author set out, in 1920 to write a history of Franklin County he discovered the following indisputable facts: Joseph Thompson Hare was born of good parentage in Chester County, Pennsylvania, in 1780. Even when very young he showed inclinations to waywardness. At the age of 16 he robbed a neighbor who lived only a mile or two from the Hare home. Soon after this, his father disowned him, and the son made his way to Philadelphia and thence to New Orleans where he enlisted in a city patrol called the Governor's Guard. While "guarding" the people, he consorted with thieves and gamblers and continued his career of crime.

His departure from New Orleans followed the robbery of a rich Cuban from whom he took five thousand dollars. With this money he made his way to Knoxville, Tennessee, purposing to return to his old home. He left Knoxville on horseback for Richmond. At Abingdon he met Robert Bumpass, a former resident of Franklin County, who was returning to his old home. They agreed to ride together as far as the old Bumpass homestead. According to Hare's testimony, Bumpass was a drover and a show-off. They traveled together until they reached a lonely spot in a deep forest, near the summit of the mountain between Turkey Cock Creek and Snow Creek. A parting boast of Bumpass about the profits of his trip ended Hare's indecision concerning the robbery he had contemplated for several days. He forced the drover to give up his money, horse and clothing. The horse was released when safely beyond the reach of its owner. Hare was then beset, according to his confessions with such a fear and panic as he had never felt before. It was now night and as he fled through the forest he said there suddenly appeared in the road before him an unmoving white horse. The apparition, said Hare, caused his mount to stop so suddenly as to almost unhorse him. Spurring failed to move the animal past the apparition. Hare turned back and came to a house near Persimmon pond on the left hand side of the road as one goes from Dickinson's to Danville. According to the late Judge A. L. Duncan of Missoula, Montana, this house was occupied at the time by a man named Young. Here Hare spent the night, and here he was arrested. Hare was arraigned before "a court held for Franklin County at the Court House on November 19, 1806 . . . charged with having on the night of Saturday the 8th of this month, feloniously taken, stolen and carried away, one eagle-colored horse, four hundred and fifty Spanish Milled Dollars and sundry wearing apparel, the property of Robert Bumpas." The Justices of the County Court who conducted the examination of Hare were: Benjamin Cook, Showers Price, Jonathan Richeson, George Turnbull, Thomas Hale, Stephen Smith, Thomas Thompson and Patrick Hix. The witnesses against him were: Robert Bumpass, Jesse Estes, Thomas Sherwood, Anderson Powell and Isaac Collins.

Hare was held for trial before the District Court of April 15, 1807. The case was tried by a jury composed of Richard Stockton, John Brown, Robert Prunty, Casimere Cabaniss, Thomas Charles, Thomas Ferguson, Nicholas Cassell, Jacob Webb, John Hill, William Jones, Thomas Arrington and John Smith.

The verdict, rendered on April 17, 1807, declared that "the said Joseph Hare, alias Thomas Hunt, is guilty of the horse-stealing aforesaid in manner and form as in the indictment against him is alleged, and they ascertain the time for which he shall undergo confinement in the penitentiary house to be eight years, and that the horse stolen hath been restored to the owner, whereupon he is remanded to jail."

Over 100 pages of Colonel Frank Triplett's book "Crimes and Criminals" are devoted to Hare. In that volume, Hare is designated as "the first noted highwayman that America produced."

In the same book, Hare is quoted as declaring he "was robbed by the Franklin County officials of over four thousand dollars, besides losing eight of the best years of my life." Hare wrote much while in the Franklin County jail. Two of his poems—"The Road" and "The Lament" are of a high order.

Upon his release, Hare went to Baltimore and engaged in harness-making for a short time, but soon "took to the road again" and roamed as far north as Canada committing robberies in many states. He was sent to the New Jersey penitentiary for five years but served only a part of that sentence. In 1817, Joseph Hare met his brother, Lewis Hare, also a robber, who was operating with a well-known criminal named Alexander. Together they robbed a mail coach at Havre De Grace, Maryland, and the three of them were hanged on September 10, 1818.

In the Calendar of State Papers (Vol. 4, page 204) it is recorded that "at a General Court held December 16, 1786, certain criminals, having been tried, were sentenced as follows: Two men from Russell Parish in Bedford and Franklin counties, three years in the penitentiary for horse-stealing; From Russell Parish, Franklin County, another for horse-stealing whose sentence had been commuted from death to life at hard labor, but who had escaped and, subsequently captured, was, by a jury, ordered to be hanged."

THE HOOK CASE

Patrick Henry delivered his celebrated speech on the John Hook case at New London courthouse in Bedford County from which Franklin County, in part, was taken. Mr. Henry appeared there as counsel for John Venable, the defendant. He excited the indignation of his audience against Hook by painting the distress of the American army, hungry, almost naked, exposed to the rigors of winter, and making blood marks on the snow with their bleeding feet. "Where is the man," asked Henry, "with an American heart in his bosom, who would not have thrown open his barns, his cellars, the doors of his house, the portals of his breast, to have received with open arms the meanest soldier in that little band of famished heroes? Where is the man?

There he stands! Whether the heart of an American beats in his bosom, you, gentlemen, are to judge." Henry concluded with a description of Yorktown surrender, the British dejection, and the patriot's triumphal cry of "Washington and Liberty"; then the discordant note, disturbing the general joy, of Hook prowling through the American camp, hoarsly howling, "Beef, beef, beef."

It hardly need be added that this suit of long standing, which the court had once settled in favor of Hook, was now settled in favor of Venable, despite the ability of William Cowan, Hook's attorney.

Hook had operated a mercantile establishment at New London with a partner named Ross, but upon the establishment of Franklin County, Hook took up residence in the new county. His name frequently appears as a litigant in the foregoing records. The legal records in his case against Venable, when Patrick Henry castigated him so unmercifully, are in the Clerk's Office of Franklin County, though one would expect to find them in the Clerk's Office in the adjoining county of Bedford where the case was tried.

When Hook removed to Franklin County in 1786, he conducted a store at Hale's Ford, about a mile from the river. That he was of a litigious nature is amply sustained by the records in this volume. If count were made, it would probably appear that he was a party to more judicial contests than any other person named in this book.

But it is not fair to judge any man of Hook's day by the standards of this day. It must be borne in mind that in the 18th century property rights commonly took precedence over what are now called human rights. Men were more grasping then than now, because any comfortable place in the social order of that day was almost wholly dependent upon material possessions.

THE WITCHER-CLEMENT CASE

The year 1860 was eventful for the little world in which Franklin County citizens lived and moved. A single local occurrence supplied Franklinites with a matter for speculation and conversation far into the 20th century. The occurrence was the killing of the three Clement brothers—James, William and Ralph—

by Captain Vincent Witcher, John A. Smith, Vincent Oliver Smith, Samuel Swanson and Addison Witcher. Addison Witcher was the son of Vincent Witcher. John and Vincent Oliver Smith were his grandsons. Samuel Swanson was his son-in-law.

The affray had its beginning in the marriage of James Clement and Victoria Smith which was celebrated on March 13, 1858. The groom was one of the ten children of Dr. George W. Clement. Dr. Clement (b. 1786, m. 1811, d. 1867) was educated in Hampden-Sidney College and in the medical department of the University of Pennsylvania. His mother, Stella Smith, was the daughter of Major John Smith of Lewis Island. Their Franklin County home was called "Mountain View." Victoria Smith (b. 1837) was the daughter of Albert G. Smith and a granddaughter of Captain Vincent Witcher.

Both Clement and Smith families appeared to be pleased with the marriage, though it was brought out in the court proceedings following the killings, that the Smith family regarded the Clement family as of inferior social station. Dr. Clement was especially proud of the beauty, wit and vivacity of his daughter-in-law. Her magnetic personality gained her many admirers. It is said that two of her old sweethearts, William P. Gilbert and Samuel D. Berger, continued their attentions even after her marriage. Though these affairs were shown to be of an innocent nature, the extremely jealous disposition of her husband led him to charge her with unfaithfulness and to humiliate her constantly.

Fearing physical violence, Victoria Smith Clement fled from her husband on the night of August 24, 1859, and found refuge in the home of Sherwood Y. Shelton who lived about a mile distant. She left behind her six months old baby (Lelia Maud, b. March 1, 1859) so great was her terror at the moment of flight. This incident was made the basis of a divorce suit. Within three weeks from her flight, the taking of depositions was begun at Dickinson's Store, the same to be read as evidence in the suit then pending between John A. Smith, next friend of Victoria Smith Clement, plaintiff, against James R. Clement, defendant. The taking of depositions continued through the fall and winter, until Saturday, February 25, 1860, when the killing of the Clement brothers ended the suit.

The depositions of S. Y. Shelton, Charles Powell, Willis Woody, G. T. Berger, W. P. Gilbert, George Samson and Edney Shelton had been taken. Elizabeth W. Bennett had been called to make her statement. Captain Vincent Witcher objected to having her qualify and make part of her statement on Saturday "and then being left in the hands of the opposite party to be picked until Monday morning." Captain Witcher made the state ment that Miss Bennett had been brought into the case by the Clements and was said to be under their control. Ralph Clement at this point said that "Whoever said that told a damned lie." Whereupon Captain Witcher replied "You had better make your remarks more direct," rose from his chair, put his hand in his bosom, drew therefrom a "five shooter," stepped toward Ralph Clement and began firing. Addison Witcher was conducting the examination for the plaintiff. Robert Mitchell was the justice of the peace before whom the depositions were being taken. His testimony in the trial of Captain Witcher, as recorded in the volume of depositions published by Dr. G. W. Clement, Sr., in June 1860, is not very impressive. He appears to have forgotten everything that transpired in his court room.

The bodies of the three brothers were not only riddled with bullets, but were horribly gashed with knives. William Clement was disemboweled. James Clement had his throat slit from ear to ear. Ralph Clement lived nearly three hours despite his fright ful wounds, and made a dying declaration before Justice Mitchell and Gresham Choice which was written down by Mr. Choice. It read as follows: "I never attempted to draw an arm. Addison Witcher caught me and held me around the waist and arms and told them to come and shoot me—a damned rascal. I was shot several times while in that fix, and he held me until I fell. Num bers of pistols were fired at me then." To this dying declaration, Magistrate Mitchell added these words: "Ralph A. Clement re quested me to tell his father that he wanted him to make the deed to his wife and child according to his will." Robert N. Powell stated in his deposition that Addison Witcher held Ralph Clement while Vincent Oliver Smith shot him. George Finney stated in his deposition that John Anthony Smith shot and stabbed James Clement. It was stated by several deponents that both James and William Clement were reclining on a bed in the counting room when the firing began. It was thought by a few that some of the early firing came from the bed. The pistols of both James and William Clement had been fired until empty, but Ralph Clement, it was testified had not drawn gun or dirk.

The bodies of the three slain brothers were carried from Washington Dickinson's counting room, in a farm wagon, and buried in a single grave near the shaded driveway which led up to the old brick house which was their boyhood home.

The trial of Captain Vincent Witcher and his accomplices was begun almost immediately in a general justices' court, commonly called a magistrates' court. Benjamin F. Cooper and Richard Parker took the depositions of the following: Jacob G. Mackenheimer, Gresham Choice, James Kemp, John C. Hutcherson, James M. Hutcherson, Madison D. Carter, Cluffee M. Brooks, George W. Finney, R. N. Powell, John B. Law, James M. Gibson, Silas W. Evans, William G. Poindexter, Gilly Ann Huffman, John C. Law, William H. Hutcherson and Alfred L. H. Muse. Names appearing in the 200-page printed volume of depositions are: Abram Hancock, Tom Keen, Samuel D. Berger, James Rice, Shack Law, Waller Wright, Silas Dudley, Samuel G. Mattox, Snead Adams, D. W. Blunt, Henry C. Mease, Mastin Williams, and John Baker, the last named being referred to as "an Englishman."

The defendants claimed self-defense as justification for their killings and the charges against them were dismissed. In June 1860, the depositions which were being taken when the killings occurred, were published in book form. After many years of searching, I found a copy and have had the same before me in writing this story. Dr. G. W. Clement, Sr., states in his foreword "To The Public" that "There were five justices on the bench of the Examining Court, three of whom were in favour of discharging the accused, and two for sending them on to further trial."

The courts record of the case shows the close of the case in the following words: "At a court continued and held for Franklin County at the Court House on the 23rd day of March 1860, for the examination of Vincent Witcher, John A. Smith, Vincent O. Smith, Samuel Swanson and Addison Witcher charged with the felonies aforesaid by them committed in this, that they did on the 25th day of February 1860, in the Counting Room of Dickinson's

Store in said county wilfully, deliberately and with premeditation murder and kill Ralph A. Clement, James R. Clement, and William C. Clement.

"Present: Richard M. Taliaferro, Robert Bush, Moses C. Greer, Jonathan H. McNeil and Isaac Cannady, General Justices.

"The said Vincent Witcher, John A. Smith, Vincent O. Smith, Samuel Swanson and Addison Witcher were again led to the bar in custody of the Jailor of this court. And the court having examined divers witnesses as well on behalf of the Commonwealth as of prisoners at the bar, who were heard in their defense by Counsel, is of the opinion that there is not probable cause for charging the said prisoners with the offense aforesaid and doth order that they be acquitted and go thereof without day."

For a half century, the acquittal of these men was pointed to by Franklin County citizens as an illustration of how extreme may be the miscarriage of justice. The Masonic fraternity in which membership was held by both the killers and the killed, did not treat the matter so lightly. After the court had, on the 23rd of March, acquitted the five men of the killings committed less than a month before, Thomas S. Muse and John P. Lovell, members of the Masonic Lodge which bore the name of Vincent Witcher, chief actor in the killings, wrote of "the unfortunate death of Brothers R. A. and James R. Clement who came to their death by the instrumentality of their brother in Masonry Vincent Witcher," and asked "that a committee of brethren be appointed whose duty it shall be to procure the evidence and make a report therefrom at our next regular communication." The reason given for "a thorough Masonic investigation," after the civil court had acquitted the killers, was stated in the following language: "The laws of a State are not the laws to try Brethren by who have offended against the Constitution and By laws of Masonry, that Civil law and Masonic law are as separate as Church and State." The Muse-Lovell document then asks "Would the Civil law punish a Brother for violating the secrets and mysteries of Masonry or its Constitution?"

Vincent Witcher Lodge No. 87 was chartered December 15, 1852, and had 39 members in 1860. The report of this lodge to the Grand Lodge for the year 1860 shows the deaths of R. A. and James R. Clement. The membership of the lodge down to

We the undersigned a minority of the Committee appointed at a Stated Communication of Vincent Witcher, on July 1654, Saturday evening the 3d of March last to look into the Case of the unfortunate death of Brothers R A & Jas R Clement who came to their death by the instrumentality of their Brother in masonry Vincent Witcher

Beg leave to Report that they Considerd a case for masonic investigation that the laws of a State are not the laws to try Bretheren by who have offended against the Constitution and Bylaws of Masonry that Civil law and masonic law are as Seperate as Church and State: Would the Civil law punish a Brother for violating the Secrets and mysteries of masonry or its constitution we think not We ask then inorder that this case may have a thorough masonic investigation that a Committee of Bretheren be appointed whose duty it Shall be to procure the Evidence and make a report therefrom at our next regular communication

all of which is Respectfully & Fraternally Submited

Thos S Muse
John P Jovell

A Masonic document relating to the Witcher-Clement feud
never before reproduced.

193

1860 includes the name of Vincent Witcher. The secretary of the Grand Lodge of Virginia, James N. Hillman, in a letter to the author writes, "I find no reference to him (Vincent Witcher) subsequent to 1860 in the list of expulsions, suspensions or membership. Evidently, something happened to him, but it is not reported in the minutes from that lodge." There were no returns from Vincent Witcher Lodge, No. 87, to the Grand Lodge, according to the minutes of 1860 to 1866. These were war years, however, and that fact, rather than the fraticidal strife, may be the explanation of the interruption of the lodge's activity. Vincent Witcher Lodge No. 87 lost its charter in 1885 for not having made a report in three years, and in 1886 is marked extinct. The number it bore is now borne by Naomi Lodge in Norfolk, but the name of Vincent Witcher, who shed the blood of his brother Masons, has not been perpetuated by Masonry.

THE LIQUOR CONSPIRACY CASE

After the illicit liquor traffic in Franklin County had become a notorious racket, the Federal Government placed men in the county to gather evidence to aid in ridding the county of the evil. Chief of these investigators was Col. Thomas Bailey of Pennsylvania.

The result of the investigation was that when a Federal grand jury sat in Harrisonburg in February 1935, thirty-four men were indicted for conspiracy against the United States Government. These thirty-four defendants were: Henry T. Abshire, Boone Mill, deputy sheriff; Edgar A. Beckett, Callaway, former state prohibition officer; Jack Bess, Roanoke; Thomas Cundiff, Penhook; Tom Cooper, Callaway; Robert P. DeHart, Shooting Creek; Leonard Davis, Martinsville; Earl Easter, Roanoke; Ferrum Mercantile Company, Inc.; Leonard L. Fralin, Union Hall; Charles Guilliams, Roanoke; C. P. Griffith, alias Cap Griffith, Ferrum; Charles Greer, Rocky Mount, deputy sheriff; D. Wilson Hodges, former Franklin Co. sheriff; Walter Hatcher, alias Peg Hatcher, Ferrum; Willard R. Hodges, Glade Hill; Posey Jones, Henry; Charles Carter Lee, Rocky Mount, Franklin County commonwealth's attorney; Howard L. Maxey, Ferrum, deputy sheriff; Grover L. Martin, Ferrum; Clifford Martin, Rocky Mount; Bu-

194

ford Nolen, Ferrum; Guy W. Nolen, Ferrum; David A. Nicholson, Ferrum, former member of the State legislature; Wilson Nicholson, Roanoke; Nick Prillaman, Prillaman's Switch; T. Roosevelt Smith, Ferrum; Claude Shively, Ferrum; J. O. Shiveley, Rocky Mount; Herman Shiveley, Ferrum; John H. Turner, Henry; Walter Turner, Henry; Will Wray, Henry, deputy sheriff; H. J. Wright, Union Hall; and Samuel O. White, former federal prohibition agent, Roanoke.

The following were named as co-conspirators but were not indicted: A. J. Bondurant, J. F. Bondurant, B. H. Bondurant, Joseph P. Hodges Jr., T. J. Richards, former deputy sheriff, deceased; Mrs. Willie Carter Sharpe, Ernest Daniels, George Dixon, Harry Dixon, T. Frank Davis, Herbert Foster, Quill Foster, Lee Guilliams, Thomas Guilliams, Willie Mason, Lewis Radford, Posey Webb, Harvey Worley, Ed. Sigmon, Norman Sigmon, Pete (J. P.) Sigmon, Esley (E. W.) Sledd, Lewis Melvin Scott, Will Stanley, Rufus Underwood, William McKinley Webb, Walter Willis, Alvin Wimmer, Owen Wimmer, Esley Wimmer, Dewey Jones, Roy Jones, Forest Dodson, Tony Ferguson, Kent Hodges, Coleman Lawrence, Leo C. Mays, alias Gummy Coleman, Cecil Steineke, Ursel Hurt, Ikey Levine, Dewey Merriman, Elmer ("Boss") Peters, Russell Steele, Melvin Nicholson, Rodney St. Clair, Ellis Sloane, Virgil Foster, Alphonso Hodges, George S. Hodges, Musco Barker, Luther Burnett, Clayton Bernard, Harry Bryant, J. P. Hodges, former sheriff, deceased, Charles L. Rakes, former deputy sheriff, deceased, and Willie Mason.

The trial began on April 22, 1935, before a jury composed of the following men: W. B. Abbott, Paint Bank; F. L. Carmell, Salem; E. H. Charlton, Christiansburg; George V. Downing, Salem; William Farrier, Sinking Creek; W. O. Goodwin, Glenvar; Herman Huffman, Newcastle; W. B. Humphries, Paint Bank; T. P. Lafon, Newcastle; W. B. Luttrell, Salem; L. E. Marshall, Indian Valley; and S. P. Mann, Newcastle. The alternates were: J. M. Peck, Fincastle, and H. E. Richardson, Meadows of Dan.

The defense lawyers included: H. Dalton Dillard, J. Bradie Allman, B. A. Davis, Sr., Henry Davis, and B. A. Davis Jr., of Rocky Mount; Joseph C. Shaffer, of Wytheville, Samuel R. Price, R. Lee Carney and T. Warren Messick, of Roanoke; Stephen O. Timberlake and J. Wesley Taylor of Staunton and John W. Carter of Danville.

The prosecutors were: Sterling Hutcheson, United States attorney for the eastern district of Virginia and special prosecutor
for the attorney general before the Harrisonburg investigation,
assisted by Frank Tavenner, assistant to Joseph H. Chitwood, of
the western district. Before the venire had been exhausted and
a jury selected, four of the defendants, W. Wilson Hodges, former sheriff of Franklin Co., Leonard L. Fralin, of Union Hall,
H. J. Wright, of Union Hall, and Thomas C. Cundiff, of Penhook, entered pleas of guilty. Pleas of nole contendere were entered for the Ferrum Mercantile Company, of Ferrum, and the
four partners in the firm, Grover L. Martin, Guy W. Nolen, C.
Buford Nolen and Herman Shiveley; Robert P. DeHart, of Shooting Creek, Nick Prillaman, of Prillaman's Switch and C. C. Greer,
of Rocky Mount.

Pleas of not guilty for the remaining twenty-three defendants, which had been entered at a continued session of the Court
March 4th, were allowed to stand.

Sherwood Anderson, one of America's noted authors, attended the trial, as did the author of this volume. He wrote a
story about the trial which appeared in LIBERTY magazine of
November 2, 1935. Fred O. Maier of Standard Brands also attended and testified that 70,448 pounds of a single standard brand
yeast was sold in Franklin county in four years. There were other
startling figures introduced by the government on the purchases
of commodities necessary to illicit liquor making, such as sugar,
33,839,109 pounds; corn meal, 13,307,477 pounds; rye meal,
2,408,308 pounds; malt, 1,018,420 pounds; hops, 30,366 pounds;
and miscellaneous grain products, 15,276,071 pounds; non-gurgling
five-gallon tin cans, 600,000.

It was the contention of the government in the conspiracy
trial that "the little fellows" had been put out of business. The
county had been divided off into sections, a big blockader and
a state officer for each section. Some of the big operators didn't
make any liquor at all. They let out the distilling to other men.
There were men running stills for "the big fellows" and turning
out liquor for a few cents per gallon. The government had two
attorneys. The indicted men had a dozen. In a United States
Court, the judge can question witnesses and make comments.
One of the lawyers pleading with the jury for his client said,

"Men, send him back where he came from: send him back to his mountain home." The judge interrupted: "You mean, send him back to keep making the same kind of mean whisky he was making."

There was a prominent business man at the trial who openly expressed his admiration for Willie Carter Sharpe, a slender black-haired woman of thirty, who had a passion for automobiles and fast driving. The business man said: "I saw her go right through the main street of our town with a federal car after her. They were banging away, trying to shoot down her tires, and she was driving at 75 miles an hour, but she got away." He liked her, as did everyone in the courtroom. She told her story frankly. "It was the excitement that got me," she said, "and most other rum-runners employed by the big shots. They were mostly kids who liked the thrill of it. There were women of aristocratic families who wanted to go along with me on a night run just for the kick of it."

One of the accused men who had pled guilty said, "I'm glad it's over. This big way of doing it had got too big and too cruel. It was bringing out too many ugly things in men. We don't want our county to be like that. This'll clean things up."

After the testimony was all in, assistant district attorney Frank S. Tavenner spent nearly seven hours in building up his argument for the prosecution from the enormous amount of evidence brought by four hundred witnesses into the case of twenty-three persons of Franklin and Roanoke counties indicted for conspiracy to violate the internal revenue laws of the United States and to defraud it of taxes due on illicitly manufactured whiskey.

Answering two questions, first, "Was there a Conspiracy?" and second, "Who are guilty of participating?" the prosecutor brought together the evidence into a compact and vigorous argument. Especial stress was laid on the enormous amount of sugar and yeast shipped into three districts of Franklin. "If the yeast shipped into three districts of the county alone were manufactured into bread," he said, "the loaves, if laid end, to end, would stretch 1245 miles, or from here to Omaha, Nebraska. "The sugar would be enough for two tons per person, while the five-gallon cans, if flattened out, would be enough tin to roof 2,900 homes of 40x40 feet."

"The tax alone on the liquor the government has shown to have been hauled out, not including the 200,000 gallons accredited to Mrs. Willie Carter Sharpe, would amount to $5,500,000."

"It is a monument of mystery," he said, but there must be

a reason for it. The shadow of that monument reaches to Roanoke, to Lynchburg. It extends from the Atlantic Ocean west to West Virginia, to Maryland. And still the officials of Franklin claim to know nothing about it. If this be true, then I say to you that it is also a monument to ignorance."

The prosecutor told how the payment of protection money for distilleries become so common in Franklin that it gained the name of "granny fee," a definition known to everyone.

"That was the picture, gentlemen, he declared, "these officers conniving with bootleggers." That nefarious business has continued until it has culminated in one of the greatest eras of crime that we know. From evil seed an evil crop will surely flourish, and it has flourished."

Each defendant was taken separately, and the evidence against that defendant was held once more up to the jury as Tavenner argued for the credibility of the government witnesses and stated that the government case had been built around testimony that had scarcely been attacked by the defense.

Tavenner pointed out that the defense claimed at the beginning the government would rely chiefly on the testimony of Bridges, Cundiff, and Bailey, but that Bridges had been referred to chiefly, that Cundiff was scarcely mentioned in his summary, and that Bailey hadn't even testified. "No investigator who worked on the case has testified because it wasn't necessary," he declared.

The trial came to an end after more than ten weeks, second longest in the history of Virginia, and two days after the case was committed to the jury.

E. H. Charlton, foreman of the jury, handed the verdict to Chief Deputy Marshal E. C. Garrard, who handed it to C. E. Gentry, Clerk of the Court. The Clerk read the verdict while hardly a sound was audible save for a gasp of surprise or relief here and there in the sweltering courtroom.

Those convicted, in order named by the jury, were: Samuel O. White, of Huntington, W. Va., under suspension from the Alcoholic Tax Unit and former Federal prohibition agent, sta' tioned at Roanoke; Edgar A. Beckett, Callaway, former State prohibition inspector; Henry T. Abshire, Boone Mill, deputy sheriff; Walter Hatcher, alias "Peg" Hatcher, of near Ferrum; T. Roosevelt Smith, of near Ferrum; Willard R. Hodges, of Glade Hill; John H. Turner, Henry; Walter Turner, Henry; David A. Nicholson, of Ferrum, former member of the General Assembly; Claude Shiveley, Ferrum; J. O. Shiveley, Rocky Mount; Jack Bess, Roanoke; Tom Cooper, Callaway; Leonard Davis, Martins' ville; Earl Easter, Roanoke; Wilson Nicholson, Ferrum; Charles Guilliams, Roanoke; Posey Jones, Henry; Clifford Martin, Rocky Mount; C. P. Griffith, alias "Cap" Griffith, Ferrum.

Those not guilty were: Charles Carter Lee, commonwealth's attorney of Franklin County; Will Wray, of Henry, deputy sher' iff; Howard L. Maxey, of Ferrum, deputy sheriff.

Eleven others stood bound by the verdict, four who had pled guilty on April 22nd and seven others, and a corporation, who had entered pleas of nolo contendere the same day.

Those who pled guilty were: D. Wilson Hodges, of Rocky Mount, former sheriff; Leonard L. Fralin of Union Hall; H. J. ("Jake") Wright, of Union Hall; Tom C. Cundiff, of Penhook, under sentence to the State penitentiary for three years for felon' ious wounding. All these testified for the government.

Those who pled nolo contendere were: Ferrum Mercantile Company, Inc.; Grover L. Martin, Ferrum; Guy W. Nolen, Fer' rum; C. Buford Nolen, Ferrum; Herman Shiveley, Ferrum; Rob' ert P. DeHart, Shooting Creek; Nick Prilliman of Prillaman's Switch; and C. C. Greer, of Rocky Mount, former deputy sheriff. The first four men were partners in the corporation.

Judge John Paul, on July 9, 1935, pronounced sentences on those convicted as follows: Henry T. Abshire, deputy sheriff, Boone Mill, 18 months and $3,000; Edgar A. Beckett, former state prohibition inspector, of Callaway, 2 years and $5,000; Jack Bess, of Roanoke, 15 months and $2,000; Tom Cooper, of Calla' way, 4 months; Leonard Davis, Martinsville, 9 months and $1,000; Earl Easter, Roanoke, 9 months and $1,000; Charles Guilliams,

Roanoke, 9 months and $1,000; C. P. Griffith, of near Ferrum, 4 months; Willard R. Hodges, Glade Hill, 15 months and $3,500; Walter ("Peg") Hatcher of near Ferrum, 15 months and $3,000; Posey Jones, Henry, 6 months and $750; Clifford Martin, Rocky Mount, 15 months and $3,000; David A. Nicholson, Ferrum, 9 months (suspended) and $500; Wilson Nicholson, Ferrum, 6 months and $750; T. Roosevelt Smith, of near Ferrum, 15 months and $3,000; Claude Shiveley, Ferrum, 6 months (suspended) and $1,000; J. O. Shiveley, Rocky Mount, 15 months and $3,000; John H. Turner, of Henry, 15 months and $3,000; Walter Turner, Henry, 15 months and $3,000; Samuel O. White, of Huntington, West Va., and Roanoke, former federal prohibition agent, 15 months and $2,000.

On the nolo contendere pleas, the following fines were imposed: Ferrum Mercantile Company, Inc., $3,000; Grover L. Martin, $500; C. Buford Nolen, $500; Guy W. Nolen, $500; Herman Shively, $2,500; Robert P. DeHart, of Shooting Creek, $3,500; Nick Prillaman, of Prillaman's Switch, $4,500.

Placed on probation were five who pleaded guilty: D. Wilson Hodges, former sheriff of Franklin; Charles C. Greer, former deputy sheriff; Leonard L. Fralin, Union Hall; H. J. ("Jake") Wright, Union Hall; Tom C. Cundiff of Penhook.

It was stated on good authority, that the trial cost the defense $12,800 for attorney fees. Very few witnesses were paid. The cost of the case to the government was in excess of $100,000.

The Roanoke Times and the World-News of Roanoke commented, in part, as follows: "The verdict in the Franklin County liquor conspiracy trial constitutes sweeping confirmation of previous allegations of the existence of an organized whiskey ring in the county. That there had been extensive moonshine and liquor-running operations in Franklin County for years was general knowledge. It was not to establish that fact that the Federal grand jury at Harrisonburg in February returned indictments against some of the best known citizens of the county, including the Commonwealth's Attorney, a former Federal prohibition agent and several deputy sheriffs. What the Government sought to prove, and succeeded in establishing to the satisfaction of a jury, was that a whiskey conspiracy had existed with ramifications reaching into the political and social life of the county.

"The trial was presided over by Judge John Paul whose high reputation for dignity, ability, impartiality and legal acumen was enhanced by his conduct of the proceedings during the past ten weeks. The prosecution was ably conducted and the defendants were represented by a distinguished array of counsel.

"More than 400 witnesses were examined exhaustively, the case being put together with great skill and thoroughness for the consideration of the jury. Judge Paul expressed high praise for the jury, saying that its members represented a high type of citizenship and that its actions renewed his belief in the American jury system.

"It was established by the evidence that sugar, malt, yeast, etc. had been shipped into the county in quantities running into several million dollars, the disclosures bringing from C. C. Lee, commonwealth's attorney, admission of his amazement at the extent of the liquor business in Franklin.

"Now that the trial is over, it is in order to express the wide-spread sympathy which is felt, no doubt, for the law-abiding citizens of Franklin in the stigma that has been placed on the good name of their county. Many of the best citizens of Roanoke have come from Franklin, contributing in marked degree to the upbuilding and development of this community. It goes without saying that a neighborly good will is felt, and with it an understanding of the peculiar problems of law enforcement under the conditions that have existed in Franklin.

"When the Treasury Department was informed that gigantic illicit liquor operations exceeding an output of 1,000 gallons a day, were going on in Franklin, Treasury Operative Thomas Bailey was selected to make an investigation. For more than a year Bailey lived in Franklin, becoming acquainted with its conditions, its citizens, and the extent to which operations in illicit liquor were carried on. His report to the Treasury Department confirmed former reports of investigators for the Wickersham Commission and went into much more detail as to the system under which illicit liquor was being manufactured and sold.

"That report the Treasury Department placed in the hands of United States District Judge John Paul, and United States District Attorney, Sterling Hutcheson. It formed the basis of

201

the prolonged grand jury investigation held at Harrisonburg, when the vast liquor operations were uncovered. It formed the basis of the ten weeks' trial in which twenty persons were convicted and eleven others entered pleas of guilty or nolo contendere. It formed the basis of the grand jury report in which many others were named as co-conspirators, but were not indicted.

"Through the preliminary investigation, through the grand jury inquiry, and through the prolonged trial, Colonel Bailey furnished to the prosecuting lawyers definite statements on which to base their interrogations of witnesses, and their orderly presentation of evidence.

"During the war, Bailey won medals as a sharpshooter. At target practice he is rated as a crack shot among government agents who are trained to shoot. But in Franklin county he went unarmed. He won the confidence of the people, and more than once was invited to stay for dinner with those whose stills had only recently been destroyed by government agents. Month after month he worked to win the cooperation of the mountain people, and today is hailed as the man who, more than any other, has rid Franklin county of the stain on its good name."

But Franklin County was not rid of the stain on its good name as the Roanoke press supposed.

Nearly one year after the famous liquor conspiracy trial, 24 persons were indicted at Harrisonburg for conspiring to influence the jury in that trial. Of the 24, Edgar A. Beckett and Samuel O. White entered pleas of guilty. Amos Rakes, Hugh Rakes, Ed Rakes, E. T. Marshall, David A. Nicholson and C. Will Ray entered pleas of not guilty.

Pleas of nolo contendere were entered by: Herman Shiveley, Henry T. Abshire, J. W. ("Peg") Hatcher, T. R. Smith, W. R. Hodges, John H. Turner, Walter Turner, Claude Shiveley, Jack Bess, Leonard Davis, Earl Easter, Charles Guilliams, M. Clifford Martin, C. Wilson Nicholson and Thomas L. Foster.

It is interesting to note that the two who pleaded guilty had been federal prohibition officers. E. T. Marshall lived at Belair, Md., and was said to be a son of L. E. Marshall, member of the jury. C. Will Ray was a former Franklin County deputy sheriff.

Of the 24 indicted, one, S. Claude Slusher, committed suicide before trial which took place in May 1936.

During the trial of the men charged with conspiring to bribe the jury of 1935, an editorial appeared in the Norfolk VIR-GINIAN PILOT reading as follows: "Somebody ought to write a book about Franklin County, Virginia. It would include sec-tions on:

1. The original unofficial investigation in prohibition days which led the investigators to characterize Franklin County as one of the worst liquor centers in the country;

2. The long-drawn-out investigation by Federal officials—itself a task of months—and the subsequent long-drawn-out grand jury action, which again was a task of months; and the eventful trial of 34 persons in the great Franklin County liquor ring which resulted in the conviction of 20, the admission of guilt by 5 others, pleas of nolo contendere for six more, and acquittal for only three;

3. The discovery by Federal Judge John Paul, months later, that a batch of those found guilty and sentenced, were, under pretense of preparing their appeals, continuing the operations for which they had been convicted and were also participating actively in political campaigns; and his summary orders that they go to jail immediately and begin serving their sentences, and the Circuit Court of Appeals' confirmation of his action;

4. The further investigation by Federal officials, which spread over many months, resulting now in indictments against 24 persons, including 17 of those previously convicted and one acquitted, on new charges of conspiring to influence the jury in the original action against them. If sustained, these charges will demonstrate that just as there were few limits to which the Frank-lin County liquor ring would not go to insure good business for itself by buying off officers of the law and cramping the style of competitors, so there were few limits to which it would not go to try to buy off the jury.

Somebody, we say, ought to write a book about Franklin County and the extraordinary revelations of these several and continuing actions. But if anybody does, it is to be hoped that he will not be merely a dramatist. He ought also to be enough the sociologist and economist to probe deep beneath the surface in an effort to understand first causes in Franklin County. For people in Franklin County were not any worse in the beginning than people in other counties. A large number of them were lured by the easy profits from illegal liquor, and some of them were shrewd enough to organize it on a business-like basis. The results are spread in the records of these court actions. It is an extra-ordinary picture of how men, once having become tangled up with such ventures, became deeper and deeper entangled."

THOMAS ARTHUR

Thomas Arthur was the stormy petrel of early Franklin County political life. The county as a judicial unit had not been functioning six months when Arthur made an attack upon its chief citizen, Colonel Hugh Innis. On May 20, 1786, Arthur wrote to Governor Patrick Henry, "opposing the appointment of Hugh Innes, Col. Commanding of that County, on the ground that his age, his being inactive, and never shew'd his Friendship to the Commonwealth in our last War, and have generally been sus-pected to disaffection, and certainly not without a Just cause . . . A large majority of the Militia and old Officers with myself con-ceive, shou'd he meet with his appointment, it might be attended with bad consequences. I hope his Excellency, for the great Trust repos'd in him for the Ease and benefit of his Subjects, will take it under consideration, &c." (1)

On February 25, 1791, County Lieutenant Peter Saunders presented to Arthur an indictment written and signed by himself and reading as follows: "Sir, you will take Notice that you are arrested as an officer of the Militia of this County for the follow-ing charges, viz: For forging the hand John Gipson to a warrant to Turn Coonroad Hartcrider, Out of Possession in January 1788. Also for Being Concerned and assisting in forging an order from Sarah Grayham to the Sheriff of Franklin County to pay the same to George Asberry; also for forging the hand of Thomas Prunty to Certain Receipts for the payment of a certain sum of money to the amount of £ 3 o s, 7½ d. dated the 20th of Janu-ary 1788; also for forging the hand of George Turnbull, Esquire; also for suppos'd Forgery in making Oath before the Judges of

1. Calendar of Virginia State Papers, vol. 4, pp. 136-37.

the District Court at New London in April, 1790, that Isaac Rentfro was not able to attend as a witness in your suit and Thomas Livsay's; also for a charge alleged against you for Bearing false witness in the suit of Mrs. Guthery against Hugh Innes; also a charge of Drawing a larger sum of money out of the Treasury when in the Assembly than you was entitled to, and for lying and not conducting yourself as an officer of the Militia." (2)

On March 8, 1791, Stephen Smith, Clerk of the Franklin County Court, sent to the Governor a copy of the court order in the trial of Thomas Arthur, reading as follows: "At a court held and Continued for Franklin County, on Tuesday, the 8th of March, 1791. Present: Hugh Innis, John Smith, Swinfield Hill, Thomas Hale, John Hook, Benjamin Cook, Daniel Brown and David Barton, Gentlemen. Ordered, that it be certifyed to the Executive that Thomas Arthur, one of the Justices of the Peace for this County, from his conduct heretofore, is by the Court thought to be of Infamous character. That he stands charged before the Hon'ble the District Court with Forgery, also for forg- ing the name of George Turnbull, Gl., to a Certificate of the Proof of Notice to Thomas Livsey in a suit then Depending in the District Court; for which the Grand Jury of this County found a True Bill, from which charges this Court conceive his char- acter to be Infamous, and refuseth to set on the Bench of Justice with him; that he frequently Intersepts the Court in the Progress of the Business of the County by Takeing a seat on the Bench." (3)

On March 29, 1791, Peter Saunders, County Lieutenant of Franklin County, wrote to Governor Randolph as follows: "Sir, I have Inclosed your Excellency a Coppy of charges against Colo. Thomas Arthur, for which I have arrested him, and Further Proceedings I shall Leave to your Determination. You will find also Inclosed the Record of the Court of this County against him. A letter lodged with Mr. James Freeland, Merchant in Manchester, will be forwarded by him to your

Hum'l Serv't." (4)

In the "Diary of Richard N. Venable, 1791-92" he records that on January 22, 1791, he went to Franklin County Court-

2. Ibid, vol. 5, pp. 278-279.
3. Ibid, vol. 5, pp. 270-271.
4. Ibid, vol. 5, pp. 278-279.

house, called on Sam Callands, visited Peytonsburg in Pittsylvania County, and thence back to his home in Prince Edward County. On March 3, 1791, he returned to Franklin County Courthouse (he was a lawyer) and "When Thomas Arthur came on the bench, the rest of the Court immediately ran off and left Arthur sitting like an owl on a chicken roost. Arthur left the bench and we proceeded to business." (5)

Arthur migrated to Knox county, Kentucky, soon after suffering this disgrace and there became active in public life. Governor Garrard appointed him a captain of Militia in 1798. He died in 1832 full of years and honors. His descendants are numerous and highly respected.

JAMES CALLAWAY

The Callaway family lived in that area of Bedford County which was cut off to help form Franklin County in 1784. The family had residence in the Bedford area even before Bedford County was formed from Lunenburg County in 1753. Among the Bedford Callaways who furnished supplies or served in the Militia during the French and Indian War were James, Richard and William. (1)

The General Assembly held in Williamsburg September 14th, 1758, passed "An act for the Frontiers of this Colony, and for other purposes therein mentioned." In the schedule to which this act refers is found the payments to the Militia of the several counties, "and for Provisions furnished by sundry Inhabitants" thereof. Under the Schedule of Bedford, James Callaway is named four times as recipient of payments ranging from eight shillings to seven pounds. In the report of "Disbursements from Auditors Office" is a list of warrants issued between 1st October 1792 and December 31st, 1792, which includes one to James Callaway for £2 5 10. (2)

William Callaway in 1761, "made a free gift of 100 acres of land in the county of Bedford, adjoining the courthouse of the

5. Tylers Quarterly, vol. 2, p. 135.

1. William and Mary Quarterly (1st series) vol. 3, p. 275.
2. Hening's Statutes, vol. 7, pp. 204, 207, 210, 211, 475 and Calendar of Virginia State Papers, Vol. 6, p. 226.

said county, to be settled into a town," known by the name of New London. During the Revolution New London contained some 70-80 houses. It is also recorded that "The Court doth order that the trustees for the county lay out the land . . . in Lotts of half acre each, as long again as wide, to be sold for £1, 1. 8 each, provided the purchaser shall build a house fraimed twenty by sixteen on each Lott within one year after purchasing, and a brick or stone chimney within four years, and that the subscribers for the said Lotts after being numbered draw "their Lotts at May Court, and that the said town be called by the name of New London." James Callaway is listed as the purchaser of Lott No. 2 of his father's 100 acre gift. Colo. John Smith who became one of the early Justices of Franklin County was the purchaser of Lott No. 11. Lott No. 10 was designated for the courthouse site. Wm. Wirt Henry, in writing the life of his grandfather, Patrick Henry, listed James Callaway as a representative of Bedford in the House of Burgesses which met November 6th, 1766, prorogued to March 31, 1768." (3)

In the Act establishing the town of New London (Nov. 1761) James Callaway was appointed trustee. In the "Act for disposing of the glebe of Russell parish" in Bedford County, (May 1779) so that a more convenient glebe might be purchased, James Callaway, Jeremiah Early, William Leftwich, John Quarles, and Richard Stith are named "gentlemen in trust." (4)

The Callaway family was also active in Campbell County which was cut off from Bedford County in 1781. A Campbell County Order Book shows that on February 7, 1782, at the house of Micajah Terrell there was read "a Commission of the Peace and Oyer and Terminer for this county under the seal of the State, bearing date the 1st day of February Instant—directed to: Samuel Hairston, Richard Stith, John Fitzpatrick, James Callaway, Charles Lynch, Francis Thorp, John Talbot, John Ward, John Hunter, George Stovall Jr., John Callaway, Robert Adams Jr., and William Henderson, Gentlemen, or any four or more of them, with authority as well to execute within the limits of the said County their duties of the said office prescribed by Law, as to be of a Court to be held for the said County." John Ward and John

3. Virginia Magazine, vol. 4, p. 380, and Hening's Statutes, vol. 7, pp. 203, 473-476.
4. Hening's Statutes, vol. 7, p. 475.

Hunter then administered the oath of a Justice of the Peace to Samuel Hairston who in turn administered the oath to James Callaway and the others aforenamed. On this same date (Feb. 7) "Francis Thorp produced a Commission appointing him Sheriff of the County" and James Callaway, John Callaway, Harry Innis and James Steptoe appeared as his securities or bondsmen. On the next day (Feb. 8) "James Callaway was recommended for appointment as County Lieutenant." The recommendation must have been tardy as he produced his commission from the Governor and took the oath of office. The same James Callaway was listed by the Court as among the citizens furnishing Supplies, Arms, Teams, &c or rendering other service to the Continental Army, and who received certificates calling for payments account thereof, at various sessions of the County Court of Campbell County, between 7th March 1782 and 4th April 1782. (5)

In the Bedford County Committee of Safety chosen May 23, 1775, the Callaway family was represented by three members, (6) James, John and William: Other members of the committee whose names appear among early Franklin County records were: Wm. Meade, John Ward, Charles Lynch, John Quarles, Haynes Morgan, George Stovall, James Steptoe, Guy Smith, Simon Miller, Wm. Trigg and Gross Scruggs.

An Act was passed in October 1782 to indemnify Robert Adams Jr., James Callaway, Charles Lynch and William Preston for suppressing "divers evil disposed persons in the year 1780, (who) formed a conspiracy and did actually attempt to levy war against the Commonwealth." (7)

An article published in the Richmond Standard for November 1, 1879, refers to Henings' Statutes at large Vol. XI pp. 134-135 in support of the connection of Charles Lynch with the lynch law. The story is that in 1780 Southwest Virginia was infested by a band of Tories who committed outrages upon defenceless inhabitants. Then, as the act recites, "Wm. Preston, Robert Adams, Jun., Jas. Callaway and Chas. Lynch and other faithful citizens aided by detachments of volunteers from different parts of the State, did by timely and effectual measures, suppress such conspiracies by measures not strictly warranted by law, although justifiable from the imminence of the danger." (8)

5. Virginia Magazine, vol. 4, p. 380.
6. William and Mary Quarterly, vol. 5, p. 253.
7. Hening's Statutes, vol. 11, pp. 134-135.
8. William and Mary Quarterly, 1st series, vol. 13, pp. 204-205.

In the Bedford-Franklin area there lingers the tradition of a song of the Revolution which contained the lines:

"Hurrah for Captain Bob, Colonels Lynch and Callaway!
They never let a Tory rest till he cries out 'Liberty!' "

A list of the Justices for Bedford County, Va., as of November 8, 1770, includes John Phelps, Robt. Ewing, Chas. Talbot, Wm. Mead, Samuel Hairston, Richard Stith, Joseph Rentfro, Jeremiah Early, James Callaway, Charles Lynch, Hugh Challis, Francis Thorp, Joel Meador, John Pate, Gross Scruggs, Robert Owen and James Donald. (9)

In an Act for forming a new county out of the counties of Bedford and Henry, (Oct. 1785) to be named Franklin, it was provided that the justices for the new county should "meet at the house of James Callaway at his iron works." (10)

An Act. (Dec. 12, 1792) reducing into one, the several acts concerning the establishment, jurisdiction and powers of District Courts, Provides that the district court for the counties of Bedford, Campbell, Franklin, Pittsylvania, Patrick and Henry, "shall be holden for the same at New London, in the late courthouse of Bedford County, now belonging to James and John Callaway, who have agreed to put the same in repair at their own expense for the use of the district court. (11) James Callaway was Clerk of the Franklin County Court from 1791 to 1813. (12) He was married three times and had twenty-two children of whom the eldest was James, Jr. The public life of James Jr., was contemporaneous with that of his father for so long a period that the activities of the two are often confused.

9. Calendar Virginia State Papers, vol. 1, p. 265.
10. Hening's Statutes, vol. 12, pp. 70-71.
11. Ibid, vol. 13, p. 429.
12. Old Virginia Clerks by F. Johnston, Lynchburg, Va., 1888, page 179.

SPENCER CLACK

So little is known of this early justice of Franklin County that some have attributed the name to a misspelling of Clark. The name Clack no longer exists in Franklin County as a surname. Recalling that a member of the Hopkins family bears it as a Christian name I wrote Colonel Walter L. Hopkins asking if the name of his brother Dr. Clack Hopkins indicates relation to the family now extinct so far as Franklin County is concerned. He replied: "My brother, Clack, (a half brother), is not related to the Clack family. He was named for his uncle Clack Smith of Penhook who was named for a Miss Clack, a governess in the Smith family."

Henry County records show that in March 1782 Spencer Clack was allowed 42 shillings three pence for 58 pounds of bacon which he supplied to the hospital at Henry Courthouse in March 1781. (1) Records in the Clerk's office of the same county show that on March 29, 1783, Spencer Clack was "appointed to take a List of Souls, the List of Tythes, and a list of Taxable Property" (2) in the Militia companies of Tully Choice and William Ryon.

JOHN DICKINSON

There are two stories of the origin of the Dickinsons of Franklin County. One story says the family is one with the Eastern Maryland family whose genealogy is given by Tilghman in his History of Talbot County. The other story says the family came from Pennsylvania and that Franklin County John was related to Pennsylvania John whose patriotic writings, published by Wm. Rind of Williamsburg, Va., made him a valued friend of Patrick Henry and Richard Henry Lee.

However that may be, the Dickinsons were in the area before Franklin County was formed. The marriage bonds of Pittsylvania County reveal that John Dickinson was bondsman in the marriage of William Letcher and Elizabeth Perkins, November 20, 1778. (1) According to the marriage bonds in the Henry County Clerk's Office, John Dickinson himself was married to

1. Virginia Magazine, vol. 10, p. 73.
2. Ibid, vol. 11, p. 92.

1. William & Mary Quarterly, 1st series, vol. 6, p. 221.

Isbell Woods on June 2, 1781. (2) He witnessed the will of Mark Payne of Pittsylvania County which was probated March 25, 1775. (3)

In a List of State Pensioners presented to the Governor by Act of General Assembly October 1782, directing courts of the several counties to make returns respecting all persons receiving pensions, Captain John Dickinson is listed as recipient of a pension of fifty pounds. (4)

JOHN EARLY

"An Act of Dec. 16, 1790 for clearing the Roanoke river from the Falls upward to the fork of Dan and Staunton rivers and up the said Dan and Staunton rivers to the heads thereof," named Henry Coleman, Richard Kennon, Samuel Hopkins, Samuel Goode, George Carrington, Thomas Watkins, Clement Carrington, William Terry, William Morton, John Wilson, JOHN EARLY, Matthew Clay, Meade Anderson, George Hairston and Archibald Hughes. (1)

On November 12, 1792, John Early of Franklin County was chosen to represent the district composed of Bedford, Campbell, Franklin, Henry and Patrick counties as Elector to vote for a President and Vice President of the United States. His name also appears among those persons to whom warrants were issued by the Auditor's office on December 31, 1792. He drew (2) £25. 5. 3.

Trustees for a town to be built on Moses Grier's 40 acres in Franklin County included John Early, Jacob Boon, John Northsinger, Daniel Barnhart, Samuel Thompson, William Wright, Jun., and William Turnbull. (3)

JOHN FERGUSON

In the "List of Land and Tithes" taken by Hugh Innes for Pittsylvania County in 1767, when the county embraced all of

2. Virginia Magazine, vol. 21, p. 278.
3. Ibid, vol. 19, p. 425.
4. William and Mary Quarterly, 1st series, vol. 20, p. 13.

1. Hening's Statutes, Vol. 7, p. 186.
2. Calendar Virginia State Papers, Vol. 6, pp. 133, 134, 215.
3. Hening, Vol. 13, p. 585.

Henry County and half of Franklin, will be found the names William Cook, John Callaway, Robert Prunty, Bragan Prunty, Abraham Motley, James Rentfro, Joseph Rentfro, Benjamin Griffith, William Griffith, Swinfield Hill and John Ferguson. (1)

The records in the Henry County Clerk's Office show that in March 1782 John Ferguson was allowed 18 shillings, 9 pence for 25 pounds of Bacon and 14 shillings for 14 diets to British prisoners and their guard enroute from the Southward to Winchester in May 1781. At the same time he was also allowed three pounds, 11 shillings and one pence for 151½ pounds pork, 12 pounds bacon and one and a half gallons of corn for Hospital at Henry Court House. (2)

JOHN GIPSON

The author has found the following only concerning John Gipson: "It having been proven That JOHN GIPSON, a Justice of the Peace for said County (of Franklin) who had removed therefrom, but in passing and re-passing through the same, continueth to act as such, the Court on this account, and from the many Illegal practices of the said Gipson, expelled him from office, and order the Clerk to certify the same to the Executive." (1)

With reference to John Gipson's expulsion, it would not be difficult to support the contention that a number of non-resident celebrities, visiting in the new county, were asked to sit with the justices as though they were actually members of the court.

MOSES GREER

On November 10, 1792 the General Assembly passed an Act "that forty acres of land in the county of Franklin, the property of Moses Grier, shall be and they are hereby vested in John Early, Jacob Boon, John Northsinger, Daniel Barnhart, Samuel Thompson, William Wright, junior, William Turnbull, and Swinfield Hill, gentlemen, trustees, to be by them, or a majority of them, laid off into lots of half an acre each, with convenient

1. Virginia Magazine, vol. 24, p. 192.
2. Ibid, vol. 10, p. 73.

1. Calendar Virginia State Papers, Vol. 4, p. 405.

streets, and established a town by the name of Wisenburgh. And that 32 acres of land lying in the County of Franklin, the property of Daniel Layman and Stephen Peters, as the same are already laid off into lots and streets, be, and they are hereby a town by the name of Germantown, and Swinfield Hill, George Turnbull, Jacob Harkrider, Daniel Pearry, Jubal Early, John Fargarson and Tobias Miller, gentlemen, constituted and appointed trustees thereof.

"So soon as the said lands of George Brent and Moses Grier shall respectively be laid off into lots, the trustees of each or a majority of them, shall proceed to sell the same at public auction, for the best price than can be had, the time and place of such sale being previously advertised two months successively in the Virginia Gazette, and to convey the said lots to the purchasers thereof in fee, subject to the condition of building on each a dwelling-house sixteen feet square at least, with a brick or stone chimney, to be finished and fit for habitation within five years from the day of sale, and pay the money arising from such sales to the proprietors of the said lands respectively, or their legal representatives.

"The trustees of the said towns respectively, or a majority of them, are empowered to make such rules and orders for the regular building of houses therein, as to them shall seem best, and to settle and determine all disputes concerning the bounds of the said lots." (1) In the disbursements from the Auditor's Office October 1, 1792 to December 31, 1792, was a warrant issued to Moses Greer for eighteen pounds. (2)

On January 23, 1800, 93 members of the Legislature and a number of other respectable persons met for the purpose of naming proper persons in the several districts to be supported as Electors of a President and Vice President. Moses Greer was named along with Henry Calloway, Benjamin Cook, Samuel Hairston and Robert Innes, all of Franklin County. (3)

On February 1, 1802, Moses Greer wrote Governor James Monroe that since a resolution had passed the General Assembly authorizing the Governor to appoint a Commission to establish the Western Boundary Line between Virginia and Maryland, he would feel himself highly honored if the Governor and Council of States would appoint him one of the Commissioners. (4)

1. Hening's Statutes, vol. 13, pp. 585-586.
2. Calendar Virginia State Papers, vol. 6, p. 203.
3. Ibid, vol. 9, pp. 74-78.
4. Ibid, vol. 9, p. 277.

THOMAS HALE

When Franklin County was formed, Thomas Hale was living in that portion of Henry County which was incorporated in the new county. He was commissioned almost immediately as a justice of the Franklin County Court. In the first list of tithables of Pittsylvania County (1767) Thomas Hale's name appears in the list taken by John Donelson. (1) Before the Henry County Court of June 1780, Thomas Hale, James Poteet, Owen Rubel, James Cowden, George Hairston and John Fontaine took their oaths as captains of the Henry County Militia. (2) Hale had been appointed in 1779 "in the room of Peter Vardeman."

In the list of Militia ordered from Henry County to the assistance of General Greene there was a company commanded by Captain Thomas Hale. His lieutenants and ensigns were Jesse Cook, Jesse Coats, Joseph Hale, Peter Anderson and Joseph Richards. (3)

The staff of Captain Hale was increased in June 1781 when Joseph Jones and Luke Standeford were commissioned lieutenants and Thomas Hill was made an ensign. (4)

In the levy made by the Henry County Court in March 1779, Thomas Hale was given 16 pounds of tobacco "for 1 Tythe over paid last year," (5) and in May 1782, the Henry County Court allowed him one shilling and six pence for three gallons of corn furnished Jesse Heard. (6)

His name is perpetuated in Franklin County by Hale's Ford, attached to both a river crossing and a post office. In the early records the name is also spelled Hail and Haile.

GEORGE HANCOCK

George Hancock was in Bedford before Franklin County was formed. He was born June 13, 1754, and married Margaret, daughter of George and Mary (Kennerly) Strother. His sojourn in Franklin County was brief. He removed to Fincastle and when his home there burned, he built Fotheringay near Big Spring.

1. Clement's History of Pittsylvania County, Virginia, p. 276.
2. Virginia Magazine, vol. 9, pp. 263, 264, 417.
3. Ibid, vol. 17, p. 193.
4. Ibid, vol. 9, p. 421.
5. Ibid, vol. 9, p. 265.
6. Ibid, vol. 10, p. 74.

He was a colonel in the Virginia line of the Revolutionary War, a lawyer and a member of the Fourth Congress. He voted for Jay's Treaty, was rejected by his constituents and withdrew from political life. He was the most noted of all the early justices of Franklin. He died July 18, 1820, and his remains lie in the vault which he himself excavated high on the mountainside overlooking what is called "Happy Valley." (1)

SWINFIELD HILL

Swinfield Hill supplied bacon to Captain John Donelson's Company on his march against the Indians in June 1778, and food for the Company on Donelson's return in August 1778. (1) He was appointed captain of the Militia of Henry County in 1779. (2) On March 29, 1783, Swinfield Hill was appointed "to take a List of Souls, Tythes and Taxable Property" in his own company of Militia. (3)

The members of Captain Hill's company are listed as of the date he was "ordered from Henry County to the assistance of General Greene" at Hillsborough, North Carolina. Other captains of companies in Colonel Abram Penn's Militia of Henry County were: Hamon Critz, John Cunningham, James Cowdin, S. Tarrant, Thomas Smith, Peter Hairston, James Tarrant, Thomas Henderson, Elephaz Shelton, Jonathan Hanby, James Poteet, Brice Martin, John Rentfro, Owen Ruble, George Hairston, James Dillard, Tully Choice, Thomas Haile, and John Fontain. (4)

Swinfield Hill was listed as buyer of four barrels of corn, of the public grain sold at Henry Courthouse in August 1780, as part of the Specific Taxes collected by Henry Lyne and Thomas Thrailkill. (5)

In 1792, Swinfield Hill was named trustee for two towns proposed for Franklin County, one to be on the 32 acres of Daniel Layman and Stephen Peters, and the other to be on 40 acres of Moses Grier. (6) There are many descendants of Swinfield Hill living in Kentucky.

1. The Johnstons of Salisbury by Wm. Preston Johnston.

1. Virginia Magazine, vol 10, pp. 357-358.
2. Ibid, vol. 9 p. 264.
3. Ibid, vol. 11, p 92.
4. Ibid, vol. 17, p. 192.
5. Ibid, Vol. 1, p. 335.
6. Hening, vol. 13, p. 585, 586.

HUGH INNES

Hugh Innes was a lawyer. He was probably the grandson of James Innes of Richmond County who came from Scotland. Maude Carter Clement says (1) that he was probably the son of this James Innis but the probability seems ruled out by the fact that the will of James Innis was probated in 1710.

In the first Vestry Book of Antrim Parish in Halifax County the name of Hugh Innes appears among the names of the seventeen men, who on June 16, 1763, signed the test oath declaring "I do declare that I do believe there is not any Transubstantiation in the Sacrament of the Lord's Supper, or in the elements of Bread and Wine, at or after the Consecration thereof by any person whatsoever." (2)

This signing of the test oath was nearly a decade before his marriage as is proven by the Virginia Gazette of January 2, 1772, which contains an item reading: "Married, Mr. Hugh Innis, one of the representatives for Pittsylvania, to Miss Hannah Eggleston of James City County." (3)

Hugh Innis, as a representative of Pittsylvania County, was among the members of the House of Burgesses who, at the Raleigh Tavern on May 18, 1769, and May 27, 1774, and August 1774, entered into Associations against the importation or purchase of British manufacturers. (4)

He was a Vestryman of Camden Parish and, with William Witcher, was instructed by a meeting held at Pittsylvania Courthouse July 14, 1769, to "let to the lowest bidder the Chappell of Ease ordered to be built near John Willcox's place the size to be 24 feet by 20 Round Loggs for the Body a clap board Roof with Benches &c." Also to "let to the lowest bidder the building of the Church ordered to be built near Snow Creek Chappell—the size of the former." (5)

As a representative of Pittsylvania County, Hugh Innes was appointed in the convention of July 4, 1776 member of a Commission "to take and collect evidence in behalf of Virginia against persons pretending to have claims for lands within the territory

1. History of Pittsylvania County, Virginia, page 94.
2. William & Mary Quarterly, 2nd series, vol. 7, p. 61.
3. Ibid, 1st series, vol. 9, p. 239.
4. Ibid, 1st series, vol. 13, p. 65.
5. Virginia Magazine, vol. 22, pp. 173, 174, 175.

thereof, under deeds and purchases from the Indians. (6) He made "A list of Land and Tithes for Pittsylvania County" in 1767. He was also a member of the County Committee of Safety. He and John Donelson represented Pittsylvania in the Convention of August 1774. (7) When Donelson left Pittsylvania for the Tennessee country in 1779, he sold his lands on Pigg River, including his iron foundry, to James Callaway and Jeremiah Early for £4,000. (8) Hugh Innes was a joint purchaser of other Donelson property. In August 1779, Innes was recommended to the Governor of Virginia as a proper person to serve in the Commission of the Peace for Henry County which had been carved from Pittsylvania County in 1776. (9)

Hugh Innes served Franklin County as Sheriff. On August 10, 1790, S. Shepard of the Solicitors Office sent to Governor Randolph "A report of Executions against delinquent sheriffs . . . with endorsements setting forth that sales could not be made for want of buyers." The name of Hugh Innes is among the 16 delinquent sheriffs. (10)

Thomas Arthur wrote to Governor Patrick Henry under date of May 20, 1786, opposing the appointment of Hugh Innes as "Colonel Commanding of that County (Franklin), on the ground of his age, his being inactive, and never shew'd his Friendship to the Commonwealth in our last war. (11)

The will of Hugh Innes was probated at the April Court of Franklin County in 1797. In the will are named sons Robert, Hugh, James and Harry Innes, daughter Elizabeth Eggleston Innes and Mrs. Turley. He directed that his lands in Bourbon County, Kentucky and Patrick County, Virginia, be sold to complete the education of sons James, Hugh and Harry and daughter Elizabeth Eggleston Innes. He named as executors of his estate son Robert Innes, friend Samuel Calland and Harry Inness of Kentucky. He left a large estate in lands and his inventory included a "Library of Books," two desks and a riding chair."

6. Calendar Virginia State Papers,, vol. 1, p. 272.
7. Virginia Magazine, vol. 24, p. 192.
8. Henry County Deed Book I, p. 300.
9. Virginia Magazine, vol. 9, p. 266.
10. Calendar Virginia State Papers, vol. 5, p. 198.
11. Calendar Virginia State Papers, vol. 4, p. 136.

ROBERT INNIS

Robert Innes was the oldest son of Hugh Innes. In the records of Donald Robertson's School in King and Queen County, he is listed as having begun Latin April 22, 1759, and as a Latin student through 1760-1764. (1)

In Richmond, January 21, 1800, "93 members of the Legislature and a number of other respectable persons convened at the Capitol for the purpose of selecting in the various districts of the State proper persons to be supported by the Republican Interest as Electors of a President and Vice President of the United States. After nominating the Electors the meeting adjourned to meet again on January 23rd. On reconvening, the meeting adopted a "Report relative to the establishment of a proper system of correspondence" for communication throughout the state. The following persons were appointed the Corresponding Committee in Franklin County: Henry Calloway, Moses Greer, Benjamin Cook, Samuel Hairston and Robert Innes. (2)

HUGH MARTIN

Following "An Act (1758) for the defence of the Frontiers of this Colony" is "The Schedule to which this Act refers" and under this schedule are payments made to the militia of the County of Augusta, and to Sundry inhabitants thereof for provisions furnished to the Militia and among the latter Hugh Martin is twice named. (1)

In the list of Virginia Officers and Men in the Continental Line in the War of the Revolution Hugh Martin is named as surgeon-mate. (2)

In the records of Henry County, Hugh Martin is listed as recipient of £1. 6. 4 for 132 pounds of beef supplied to Revolutionary soldiers. (3)

THOMAS PRUNTY

Thomas Prunty is listed among "the Inhabitants of Henry County . . . that hath taken the oath of allegiance, Sept. 13,

1. Virginia Magazine, vol. 33, pp. 198, 289, 290, 291 & vol. 34, pp. 141, 142.
2. Calendar Virginia State Papers, vol. 9, pp. 78. 84.

1. Hening, vol. 7, pp. 197, 199.
2. Virginia Magazine, vol. 2, p. 256.
3. Ibid, vol. 10, p. 141.

1777." (1) The first person of record in Franklin County bearing the name Prunty was this same Thomas who was granted 354 acres of land "On the headwaters of Snow Creek, adjoining the land of Jeremiah Morrow" on October 20, 1779. (2) Robert and James, sons of Thomas Prunty, received grants of land on Pigg River and on Snow Creek respectively on September 1, 1780 (3) and December 2, 1785 (4) Thomas Prunty also served Franklin County as deputy of sheriff Robert Wood in 1789. It appears he had considerable difficulty in collecting the taxes for which he was responsible. His period of service as justice was brief. Members of the Prunty family were numerous and prominent in Franklin County for more than a century. William Prunty, last Franklin county member of this family bearing the name, died in 1934, on the homestead originally granted to his ancestor, Thomas Prunty. The name Prunty still survives in Kentucky and Missouri where members of the Franklin County family settled about 1830.

JOHN RENTFRO

John Rentfro became a Justice of the Franklin County Court at the Court's institution in February 1786. He is listed in Henry County records as one of 37 men who subscribed the oath of allegiance to Virginia as directed by an Act of the General Assembly. (1) At a meeting of the Committee of Pittsylvania County, September 27th 1775, John Rentfro was "nominated an ensign of the Militia, Agreeable to the Ordinance of Convention." (2)

In July 1780, John Rentfro was "appointed captain of the upper part of Captain Thomas Hale's Company," with Thomas Jones as his first lieutenant, Joshua Rentfro, second lieutenant, and William Standifer, ensign. (3) He is listed as having supplied 700 pounds of beef to the Commissioner of Provisions of the Militia in the year 1781, (4) and as having received 45 pounds paper currency for a shot-pouch supplied to the Militia May 26,

1. Virginia Magazine, vol. 9, p. 139.
2. Land Book A. p. 14, in Land Office at Richmond, Va.
3. Ibid, D. p. 160.
4. Ibid, U. p. 572.

1. Virginia Magazine, vol. 9, p. 14.
2. Ibid, vol. 19, p. 307.
3. Ibid, vol. 9, 417.
4. Ibid, vol. 10, p. 357.

1781 (5) On March 29, 1783, John Rentfro was appointed "to take a List of Souls, the List of Tythes and a list of Taxable Property, in Thomas Hale's Company of Militia. (6)

John Rentfro's Company of Militia which was ordered from Henry County to the assistance of General Greene, was drawn from that area of Henry which became a part of Franklin upon the formation of the new county, and contains family names still represented in Franklin. (7)

WILLIAM RENTFRO

The Rentfroe family settled early in Lunenburg County. In the records of Cumberland Parish for 1751, William Cook is listed as "Reader on Blackwater at the House of Joseph Rentfroe," (1) which was embraced in Franklin County when that county was erected. A Reader was a layman who conducted religious services during the scarcity of regular clergymen of the Established Church. They were paid for their services from the county tobacco levy.

Of William Rentfro but little biographical data has been un-covered. He is listed in June 1781 as a "2nd lieutenant in Captain Poteet's Company, (2) and appears along with John Rentfro as having supplied "300 pounds of beef, ½ bushel of corn and 4 diets" to the same Commissioner of Provisions for the Militia. (3)

JONATHAN RICHARDSON

Little information is available concerning Jonathan Richard-son, though he served Franklin County as justice and sheriff. The General Assembly held in Williamsburg September 14, 1758, passed "An Act for the Frontiers of this Colony, and for other purposes therein mentioned." In the Schedule to which this Act refers is found the payments to the Militia of the several coun-ties, "and for Provisions furnished by sundry Inhabitants" thereof. Under the Schedule of Bedford County Jonathan Richardson is named for three pounds and eight shillings. (1)

5. Ibid, vol. 11. p. 91.
6. Ibid, vol. 11. p. 92.
7. Ibid, vol. 17. p. 192.

1. Cumberland Parish by Landon C. Bell, Richmond 1930, p. 338.
2. Virginia Magazine, vol. 9, p. 421.
3. Ibid, vol. 10, p. 357.

1. Hening's Statutes, vol 7, p. 205.

On November 12, 1792, Jonathan Richardson, then Sheriff of Franklin County, joined John Hopkins Otey of Bedford, James Clark of Campbell, Wm. King of Henry and Wm. Mitchell of Patrick, in certifying that John Early had been duly chosen "to Represent the said District as an Elector to vote for a President and Vice President of the United States. (2)

PETER SAUNDERS

The Saunders family had residence in Pittsylvania County before the Revolution. Peter Saunders was a member of the Pittsylvania County Committee of Safety set up January 26, 1775, of which Robert Williams was chairman. (1)

On January 19, 1778, Peter Saunders named 37 men of Henry County certifying that they had "taken and subscribed the oath or affirmation of allegiance and fidelity as Directed by an act of General Assembly Intitled an act to oblige the free male Inhabitants of this State above certain age to give assurance of allegiance to the same and for other Purposes." He then adds that "Dennis O'Bryant, John Bryant and Daniel Brilliman refuseth to take and subscribe the oath or affirmation of allegiance." (2)

Born September 20, 1748, Peter Saunders was married October 31, 1767, to Mary Sparrell. They had issue: Judith, (b. 1769); Lettie (b. 1770); Elizabeth (b. 1772); Peter (b.1776); Fleming (b. 1778); Robt. (b. 1781); Samuel (b. 1783); and Polly. (3)

On removing from Pittsylvania to Franklin County, Peter Saunders settled on the headwaters of Pigg River. He called his home place "Bleak Hill." His son Fleming who married a Miss Watts was the grandfather of Judge Edward Watts Saunders of the Virginia Supreme Court.

In March 1782, the Henry County Court recommended Peter Saunders, Esq., to the Governor as a proper person to serve as Colonel of Militia, (4) and in July 1782, he produced before the

---

2. Calendar Virginia State Papers, vol. 6, pp. 133-134.

---

1. William and Mary Quarterly, 1st series, vol. 5, p. 247.
2. Virginia Magazine, vol. 9, p. 14.
3. Genealogy of the Saunders Family in William and Mary Quarterly, 1st series, vol. 14, pp. 145-148.
4. Virginia Magazine, vol. 10, p. 72.

same court a commission as lieutenant-colonel and was qualified. (5)

In the "Account of publick Grain received of Henry Lyne and Thomas Thrailkill, Com'rs of the Specific Tax in Henry County, August 1780, and sold at Henry Court House" Peter Saunders is named as the purchaser. A memorandum states "Patrick Henry Esqr is indebted to this Common Wealth in the County of Henry Seven Barrels Corn and three Bushels Corn for year 1780 purchased of Peter Saunders at 40 shillings a Barrel." Henry Lyne notes on the memorandum "The above Colo. Peter Saunders refuses to take." (6)

Peter Saunders was recommended to the Governor in August 1779 as a proper person to serve Henry County in the Commission of the Peace. Among others recommended for the same honor at the same time were Patrick Henry, Robert Woods, Hugh Innes, Frederick Rives and William Cook. (7) The two representatives of Henry County in the House of Delegates in 1781 were Peter Saunders and Patrick Henry. (8) Henry County's first Court was held on April 20, 1778, and was composed of justices Peter Saunders, Abraham Penn, Edmund Lyne and George Waller. (9)

On December 9, 1793, Peter Saunders wrote Governor Henry Lee stating he had heard that the Legislature was about to pass a law for appointing "Agents to superintend the collection of arrearages" and that, being well acquainted with the collection business he was making a tender of his services for the district in which he had residence. He closed with the words, "I reside in Franklin County." (10)

JOHN SMITH

John Smith was from Pittsylvania County. He was born on a plantation called "The Pocket" on Staunton River, married Camelia Thurman and lived on Pigg River. (1) His sister Elizabeth married Samuel Callands of Pittsylvania Courthouse. His sister

5. Ibid, vol. 10, p. 240.
6. Ibid, vol. 1, p. 335.
7. Ibid, vol. 9, p. 266.
8. Ibid, vol. 5, pp. 216-217.
9. Ibid, vol. 9, p. 262.
10. Calendar Virginia State Papers, vol. 6, p. 675.

1. Clement's History of Pittsylvania County Virginia.

Anne married Captain William Callaway, son of Colonel William Callaway of Bedford. In 1801, the General Assembly of Virginia named John Smith among the 19 trustees of Banister Academy whose first principal was the Rev. Wm. L. Turner, Presbyterian minister of Bedford County.

STEPHEN SMITH

Stephen Smith, early justice and clerk of the Franklin County Court from the formation of the county to 1791, was the son of Bowker and Judith Smith of Russell Parish in Bedford County. His five brothers were, John, Bowker, Guy, William and Achilles. His two sisters were Judith and Elizabeth. (1)

The family had residence in Lunenburg prior to the formation of Bedford. Stephen Smith appears as surety on the marriage bond of John Russell and Pheby Hudson of Lunenburg County June 30, 1787. (2) His son Stephen married Agnes Hix of Lunenburg on November 19, 1795. (3)

GEORGE TURNBULL

George Turnbull, Gl., is named in a certificate dated March 8, 1791, from Stephen Smith, Clerk of Franklin County Court, as one whose name Thomas Arthur had forged "to a certificate of the Proof of Notice to Thomas Levsey in a suit then Depending in the District Court." (1)

An Act of Assembly in 1762, adding 26 acres of land of Peter Jones to the city of Petersburg, named George Turnbull as one of the trustees cf the enlarged town. (2)

An act of November 10, 1792, for establishing Germantown on 32 acres of the land of Daniel Layman and Stephen Peters in Franklin County, names George Turnbull as a Trustee of the town. His brother, William Turnbull, was named as trustee of a town to be built on 40 acres of the land of Moses Grier in Franklin County. (3)

1. William and Mary Quarterly, 1st series, vol. 10, p. 62.
2. Old Free State by Landon C. Bell, vol. 2, p. 393.
3. Ibid, vol. 2, p. 437.

1. Calendar Virginia State Papers, vol. 5, pp. 271 and 279.
2. Hening, vol. 7, p. 602.
3. Ibid, vol. 13, p. 585-586.

ROBERT WILLIAMS

Robert Williams was a lawyer and a representative of Pitt-sylvania in the Virginia Convention held in Williamsburg May 6, 1776 of which Professor Henry Augustine Washington said, "This convention framed the first written constitution of a free state in the annals of the world." (1) Commenting on this statement, Hugh Blair Grigsby declared Professor Washington "has said truly." (2)

Robert Williams and his brother Colonel Joseph Williams lived in North Carolina for a while, prior to the Revolution. (3) On October 10, 1774, Robert was married to Sarah Lanier, a daughter of Thomas Lanier, an early justice of Lunenburg County, before his removal to North Carolina. Colonel Joseph Williams married Rebecca Lanier, a sister of his brother's wife. Robert Williams and his wife settled near Sandy Creek of Banister River. He served both Pittsylvania and Henry Counties as common-wealth's attorney before he became a justice of the Franklin County Court. (4) He represented Pittsylvania County in the House of Delegates in 1776 and was chairman of the County Committee of Safety which was set up January 26, 1775.

On March 14, 1776, the State Auditor issued a warrant "to Joseph Akin for use of Robert Williams for £300 upon account, for the purchase of arms for use Pittsylvania Regulars." (5) On May 8, 1776, another warrant was issued "to Robert Williams, Esquire, for £139. 10. 6 for the ball'ce of his acc't for arms and other necessaries to ye Pittsylvania Comp. of regulars." (6) On May 15, 1776, warrant "to Robert Williams, Esquire for use Lt. Col. Haynes Morgan for £422. 15. 0. for one month's pay of 3 companies from Pittsylvania Co. to No. Carolina: Also £4. 8. 6 for express hire." (7)

On June 6, 1776, a warrant was issued to Robert Williams "for use Samuel Calland & Co. £12. 10. 0. for Leggins furnished Capt. Hutchings' Comp'ny, Pittsy. Va." (8) On June 13, 1776,

1. Address before the Virginia Historical Society in 1852. Virginia's Historical Register, Vol. 5, pp. 51-52, 107-110.
2. Discourse on the Virginia Convention of May 6, 1776, Tyler's Quarterly, Vol. 6, p. 70.
3. Reminiscences of North Carolina by John H. Wheeler, Columbus, Ohio, 1884, p. 418.
4. Clement's History of Pittsylvania County, Virginia, p. 139.
5. Calendar Virginia State Papers, vol. 8, p. 122.
6. Ibid, vol. 8, p. 173.
7. Ibid, vol. 8, p. 177.
8. Ibid, vol. 8, p. 189.

a warrant was issued to Robert Williams for the use of James Roberts for £4. 0. 6 for provisions furnished Captain Hutchings' Company. (9)

On June 15, 1776, "25 Commissions for officers Mil. Pitt-sylvania were issued and delivered to Robert Williams Esq'r." (10)

On June 19, 1776, a warrant was issued to Robert Williams, Esquire, for £13 advanced by him to the Minute Men ordered from Pittsylvania County to North Carolina. (11)

On July 2, 1776, a warrant was issued "to Robert Williams for £21. 2. 6 for use John Morton, for waggonage to Capt. Dil-lard's Min. Men Comp. Pittsylvania; for use Jesse Duncan £2. 10. 0 for do. to Ballard's Comp. Mecklenburg, and for himself £174. 17. 9 ballance of his acct for arms purchased for the public." (12)

HUGH WOODS

In the early years of Henry County, as in all other counties, the County levies were laid in terms of tobacco. In the levy made in March 1779, Hugh Woods was given 200 pounds of tobacco "for going after witnesses" (1) and 500 pounds "for 10 young wolves' heads." The Marriage Bonds of Henry County record the marriage of Hugh Woods to Sarah Ann George on August 5, 1779. (2)

ROBERT WOODS

Robert Woods, the first sheriff of Franklin County, was a native of Pittsylvania C inty. The Committee of Safety of that county on September 2', 1775, nominated him as captain of the Militia "agreeable to the ordinance of convention." (1) He is listed among the persons who took the oath of allegiance before Edmund Lyne August 30, 1777. (2)

9. Ibid, vol. 8, p 203.
10. Ibid, vol. 8, p. 206.
11. Ibid, vol. 8, p. 212.
12. Ibid, vol. 8, p. 232.

1. Virginia Magazine, vol. 9, p. 265.
2. Ibid, vol. 21, p. 280.

1. Virginia Magazine, vol. 19, p. 307.
2. Ibid, vol. 9, p. 17.

In August 1779, Robert Woods was recommended to Governor Thomas Jefferson as "a proper person to serve in the Commission of the Peace" for Henry County. (3) He and William Tunstall were allowed fifteen shillings each "for assessing the Commrs Lands in the North Battalion." (4)

Robert Woods was allowed pay 15 days pasturage for 66 beeves, 36 forages and 45 diets. When Captain Heard marched to join General Sumner in North Carolina, Robert Woods supplied 23 Diets and pasturage for 55 horses. On Heard's return, Woods supplied 35 Diets and forage for 34 horses. In addition to compensation for these items, he was allowed pay for 160 pounds of fresh pork, 43 pounds of bacon and 3 bushels of oats furnished hospital at Henry Court House in March 1781. (5)

Woods became sheriff of Franklin County in 1786 and served to August 1787. An execution was issued against him for failure to collect taxes of the year 1786. On October 15, 1788, he petitioned for relief from the execution stating that "The Burden of the said tax on the poor inhabitants of the county and the amazing Scarcity of money were responsible for the default." (6)

In the closing years of the 18th century, most eyes were turned westward. Robert Woods was looking west. The Act of December 9, 1791, to establish several new ferries across the New and Ohio Rivers refers to "the land of Robert Woods on Fishing Creek in the County of Ohio," (7) which is now in West Virginia.

Robert Woods was still interested in feeding the Militia. On June 4, 1792, he signed a paper acknowledging himself bound to Governor Henry Lee in the sum of 1000 pounds in connection with "contracts to furnish such of the volunteer Militia now in the County of Ohio or who may be hereafter stationed in the County . . . each Ration to consist of one pound of beef or three quarters of a pound of pork, one pound of Bread or Flour, Half a Gill of Rum, Brandy, or Whiskey, and one quart of salt to every hundred rations: the price of a Ration to be Eight Cents." (8)

3. Ibid, vol. 9, p. 266.
4. Ibid, vol. 10, p. 143.
5. Ibid, vol. 9, p. 420.
6. Calendar Virginia State Papers, vol. 4, p. 499.
7. Hening's Statutes, vol 13, p. 283.
8. Calendar of Virginia State Papers, vol. 5, pp. 570-571.

GLOSSARY

Ab ante. In advance.

Ab initio. From the beginning.

Ab invito. Unwillingly.

Accedas ad curiam. That you go to the court.

Accedas ad vicecomitem. That you go to the sheriff.

Accordg., Accorg., Accg., Accog., Accordl., Accol., Ac'd . According and accordingly.

Ack'd., Ackn'd., Acknow'g'd., Ac'd. Acknowledged.

Acta publica. Things of general knowledge and concern.

Ad culpam. Until misbehavior.

Ademption. A taking away.

Adeu. Without day.

Ad idem. To the same point.

Adj'd. Adjourned or adjudicated.

Ad largum. At large.

Ad libitum. At pleasure.

Ad litem. For the suit.

Ads. Adsectam. At the suit of.

Ad valorem. According to the valuation.

Adms., Admrs., Admr., Admin. Administrators or administration.

Af'd. Aforesaid.

Afect. Reliated. Meant for effects released.

A fortiori. With the stronger reason.

Agard. Meant for award.

Agens. To conduct. A manager of affairs.

Ags., Agt., Agst. Against.

Alia. Other things.

Alia enormia. Other wrongs.

Alias. Another. An alias writ is a writ issued where one of the same kind has been issued before in the same cause.

A. Cap., Alis Capt., Alias Caps., A.C., AC. Alias Capias. A writ to re-arrest or re-take the body of the person named.

Alias Dictus. Otherwise called.

Alienate. To transfer or convey.

Alienor. One who makes the grant.

Alienee. One to whom the grant is made.

Al plee. Meant for Alias Pluries or a third arrest.

Am'd. Amend.

Amicus Curiae. A friend of the court.

Ancillary. Auxiliary or subordinate.

Animo. With intention.

Animus. The intention with which an act is done.

Animus testandi. With the intention of making a will.

Apoca. A writing acknowledging payments.

A posterioro. From the effect to the cause.

Appelor. A criminal who accuses his accomplices or one who challenges a jury.

Appo'., App'd., Appoin'g. Appointee, Appointed, Appointing.

A priori. From the cause to the effect.

Approb. Approbation.

Arbitrium. Decision, award, judgment.

Arguendo. In the course of arguments.

Arles. Earnest.

Assee. Assignee.

Assi. Assidere. Originally a court; then the enactment of a court.

Assu. Assumpsit. He has undertaken; he undertook. The name of a common law action to recover damages for the breach of a contract not under seal.

Assize. To sit by or near. A writ to the sheriff for recovery of immovable property.

Assizes. Sessions of the justices of Assize.

Atta. Attachment or attainder.

Atta with proelem. Meant for attachment with pro laesione fidei for breach of faith.

Atte. Attestor.

Atto. Attorney.

Att., Attce., Attg. Attendance and attending.

Aw'd. Awarded.

Bl. Bill or Bail.

Capias ad satisfaciendom or Ca Sa. That you take to satisfy.

Capias in withernam. That you take again.

Chose in action. A thing to which one had the right but not the possession.

Chy. Chancery.

Cognovit actionem. He has acknowledged the action.

Certiorari. The name of a writ directed by a superior court to one of inferior jurisdiction commanding the latter to certify to the former the record in a particular case.

Clk., clks. Clerk, clerks.

Con'd., cond., cont'd., cont., conin. Continued.

Condemna., condim'a., conda. Condemnation.

Conf'd. Confirmed.

Conf't., Confst. Confessed.

Com. Wealth., C. Wealth. Commonwealth.

Com'g & ret'g. Coming and returning.

Com't., comtd. Commitment and committed.

Compt., Compl. Complaints.

Com., Comm., Comn., Com'n. Commission.

Coram nobis. In our presence. A writ issuing from and returnable to the Circuit Court for the correction of errors of fact alleged to have occurred in a former trial in that court.

Const. Constable.

Debene. Bebenture. Money or debt due.

Debene esse. Taking testimony in advance for fear witness might die before court.

De bonis non. Of goods not administered. One who completes a dead administrator's task is called Administrator de bonis non.

De bonis asportatis. Concerning goods carried away.

Dec'd., des'd. Deceased.

Decl. Declare or declaration.

Ded's., dedim's. Dedimus.

Dedimus potestatem. We gave, or have given, the power.

Def., defdt., deft., defdts. Defendant or defendants.

De injuria. By reason of the injury.

Depo., depo's. Deponent or deposition.

De Novo. Afresh, anew.

Detn'd. Detained.

Detr. Determination or detainer.

Detinue. Withholding the possession of name of an action.

De retorno habendo. Concerning the return to be had.

Devastavit. He has wasted the assets. Said of an administrator or executor.

Dis., dismd., dis'd., dism. Dismissed.

Do. Ditto.

Dpy. Deputy.

D. S. Deputy Sheriff.,

D. S. A. District States Attorney.

Duces tecum. That you bring with you.

Esta. Estate.

Et us. And wife.

Ecor., exors., exo., exeu., exon'x., exuer., exeon., ex'x., exrs., exorship., exon. Executor, execution, executorship, executed, executrix.

Excudg. Excluding.

Ex parte. Proceedings are ex parte when relief is granted without opportunity for the defendant to be heard.

Ex officio. By virtue of the office.

Ex mora. From the delay.

Ex post facto. By an after act.

Gam'g. Gambling.

Gaol. Jail.

Garshee., garn., g'shee., gshee., garsee., gshee. Garnishee.

Gen., Genel., Gen'l., Gl., Gent., Gt. Gentlemen and general.

Grn. Granted.

Impl. Implementing.

Ind., Aul. Individual indorsers.

In Chy. In chancery.

Indg., indt. Indicting, indictment.

Inform. Information.

Inst. Instituted.

Injo. Injunction.

Is. a. Issued a.

Jud., judgt., juddg., judgl., ju. Judgment, Judging.

Jus. Justice.

Mot. Motion.

Neat. Net.

Net Debett Issue. Meant for nil debit issue.

Nihil driet. Didn't show up.

Nil debet. He owes nothing.

Nihil dicit. He says nothing.

Nihil habet. He has nothing.

Nisi prius. Unless before.

Nolo contendere. I do not wish to contest.

Nolens volens. Whether willing or unwilling.

Nole prosigue., nole proseque. Meant for Nolle Prosequi, unwilling to proceed.

Non pros. Non prosequitur, meaning the plaintiff does not pursue.

Non asse Non assumpsit. Didn't make the contract.

Non facit. He did not make it. The name of a plea in an action of assumpsit on a promissory note.

Nunc pro tunc. Now for then. A thing done at one time which should have been done at another.

Nul'd. Nullified.

N. Sl. Probably meant for non suit.

N. P. Notary Public.

N. Sum., N. Summon. Non assumpsit.

O. C., Ord. Ca. Ordered set aside.

O. Re., O. R. Ordered Recorded.

O' Condema. Order of condemnation or sale.

Off'g. Offering.

Ord., Ord'd. Ordered.

Ovs'r. Overseer.

Oyer and Tummener. Meant for Oyer and Terminer, a trial court of criminal jurisdiction.

Pendente lite. The suit pending or during the pendency of the suit.

Pention. Pension.

P., per. Public or percent.

Post. Afterward.

Posse comitatus. The power of the county.

Plu. Caps. Pluries Capias. The write that issues after an alias ordering another arrest.

Prest. Presentment.

Pris. Prisoner.

Prcedg., proceedg. Proceeding.

Pr'd., Pv'd. Proved.

Prima facie. On the first face—at the first view.

Procedendo. By proceeding.

Prochein Ami. Nearest or next friend.

Pro confesso. As confessed.

Ptf., Pllfs., Plfs., Pltf., Plf., Pltfs. Plaintiff.

Qtm. Quartermaster.

Qual. Qualify or qualified.

Quasht. Abated, nullified or made void.
Qty. Quantity.

Rec'd. Recorded. Received.
Relesmt. Releasements.
Relingst., reling'd. Relinquishment, relinguished.
Repy., repley. Replevy bond or replecation.
Repl. Replesation. Reply of plaintiff to defendant's plea.
Ret. Returned or retained.

Shf., shef., shiff. Sheriff.
Sec'y., secuy., sec'ty., su'ys., su'ry., sur'y., sey., su'y., sut'y. Surities
    or securities.
Specee. Meant for specie. Money.
Sp. Bl., Spl. Bl. Special bail.
Spl. Impl. Special impleading, or special implementation.
Spl. Bl. Impl. Special bail and implementation.
Spy. Specialty, a bond with a specific condition.
Sply & costs. Specialty and costs.
Sum. Summoned.
Surv., sur. Surveyor.
Swo. Sworn.

Tom. Tomorrow.

Verd., verdt., vd. Verdict.
Vs. Versus, against.

Wits. Witnesses.
Whip'g. Whipping.

INDEX

INDEX

A

Abbott
W. B., 195.
Abshire, Absher
Abram, Abraham, 51, 101, 131, 160, 168.
Henry T., 194, 199, 202.
Luke, Lute, 14, 19.
Adams
Robert, Jr., 207, 208.
Snead, 191.
Aday, Adey
N., 79.
Walter, 44, 100, 103.
Adkins, Atkins
Jacob, 65.
Joel, 73.
Tom David, 48.
Agee
Matthew, 89.
Akers
James, 166.
Jean, 166.
Wiliam, 17, 68, 70, 84, 104, 123, 124, 125, 126, 128, 134, 139, 157, 170.
Akin
James, 101.
Joseph, 224.
Allen
Drury, 9.
Allman
J. Bradie, 195.
Altick
John, 7.
Anderson, Anduson
Charles, 126, 127.
John, 152, 155.
John P., 75, 96.
Meade, 211.
Milley, 72.
Peter, 214.

Robert, 152, 155, 161.
Sherwood, 196.
William, 44, 62.
Anglan
Samuel, 114.
Anthony's Ford, 38.
Archer
Eliza, 10.
Will, William, 10. 24, 50.
Arrington
Samuel, 172.
Thomas, 186.
Arthur
Barnaba, Barnabas, 88, 153, 178.
James, 27.
John, 56, 74, 112, 116, 130, 153, 176, 179.
Lucy Ann, 88.
Sarah, 157.
Tabitha, 26.
Thomas, 8, 10, 11, 12, 13, 14, 15, 16, 17, 21, 22, 23, 26, 27, 29, 31, 33, 36, 39, 42, 43, 44, 45, 47, 49, 50, 51, 53, 55, 60, 61, 63, 68, 69, 71, 73, 74, 75, 77, 78, 81, 82, 83, 86, 87, 88, 92, 93, 96, 106, 107, 108, 110, 112, 113, 115, 116, 117, 119, 120, 122, 123, 125, 127, 128, 129, 130, 131, 132, 133, 134, 136, 138, 140, 142, 146, 147, 148, 150, 152, 155, 156, 157, 160, 161, 162, 163, 164, 166, 168, 171, 174, 175, 176, 204, 205, 206, 217, 223.
Asberry
George, 25, 34, 35, 39, 40, 51, 54, 58, 59, 61, 86, 87, 90, 96, 113, 127, 128, 136, 141, 142, 143, 144, 145, 146, 147, 163, 173, 179, 204.
John, 146.
Ashurst
Wiliam, 83.
Austin
William, 39, 93, 122, 168, 177, 179, 180.
Aylett's Creek, 19.

B

Bailey
Phillip, 130.
Richard, 25, 74, 89, 92, 126, 127, 130.
Thomas, 194, 201.
Baker
James, 150.
John, 191.
Ballard
Harris, 159.
James, 138.
Mary, 151.
Richard, 35, 43, 101, 144, 151.

Bandy
Richard, 79, 84, 149, 156, 158.
Banks
John, 39.
Barker
Musco, 195.
Barnet, Barnott, Barnett
Allen G., 48.
Ann, 64.
John, 31, 32, 47, 48.
Nathan, 64.

235

236

C

Cooper
  Arthur, 91.
  Benjamin F., 191.
  Isles, 85.
  John, 54. 91. 116, 134, 149
  Tom, 194, 199.
Copeland, Copland
  Richard, 113, 128, 137, 178.
Cowden, Cowin, Cowdin, Cowan
  James, 103, 109, 122.
  Robert, 122.
  William, 26, 28, 77, 81, 100, 122, 124, 155, 159, 188.
Cowl's Cabins, 66.
Cox
  John, 31, 54, 72, 75, 103, 143, 155, 177, 181.
Cradle
  Jacob, 9.
Cragg, Craig
  Thomas, 85, 122, 123, 178.
  Tolliver, 149, 156, 162.

Craghead, Craighead
  John, 52, 64, 88, 103, 105, 125, 126, 127, 128, 140, 161 165.
  Mary, 34, 52, 88, 137.
  Peter, 34, 137.
Crawford
  Isabella, 170.
Crow, Crowe
  William, 88, 95.
Crump
  John, 54.
  Thomas, 95, 122, 164.
  Will, Williams, 43, 67, 81, 152, 158, 159.
Crutcher
  Sebret, 48.
  Thomas, 48, 75, 101, 164.
Cundiff
  Thomas C., 194, 196, 199, 200.
Cunningham
  John, 215.

D

Daniels
  Ernest, 195.
David
  Isaac. 130.
Davis, Davies
  B. A. Jr., and Sr., 195.
  Henry, 195.
  James, 57.
  John, 27, 64.
  Jonathan, 96, 112, 139, 141.
  Joseph, 11, 15, 39, 54, 66, 105, 173.
  Leonard, 194, 199, 202.
  Lewis, 14, 27, 42, 43, 48, 57, 62, 68, 72 73, 82, 84, 86, 87, 99, 113, 115, 126, 128, 129, 131, 141, 142, 143, 144, 145, 148, 155.
  Samuel, 159, 170.
  Solomon, 38, 130.
  T. Frank, 195.
  V., 137.
  William, 17, 46, 57, 62, 65, 68, 94.
  Zachariah, 80, 148, 156, 172.
Dehart
  Robert P., 194, 196, 199, 200.
Delany, Delancy
  Martin, 124, 126, 139.
Demoss, Dimoss
  Thomas, 86, 87, 100, 112, 113, 139, 176.
Demsey, Dempoy
  Nathan, 148, 164.
Dent
  Samuel, 130.
  Walter, 93, 180.
Derest, Drists, Durst
  Samuel, 31, 32, 53, 87.

Derby
  Samuel, 146.
Dickinson, Dickerson, Dickirson, Dukinson
  J., John, 8, 10, 11, 13, 18, 19, 20, 27, 36, 38, 39, 48, 53, 65, 67, 100, 102, 106, 108, 110, 113, 115, 118, 119, 120, 121, 123, 127, 129, 130, 131, 136, 145, 146, 152, 154, 155, 156, 162, 163, 164, 166, 174, 180, 181, 184, 211.
  Washington 191.
Dillard
  H. Dalton, 195.
  James, 215.
Dillingham
  Absalom, 184.
  Joshua, 76, 105.
  William, 12, 47, 57, 76, 82, 141.
Dillon, Dillion
  Elizabeth, 34.
  Jacob, 7, 34, 36.
  James, 13, 42, 76, 122, 148.
  Jesse, 37, 117, 119, 105.
  J., 105.
  Mary, 122.
  Samuel, 40, 76, 116, 128.
  William, 122, 183.
Dillon's Mill, 13, 14, 23, 116.
Dillmon
  Daniel, 149, 151.
Divine
  Daniel, 108.
Divers
  John, 14, 52, 64, 74, 100, 139, 158, 159, 160.

E

F

G

Gamble
  Joan, 100.
  Samuel, 100.
Garrard
  Governor, 206.
  E. C., 198.
Garret
  James, 110.
Garst
  Samuel, 51.
Gee
  P., 118.
Gentry
  C. E., 198.
George
  Sarah Ann, 225.
Gearheart, Geerheart
  Leonard, 119, 130.
  John, 168, 172.
  Peter, 25, 39, 47, 54, 66, 70, 71, 72, 79, 130,
    155, 160, 164, 168, 179.
Gibson, Gipson
  James M., 191.
  John, 8, 10, 11, 17, 22, 39, 42, 46, 105, 106,
    204, 212.
Gilbert
  Michael, 149.
  William P., 189, 190.
Gill, Guild
  Walton, 110.
Gill's Creek, 7, 9, 14, 41, 100.
Gillaspy, Glaspy
  Daniel, 84, 87.
  John, 37.
Gilliam, Gilliams
  Peter, 38, 52, 58, 134.
Glade
  Terry, 101.
Glover
  Richard, 75.
Godsey
  William, 100, 115, 160.
Goff
  Ambrose, 75.
Goggins, Goggin
  Stephen, 121, 122.
Goodall
  David, 18.
Goode
  Samuel, 211.
Goodson
  Thomas, 113.
Goodwin
  W. O., 195.
Gordon
  Archibald, 173, 177.

Graham, Grayham
  Archibald, 111.
  Arthur, 76, 146, 147, 148, 149.
  Daniel, 135.
  Jonathan, 164.
  Michael, 111.
  Robert, 164.
  Sarah, 204.
Graves
  Frances, 13, 171, 175.
  Frank, 89.
  William, 11, 38, 66, 89, 110, 120, 149.
Gravet, Gravit
  Obediah, 47, 64.
Green, Greene
  General, 220.
  William, 108.
Greer, Grier
  Acquila, 62, 93.
  Benjamin, 11, 66, 68, 129, 148.
  Charles, 194, 200.
  C. C., 196, 199.
  Cox, 142.
  Capt., 130.
  Eliza, 152, 153.
  Granberry, 177.
  James, 11, 18, 37, 47, 54, 66, 76, 85, 92, 110,
    126.
  Joseph, 160, 161, 173, 183.
  Martin, 129.
  Mary, Maryann, 108, 129.
  P., Philemon, Phillman, 108, 119, 143, 172,
    173.
  Moses, 8, 10, 11, 12, 13, 14, 15, 16, 21, 22,
    24, 31, 35, 36, 40, 42, 43, 44, 47, 48, 50,
    53, 54, 55, 59, 61, 63, 64, 65, 67, 68, 69,
    71, 73, 75, 77, 78, 80, 81, 84, 85, 86, 87,
    88, 90, 93, 95, 97, 98, 102, 103, 104, 106,
    107, 108, 113, 115, 116, 118, 123, 125, 127,
    129, 132, 133, 134, 136, 138, 139, 140, 147,
    148, 150, 152, 155, 156, 158, 160, 163, 164,
    165, 166, 168, 169, 172, 175, 176, 178, 181,
    184, 192, 211, 212, 213, 215, 218, 223.
  Thomas, 85.
  Will, William, 37, 72, 77, 90, 93.
  Writ, 119.
Griffith
  Benjamin, 79, 92, 134, 155, 160, 166, 212.
  C. P., 194, 199, 200.
  Cap., 199.
  George, 9, 20, 34, 58, 97, 98.
  James, 158.
  John, 42, 80.
  Joseph, 57, 62, 173.
  Susannah, 148, 155, 184.
  William, 37, 60, 62, 68, 76, 90, 114, 148, 155,
    163, 171, 172, 173, 175, 178, 180, 184, 212.

H

243

244

I

J

Cox, 26.
Daniel, 37, 50, 92, 157.
Dewey, 195.
Edith. 17.
Elijah, Elish, 74, 75.
Ellenor, 17.
Gabriel, 33.
Henry, 54, 72, 94, 117, 173.
Howell, 164.
Isaac, 39, 93.
J., 79.
James, 70.
John, 37, 89, 167.
John Howel, 63, 165.
John H., 107.
Joseph, 67, 214.
Mavey, 80.
Miles, 26.
Peter, 223.

Posey, 194, 199, 200.
Rachel, 24, 50, 72, 93.
Ray, 195.
R., Robert, 52, 72, 84, 116, 124, 125, 127.
Samuel, 157.
Tabitha, 138.
Thomas, 43, 44, 68, 69, 70, 72, 74, 79, 80,
    81, 84, 85, 90, 91, 94, 95, 96, 105, 107, 108,
    110. 111 112, 114, 125, 126, 127, 139, 140,
    141, 151, 155, 173, 178, 183, 219.
William, 186.
Zachariah, 101.
Jordon, Jourdin, Jurdin
    Absalom, 156.
    Jonas, 44, 48, 51.
    Thomas P., 134, 157.
Josith
    Booker, 61.

K

Kay, Keay
    John, 139
    Thomas, 128.
Keen, Kean
    Elisha, 38, 71, 123, 124, 130, 144, 145, 155,
        159.
    John, 38, 63, 64, 159.
    Tom 191.
Kee
    George, 52.
    William, 52.
Keele
    John, 148, 149.
Keith
    Samuel, 76.
Kellor
    Francis, 88.
Kelly, Kelley, Keeley
    Eliza, 125, 139, 157, 170.
    George, 14, 93. 134, 150.
    Jesse, 37.
    John, 37, 46, 70, 82, 95, 121, 126, 146, 147,
        148, 171.
    Rachel, 170.
    Will, William, 17, 18, 49, 55, 61, 67, 68,
        69, (Sen) 70, 80, 94, 109, 122, 140, 142,
        145, 158, 180, 181, 182.
Kemmis
    Robert, 39.
Kemp
    James, 191.
    John, 122, 124, 126, 139, 140, 153, 178.
Kennedy
    James, 90.

William, 48.
Kenney
    Eliza, 71.
Kennon
    James, 87.
    Richard, 211.
Kerby, Kearby, Kerbey, Kierby
    David, 92, 93.
    Elizabeth, 92.
    Francis, 33, 52, 122.
    Jesse, 24, 89.
    John, 15, 52, 108, 140.
    Joseph, 64.
    Samuel, 69, 70, 71, 72, 73, 81, 84, 85, 86,
        87, 96, 87, 96, 97, 98, 112, 141, 142, 143,
        144. 145, 146, 147.
    William, 65, 109.
Key
    John, 172, 181.
    Martin, 167.
Keyley
    John, 138.
Kidd
    Mathew, 134.
King
    Joseph, 25.
    William, 221.
Kingery
    Jacob, 17, 128, 170, 178.
    Peter, 169.
Knight
    Augustin, 98.
Kyle
    John, 141, 142.

L

Lafon
  T. P., 195.
Lamb
  George, 78, 107, 114, 165.
Landes
  Ira, 7.
Laney
  Elizabeth, 63.
  William, 63.
Lanfield
  Peter, 162.
Langdon
  John, 17, 35, 101.
  Samuel, 85, 109, 112, 114.
Lanier
  Rebecca, 224.
  Sarah. 224.
  Thomas, 224.
Lason
  Gen., Lason's Brigade, 142.
Lavine. Lavoir, Levine
  H., Henry, 28, 79.
  Ikey, 195.
Law
  Henry, 14.
  Jesse, 14, 25, 33, 52, 149.
  John, 14, 27, 38, 75, 77, 101, 131, 147, 164,
    166. 182.
  John B., 191.
  John C. 191.
  Nathaniel, 76, 91.
  Shack, 191.
  Stephen, 64.
Lawrence
  Coleman. 195.
Layman, Laymon
  Daniel, 73, 213, 215, 223.
Lee
  C. C.. 201.
  Charles Carter, 194, 199.
  Henry, 222, 226.
  Stephen, 169, 171.
Leftwich
  John, 127.
  Littleberry, 158.
  William, 207.
Lemmon
  Isaac, 74.
Lesane, Lisaney
  John, 75.
  Lawrence, 24.
Letterall, Letter, Lutterel, Litteral, Luttrell
  John, 153.
  Samuel, 37, 50, 84, 153.
  W. B., 195.
Levison
  Aaron, 34.

Lewis
  James, 67, 104.
  Joseph, 66.
  Thomas, 124, 139, 147, 158.
Likins
  Marcus, 17.
Lilley
  Robert, 17.
Little Creek, 7, 92, 138.
Livesey, Levisey, Leysey, Livsey, Liveys
  Edmund, 79.
  George, 67, 80, 97, 114, 168.
  John, 14, 23, 44, 58, 80, 84, 111, 116, 127,
    128.
  Peggy, 61.
  Peter. 67.
  T., and Thomas, 19, 57, 88, 89, 110, 145,
    148, 150, 205, 223.
Long
  Christian Charles, 7, 14, 82.
  Thomas, 176.
  William, 89.
Lovell
  John P., 192.
Loyd
  John, 76.
Luke
  Faithful, 160.
Lukmon
  Peter, 14.
Lumpkin
  Thomas, 84, 95.
Lumsden, Lumdson
  Charles, 13, 105, 116.
  Jeremiah, 151, 153, 161.
  John, 23, 38, 151, 153, 160.
  Willmouth, 151.
Lynch
  Charles, 207, 208, 209.
Lynn
  James, 132, 133.
Lyon, Lyan, Lyne
  Eda, 142.
  Edward, 87, 93, 97, 112, 113, 115, 121, 151,
    164, 165.
  Edmund, 22, 225.
  El.. 160.
  Elijah, 183.
  Elisha, 92, 106, 115, 117, 141, 149, 158, 160.
    162, 165, 180, 183.
  Henry, 106, 181, 215, 222.
  James, 132.
  M., May, Mary, 97, 106, 112, 113, 115, 121,
    142, 147, 160, 165.
  Stephen, 104.

M

Maberry
Lebanus, 15.
Jacob, 191.
Maggotty Creek, 7, 35, 88, 131.
Mahoon
Daniel, 66.
Sally, 66.
Maier
Fred O., 196.
Majors
James, 21.
Mann
S. P., 195.
Mannin
Samuel, 132.
Mapleswamp, 116.
Marcum, Markum
Agness, 97.
Edwards, 45.
James, 63, 131.
John, 79.
Josiah, 22, 37.
Thomas, 17, 25, 62, 87.
William, 150.
Marr
John, 31.
Marshall
E. T., 202.
L. E., 195, 202.
Martin, Marin
Brice, 215.
Clifford, 194, 199, 200, 202.
Grover L., 194, 196, 199, 200.
Hugh, 36, 50, 51, 56, 59, 63, 67, 73, 78, 93, 95, 97, 115, 127, 154, 156, 167, 174, 218.
James, 22, 35, 56, 105 118, 158, 159, 165.
Jesse, 166.
John, 13, 18, 39, 51, 56, 60, 67, 68, 127, 136, 145, 174, 177, 179.
Thomas, 54, 91.
William, 7, 64, 74, 79, 84, 85, 137, 151, 162, 183.
Mason
James, 54, 64, 67, 69, 86, 87.
Nathaniel, 151.
Robert, 18, 25, 44, 48, 56, 85, 141, 142, 144, 145, 151, 155.
Willie, 195.
Matthew
George, 144.
Samson, 144.
Mattox
John, 161.
Samuel, 191.
Maviety, Mavity, Maveaty, Maevity
Robert, 42.

Will, William, 8, 17, 19, 42, 44, 48, 62, 89, 97, 100, 111, 112, 113, 124, 126, 127, 139, 140, 142, 143, 144, 145, 146, 147, 153, 155, 169, 170, 171, 178.
Maxcey, Maxey
Howard, 94, 199.
Josiah, 89.
Mays
Leo C., 195.
McCary, McClary, McLary
John, 71.
Richard, 7, 91.
McClure
Isabella, Isbell, 94, 125, 139.
Phebey, 125, 139, 170.
McCoge
William, 70.
McCoy
John, 15.
Samuel, 115, 137.
William, 69, 107, 137.
McCutcher, McCutchin
James, 132, 133.
McGee, McGhee
Holden, 10, 96, 114, 141.
McGeorge
Law, Lawrence, 25, 95, 123, 124, 126, 127, 128, 129.
Thomas, 114.
McGrady
Lochlan, Laughlin, 24, 25, 118.
McKennon
William, 151.
McKinsey, McKinzey
James, 150, 169.
McLain
Isabella, 157.
Phebey, 157.
McNeal, McNeil
Jacob, 7.
Jonathan, 192.
McVay, McVey
James, 9, 60, 61, 62, 68, 70, 77, 98, 101, 110, 111, 112, 123, 124, 125, 126, 127, 128, 129, 137, 141, 142, 169, 173, 175.
Mary, 80, 124, 139, 157, 170.
Samuel, 73.
William, 60, 72, 73.
McWilliams
James, 105.
Mead, Meed
James, 36, 38, 51.
Rice, 156.
Robert, 135, 170, 175, 178, 180, 181, 182, 183.
James, 104.
William, 25, 42, 80, 170, 208, 209.

Meador, Meadow, Medor, Medow
  James, 104.
  Job, 93.
  Joel, 9, 22, 131, 166, 209.
  Road, 131.
Mease
  Henry C., 191.
Medley
  George, 100, 115, 164.
Menefee, Menifee
  Eliza, 179.
  William, 38, 48, 57, 61, 81, 101, 127, 128,
    136, 141, 143, 145, 152, 165.
Merriman
  Dewey, 195.
Messick
  T. Warren, 195.
Miles
  Enos, 126.
  Samuel, 110, 126, 127.
Miller, Milla
  Elizabeth, 91, 101.
  Isaac, 130, 160.
  Js., 99.
  Jacob, 17, 52.
  John, 115.
  Joseph, 20, 33, 49, 155..
  Kelley Y., 28.
  Martha, 42, 70, 82, 121.
  Mary, 125 154, 157.
  Mathew, 140.
  Peter, 90, 115, 164.
  Phillip, 82.
  Sarah, 90, 115.
  Simon, 208.
  Thomas, 17, 20, 26, 33, 42, 43, 44, 56, 62,
    63, 70, 71, 86, 87, 91, 95, 97, 101, 104, 109,
    114, 124, 125, 126, 127, 128, 136, 139, 142,
    154, 157, 158, 166, 170, 181.
  Tobias, 7, 99, 131, 213.
  William, 19, 21, 25, 27, 33, 42, 43, 44, 68,
    70, 76, 80, 94, 100, 109, 121, 123, 141, 157.
Mills
  James, 18.
Minnix, Menis

Catherine, 91, 101, 104.
Charles, 91, 104, 160.
Chastin, 101.
Secily, Sicily, Seicily, 91, 101, 104.
Mitchell
  Robert, 190.
  William, 221.
Monroe
  Gov. James, 213.
Moody
  Thomas, 85, 91.
Moore
  George, 114.
  Lucy, 114.
  Sarah, 114.
Morgan
  David, 27, 35, 42, 51, 60, 101, 131, 158.
  Haynes, 182, 208, 224.
Morrow
  Jeremiah, 219.
- Morton
  John, 225.
  William, 211.
Moseby, Moseley, Mosley
  Mordecai, 71, 123, 124, 126, 127, 128, 136,
    181.
  William, 147.
Motley
  Abraham, 212.
Mullindon
  Jacob, 118.
Mullins
  William, 35, 36, 37, 142, 143, 144, 149.
Murph, Murphy
  John, 55, 56, 68.
Muse
  Alfred, L. H., 191.
  John, 64.
  Thomas, 192.
Musgrove
  Alley, 11.
Myer
  James, 130.
Mykepe
  Colo., 50.

N

Napier
  Ashford, 37, 39, 52, 72, 73, 74, 85, 92, 94, 97,
    121, 134, 135, 136, 140, 143, 145, 159.
  Champion, 110, 150.
  Charles, 110.
  James, 100.
  Patrick, 119.
  Robert, 22, 37, 76, 87, 97, 110, 139, 141, 143,
    147, 160, 179.
Neal
  Ann, 165.
Newton

Richard, 43.
Nichols, Nicholas, Nicholes, Nicholls
  Frale, Fraggle, Frayl, Flails, 68, 85, 126,
    147.
Nicholson
  David A., 195, 199, 200, 202.
  Melvin, 195.
  Wilson, 195, 199, 200, 202.
Noals, Noles, Noales
  Joshua, 48, 51, 164, 177.
Noftsinger, Nofsinger, Naufsinger, Knauf-
    singer, Northsinger

Polson
Andrew, 104.
Poteet
Benjamin, 24, 74.
Capt. 220.
James, 214, 215.
Thomas, 64, 66, 72.
William, 139, 153.
Potter
Benjamin, 116.
Stephen, 7.
Susannah, 89.
Thomas, 89.
Powell
Anderson, 186.
Charles, 190.
Robert, 25, 190.
R. N., 191.
Praddy
Ann, 15, 51.
Prater's Run, 17, 91, 134, 149.
Prathon
Edmond, 137.
Pratt
Jonathan, 52, 64.
Preston
David, 140.
Thomas, 100.
Wiliam, 208.
Prewit, Pruit
David, 18.
John, 177, 183.
Price, Peice
Amy, 91.
Anna, 38.
Evan, 91, 165.
George, 7.
James Shores, 94.

John, 70, 93.
Jonathan, 38, 151, 165, 178.
Joseph Shores, 35, 39, 54, 67, 68, 134, 164, 166.
Samuel R., 195.
Shores, 178.
S. & Shores, 7, 101.
Showers, 186.
Prillaman, Prillamon, Prillimon
Daniel, 221.
Jacob, 52, 65, 90, 92, 153, 155, 158, 166, 173, 178, 179.
Nick, 195, 196, 199, 200.
Presley
Robert, 64.
Procer
Oaty, 129.
Prunty
Bragan, 212.
James, 9, 11, 16, 74, 75, 82, 85, 91, 109, 130, 140, 148, 158, 160, 169, 172, 171, 181, 182, 219.
Mary, 91.
Robert, 15, 33, 34, 39, 66, 68, 79, 85, 94, 106, 130, 131, 138, 140, 144, 145, 149, 161, 186, 212, 219.
Thomas, 8, 10, 13, 19, 27, 30, 36, 43, 47, 48, 65, 66, 67, 69, 70, 73, 74, 75, 77, 80, 86, 88, 90, 95, 107, 110, 115, 119, 120, 123, 124, 139, 148, 149, 152, 156, 160, 162, 163, 165, 167, 168, 171, 173, 174, 175, 177, 178, 183, 204, 218, 219.
William, 219.
Puckett
Jeremiah, 93, 94, 104.
Pursel, Persel, Parsel, Pursill
Rubin, Reuben, Ruben, 132, 133, 164, 165.
Pyatt
Ebenezer, 20.

Q

Quarles
Francis, Frances, 15, 27.
John, 207, 207.
Quartee

Colo. Gordon, 13.
Quigley
Ellenor, 37.
Thomas, 37, 168.

R

Radford
George, 144, 145, 160, 162, 172.
James, 84, 99.
Lewis, 195.
Richard, 34, 52, 74, 95, 96, 101, 123, 124, 128, 160, 162, 172.
Radford's Ford, 7, 10, 65.
Raines
Ambrose, 56, 62, 69.
Rakes
Amos, 202.
Charles L., 195.

Ed., 202.
Hugh, 202.
Raley, Rasley
Philip, 42, 68, 105, 165.
Ramey
John, 25.
William, 36, 38.
Ramsey
George, 15, 31, 32, 33, 57, 174, 175.
James, 85, 113, 174.
John, 127, 159.
Susanah, 33.

252

Christopher, 104.
Owen, 10, 18, 25, 39, 47, 48, 51, 54, 79, 118, 119, 130, 140, 153, 165, 214, 215.
Thomas, 166.
Rudy
Daniel, 7, 73.
Russell
John, 223.
Ryan, Rayan, Ryon
Capt., 106.

Cabbins, 52.
Daily, 33.
Darby, 37.
Elizabeth, 130.
Nathan, 27, 38, 92, 116.
William, 9, 13, 18, 27, 38, 51, 55, 67, 69, 71, 74, 77, 79, 80, 82, 86, 88, 90, 92, 99, 107, 109, 115, 117, 119, 131, 152, 157, 160, 163, 168, 172, 174, 182, 210.

S

Samson
George, 190.
Sandford
George, 164, 177.
John, 116.
Sands
Henry, 129.
Saulsberry, Salsberry
Jeremiah, 101, 103.
Richard, 73.
Saunders
Edward Watts, 219.
Elizabeth, 221.
Fleming, 221.
Judith, 221.
Lettie, 221.
Peter, 8, 10, 11, 12, 15, 16, 17, 20, 21, 23, 24, 27, 29, 31, 36, 37, 39, 41, 42, 43, 44, 47, 48, 50, 51, 63, 64, 65, 66, 68, 71, 74, 81, 83, 85, 108, 109, 110, 111, 113, 115, 116, 117, 118, 86, 88, 90, 93, 95, 97, 102, 103, 104, 106, 107, 120, 129, 130, 131, 136, 138, 139, 140, 143, 145, 146, 148, 150, 152, 158, 164, 169, 170, 171, 172, 173, 178, 184, 204, 205, 221, 222.
Philemon, 176, 177.
Robert, 221.
Samuel, 221.
Savers
B., 98.
Scott
Lewis Melvin, 195.
Scruggs
Gross, 208, 209.
John, 37, 76.
Rebecca, 100, 125.
Susannah, 37.
Sebret
Charles, 152, 162, 181.
Sellers
Jean, 44.
Nathan, 119, 131, 140, 153.
Shaffer
Joseph C., 195.
Sharp
Richard, 153.
Willie Carter, 195, 197, 198.

Sheaster
Lodewick, 104.
Shelton
Edney, 190.
Elephaz, 215.
Sherwood Y., 189, 190.
Sheridan, Sheredon, Sherdan
Joanah, 68.
Philip, 35, 68, 87, 88, 165.
Shewood, Shearwood, Sherewood, Sherwood
Robert, 21, 104, 108, 153.
Thomas, 186.
William, 34, 162.
Shoat
Edward, 80.
Shockley
David, 14, 73, 88, 91.
Levi, 14, 37.
Shooting Creek, 18, 90.
Short
Ann, 105.
John, 32, 127, 164.
Shrewsberry
Jeremiah, 55.
Shiveley, Shively
Claude, 195, 199, 200, 202.
Herman, 195, 196, 199, 200, 202.
J. O., 195, 199, 200.
Shumate
Berryman, 47.
Daniel, 17.
Sigmon
Ed, 105.
Norman, 195.
Pete (J. P.), 195.
Simmons, Semmons
Charles, 44, 45, 57, 89.
George, 79, 85, 86, 127, 128, 136, 153, 171.
John, 166.
Joseph, 26.
Nathaniel, 104, 177.
Samuel, 78.
Thomas, 79, 183.
Williams, 89.
Skelton
Rhody, 108.

T

255

Thor
Francis, 49.
Thornton
John, 64, 180.
Luke, 47, 93.
Thorp
Frances, Francis, 23, 33, 58, 92, 207, 208, 209.
John, 52.
Richard, 52.
William, 35, 114.
Thrailkill
Thomas, 215, 222.
Thurman
Camelia, 222.
Thurston
Plummer, 123.
Timberlake
Stephen O., 195.
Toney
Ducker, 109.
John, 159.
Thomas, 85.
William, 52, 54, 58, 76, 93, 95, 144.
Townshend, Tounsend, Townson
Thomas, 63, 66, 106, 169, 180.
Trent
Bryant, 25.
John, 69.
Joseph, 94.
Obediah H., 39, 54, 82, 86, 96, 111, 112, 138, 140, 158, 166.
William, 52, 60, 85.
Trigg
William, 208.

Tripletts
Frank, 186.
Troup
Jacob, 76, 106, 143.
Mary, 76, 106, 142.
Tuggle, Tygle
Lodowick, 11, 89, 91.
Tunstall
William, 226.
Turley
James, 79, 81, 95.
John, 116.
Sarah, 116.
Turner
Isaiah, 100, 135, 154, 165.
James, 54, 73.
John, 75, 94, 101.
John H., 195, 199, 200, 202.
Josiah, 136, 154.
Nathan, 80.
Walter, 195, 199, 200, 202.
William L., 223.
Turnbull, Tumball
George, 7, 13, 27, 36, 37, 51, 52, 63, 73, 74, 88, 90, 93, 97, 98, 100, 101, 102, 104, 107, 111, 113, 115, 118, 119, 120, 129, 132, 136, 145, 156, 158, 164, 174, 175, 183, 186, 204, 205, 213, 223.
William, 151, 211, 212, 223.
Turpin
James, 9.
Jesse, 9.
Tusley
James, 60.

U

Underwood
Rufus, 195.

Samuel, 70.
Joseph, 149, 163.

V

Vandevender, Vanwindee
Abram, 34, 74.
Van Maple, Meapell
John, 50, 73, 128, 139, 157, 170.
Vanover
Cornelius Sr., 28.
Vardeman
Peter, 214.
Venable, Veneble
John, 187.
Richard N., 33, 108, 151, 171, 172, 174, 181,

205.
Richard, 49, 51, 75, 91, 96.
Vest
J., 114.
Richard, 114.
Sally, 114.
Vincent, Vinson
Henry, 31.
Martha, 46, 49.
William, 15, 51, 116.

W

Wade
Bartlett, 21, 67, 76.

Hampton, 88.
Royal, 167.

257

Y

www.ingramcontent.com/pod-product-compliance
Lightning Source LLC
Chambersburg PA
CBHW050416280326
41932CB00013BA/1888